Tribe

Tribe

Why Do All Our Friends Look Just Like Us?

Sandra Mayes Unger

FORTRESS PRESS
MINNEAPOLIS

TRIBE
Why Do All Our Friends Look Just Like Us?

Cover design: Brice Hemmer

Print ISBN: 978-1-5064-4626-4
eBook ISBN: 978-1-5064-4627-1

This book is dedicated to Ernest B. Johnson, one of my best friends, cheerleaders, challengers, mentors, and defenders. His words live in my head and on these pages. Ernest, may you rest in peace and breathe easy.

Contents

Acknowledgments

This book is the product of over a year of work on my dissertation, and then several additional months to turn it into a "normal" book. I would never have made it through if it were not for the patience of my husband Dave, who never once complained about all of the things left undone while I wrote instead, nor about the giant stacks of books piled on his side of the bed—and sometimes on top of him.

Thank you to my wonderful kids, Connor, Hadley, and Rikkia, and son-in-law Kamal, who are more compassionate and generous in their twenties than I ever thought of being at that age. I am indebted to Connor, who used his writing, storytelling, and editing skills over many hours to make this book much better than it would otherwise have been. He refused to allow me to leave leaps of logic and non sequiturs unaddressed. Hadley's compassion for homeless people, and for anyone whose story reminds her of Ernest, continues to humble and inspire me. And Rikkia, who has been with our family since she was thirteen, has fought and won more battles by age twenty-one than I have in my whole life. She has truly put to the test the things I say I've learned over the past fifteen years.

I am grateful to Keshia, Connie, Ricky, Wesley, and Cortez, who sacrificed many hours to patiently walk down memory lane with me and answer questions about the past fifteen years.

Thank you to my good friends Aaron Day, Deynn Hampton, Julie Wright, Kris Johnson, and Stephanie Crane, who encouraged me all along. A special shout-out to Julie, who kept me supplied with giant buckets of Diet Coke on all my writing days.

To my entire Lift community: whether your name is on these pages or not, you are part of my story, and I am grateful to be on this journey with you. Everyone should have the opportunity to be part of a community where we know and are known, love and are loved, forgive and are forgiven.

I can't thank my mom, Nancy Mayes, enough for many years of supporting whatever crazy thing I happened to be doing at the moment—and praying for me through all of it. My five siblings (Curt, Craig, Gerry, Laurie, and Jim) and their families, with whom I have gathered regularly over the years, provided needed breaks and laughter for the many years I have been in school and writing. We have all journeyed differently through the narrow theological waters in which we were raised, and I respect all of you for keeping at the hard questions.

The first version of this book was my dissertation for my EdD in leadership at the University of St. Thomas. My classmates in Cohort 21 were the best ever. We laughed, we cried, we wrote. And then we wrote some more. I am especially grateful to Diane Fittipaldi and Nate Schurman. We met throughout the dissertation process to give whoever needed it a kick in the pants. So often it was me, and I am grateful for the "encouragement."

Dr. Paul Eddy and Dr. Tom Fish were on my dissertation committee for the genesis of this project. I had Tom for a few classes, and he was ever gracious while at the same time pushing me to be the best I could be. Paul has been a friend for over twenty years and has been my cheerleader for one thing or another for that entire time.

My dissertation advisor, Dr. Stephen Brookfield, was wise, responsive, and patient with me as I worked to remember what I had learned and relate it to the five hundred books he made me read! He expressed genuine interest in my topic and provided wonderful affirmation and constructive feedback. He really is the kind of ideal adult educator that graces the pages of his many books.

And finally, a big thank you to J. Andrew Edwards, who completed the final edits on this manuscript. From correcting my split infinitives to suggesting words that brought a great deal more clarity, he has made it much better than it otherwise would have been.

Introduction: Everyone Looked Just Like Me

> And yet in our world everybody thinks of changing humanity, but nobody thinks of changing himself.
>
> —Leo Tolstoy[1]

The moment I realized nothing would ever be the same was when I saw that crappy little pile of candy. It was Halloween the year after I moved with my husband and two children from the suburbs to the city. The kids went out with the neighbors to go trick-or-treating. An hour later, they returned from the cold to a house full of friends, noise, and candy. In the midst of the chaos, my son Connor whispered to me, "Mom, I didn't get a lot of candy." I brushed off his concerns and continued to socialize. Later, when he was in bed, I went into his room and saw the pile of candy on his desk. In the past, we lived in large suburban neighborhoods and the kids came home with pillowcases that would be sorted into piles of, for instance, ten peanut butter cups, thirty-two candy bars, fifteen bags of M&Ms, and twenty quarters. In contrast, this year's haul was a small pile of penny candy, mints, a used pen, a half-full bottle of dollar-store cologne, and a handful of miniature candy bars. I looked at the detritus of my son's first urban Halloween and burst into tears. I don't cry easily and was disturbed at what felt like a ridiculous overreaction to a trivial matter. I couldn't shake the feeling, though, and every time I walked past his room the next day and saw that pile on his desk, I started to cry.

Why was I crying about Halloween candy? I had a wonderful family and a great life. For ten dollars, I could fill Connor's plastic pumpkin with whatever candy he wanted. The tears surprised and baffled me.

With some reflection, I started to see that pile of candy as a microcosm of the changes our family was entering. We were exchanging our comfortable lifestyle for a very different one, the profound meaning of which I was barely beginning to grasp. We had given up some things when we moved from a safe suburban community to an urban neighborhood. We had decided to live in solidarity with people very different from ourselves for reasons of faith that I could not yet clearly articulate. We had a very old house in disrepair, a small pile of candy, and no idea at the time of the radical reorientation that would ensue, guided by new friends who did not look just like us.

To anyone looking to live a life in which everyone does not look just like you, this is my invitation to get out of your comfort zone, expand your map, take some risks, and learn to see the world through a different lens. There is so much to be gained when we reach out across lines of difference and build authentic relationships. Not only do we as individuals win, but *everyone* wins. For me, it all started just a couple of months before that pile of Halloween candy appeared in Connor's bedroom. Today, I am living a life that could not have been predicted from my sheltered and conservative past.

My Sheltered and Conservative Past

I grew up in almost exclusively white neighborhoods and attended an almost exclusively white fundamentalist Baptist church three times a week while living in a slightly less fundamentalist home. Everyone looked like me and most everyone believed like me. Among the many sins my church warned against were the following: playing cards, dancing, smoking, drinking, gambling, attending movies, saying words like "gosh" or "golly" that were presumed to be a stand-in for taking the Lord's name in vain, and being anything other than Baptist. Among the many additional sins a Baptist *woman* could commit were wearing a two-piece bathing suit, wearing pants to church, not obeying her husband, leading any group that included men, serving in positions of leadership, serving communion, having a job outside the home, or doing anything that resembled teaching or preaching in the church. In eighth grade, I began attending a Christian school that stood theologically about midway between the relatively moderate beliefs of my parents and the extreme beliefs of my church. My world of faith mostly revolved around things I could *not* do.

And it was *not* in this context that my passion for social justice blossomed. I recall as a teenager hearing about the heresy of the "social gospel" experiencing a resurgence in the church world. When I inquired what the social gospel was, I was told it was when churches got involved in what we would now call ministries of social justice: feeding the poor, housing the homeless, visiting the prisoners, and providing for people's basic needs. This movement was originally popularized by the Baptist pastor Walter Rauschenbusch in the early twentieth century. The social gospel of that day focused on economic justice, reform in public policy, and fair labor laws.[2] I must admit that the point my church was making against the social gospel was lost on me.

Because my two brothers, Curt and Craig, who were over a decade older than I was, attended a Bible college our church saw as theologically suspect, I was privy to conversations that would, generally speaking, not be in the interests of a child. I recall reviewing the five points of Calvinism with Craig when I was about ten years old and trying to decide how many I agreed with. My church had other issues with my brothers that went beyond suspicions about their theology. Craig grew a beard, which was apparently another sign that he had gone astray. In the end, he had to decide between keeping his beard and singing in the choir. He chose the beard. Both Curt and Craig were told at different times that they needed to cut their hair short in order to volunteer in the youth ministries. When Craig asked the pastor what he meant by "short," he was told that his hair could not touch the tops of his ears when it was wet.

This was the mid-1970s, and during this time of social upheaval an evil breed of what my pastor called "neo-evangelicals" was emerging in the conservative church, and it seemed our pastor was worried my brothers were headed hell-bound in that direction. The neo-evangelicals of the 1970s were pushing elements of the social gospel.[3] Since these activities and issues were considered the province of Catholic and mainline denominations, my church would not embrace them, regardless of what the Bible had to say.

Religious historians have long recognized a significant shift in American religion during this time, some calling it a fundamentalist "resurgence" and others a "contraction." Church historian Chris Armstrong describes "a new sort of fundamentalism" in which "the crusade was not primarily denominational and theological but cultural and political."[4] Indeed, my own church was fighting anything labeled neo-evangelical or the social gospel, but they did not engage in a substantive way with the actual theological issues aligned with those labels. They were more concerned about beards and hair length. Throughout my childhood and young adulthood in conservative churches, I never heard one sermon about feeding the hungry or helping the poor. I never heard of a church or organization that engaged in these kinds of ministries. We occasionally heard from missionaries who were feeding the hungry in Africa and destitute nations while also preaching the gospel. (It was apparently not heretical to work for social justice abroad; only here at home were such efforts forbidden.) Even as I moved into slightly less theologically conservative circles, caring for the poor did not seem to be on anyone's radar.

Caring for the poor, however, was not the only important biblical topic my church missed out on. I also never heard about racial reconciliation. I did not notice that everyone in my church looked just like me, probably because we all looked just like everyone else in my neighborhood and in my school. There was some socioeconomic diversity, but for the most part everyone in my church had similar houses and incomes, and we all lived in conformity with white middle-class culture. The idea that every tribe and nation has been invited to participate in the kingdom of God or that all people bear the image of God was not discussed. Another thing that was never discussed was justice around our nation's history of genocide and slavery. I cannot even imagine a person in my church raising the question of reparations for these national sins. Or in my home. Or neighborhood. Things were just fine as they were, thank you very much.

As I grew into adulthood, I spent many years attending church on Sundays to see our friends and make sure our children learned the Bible. I had a personal faith that was important to me, but it was not much attached to Sunday morning church. Through most of those years, if I'm honest, I went to church on Sundays because I was supposed to, not because I wanted to. In the mid-1990s, I was wrestling with how my personal faith was or was not connected to Sunday church services. I had mostly decided there was not much connection, and I was about to give up on church altogether.

At this time, our family moved to the Twin Cities. As we visited various churches, something or other would rub me the wrong way and I would get up and walk out, waiting in the car until the service was over. It didn't take much to send me to the parking lot, since I was looking for reasons to take offense. Usually, it was songs with theologically suspect lyrics. One time, I looked around the sanctuary and decided for reasons I don't remember that these were not my people. I retreated to the parking lot. I was in crisis and was not sure where to turn. I made one last-ditch effort to make church work for me when we attended Woodland Hills Church, which, contrary to its name, met in an urban high school. Over the next few months, I heard a message of faith that was all about love and the social gospel, and it turns out it is this active and engaged gospel that had been laid out in the pages of my Bible all along. In fact, when Jesus was here on earth and started his ministry, he actually announced that he had been anointed to "proclaim good news to the poor . . . proclaim liberty to the captives and recovering of sight to the blind, to set at liberty those who are oppressed, to proclaim the year of the Lord's favor" (Luke 4:18–19). He was quoting from the Old Testament prophet Isaiah, who had announced at least seven hundred years earlier that the promised messiah would do these things. Even though I had actually read my Bible through from cover to cover, it was only at this church that I realized that the whole Bible is about social justice, with love as its motivation.

This was a faith I could embrace, and I was brought to tears more than once as I learned what I had been missing. The leadership at Woodland Hills cast a vision for caring for those in any kind of need, working toward healing the divide between people of different backgrounds, and making faith something you could actively live out every day, rather than something you just dressed up for at 11:00 a.m. each Sunday. Over the next seven years, I tried to live out this new-to-me gospel from my suburban base. I went from being about to give up on church to graduating from seminary. We moved from the Twin Cities to Chicago and then back to suburban Detroit, where I was from. I helped feed the hungry, passed out backpacks to students who needed them, worked with prostitutes on the streets of Detroit, and built relationships with people who were different from me. This loving social gospel became my gospel, and I held onto it with both hands.

In 2003, I was living in a suburb of Detroit and serving on the pastoral staff of a very rich and very white church. I was also spending many evenings in one of the worst neighborhoods in Detroit passing out food, condoms, and other basic needs to the prostitutes who worked those streets. I couldn't reconcile these two worlds and found myself becoming angry—at white people, at the church, at God, and at myself. A prostitute I'll call JoJo was covered with burn scars after trying to commit suicide by lighting herself on fire. I met people living in abandoned homes with no water or electricity, not to mention food and other basic necessities. There was a tragic story every week.

In August of that year, I came across Psalm 146:7, which says that God "executes justice for the oppressed" and "gives food to the hungry." I was frustrated thinking of JoJo and others like her on the streets of Detroit. When would justice and food come for them? The answer, I concluded, was rather simple. God would have to use something besides his own hands and feet to do these things. I realized he was asking for mine. What if he intended the church to be his army of hands and feet bringing justice to the world, but the army was busy with other things? What if people who identified closely with Jesus were not available to bring food and justice? I decided at that point that I either had to sign on or sign off, but I could no longer be part of any church that did not prioritize God's call to actively work for justice.

Movement

Within two months of that conversation with God, I moved with my husband and two school-age children back to Minnesota. I had spent a lifetime in the suburbs and the middle class, and now I was moving into a diverse, under-resourced neighborhood on the east side of St. Paul. When people asked about our decision to relocate to the city, we had a few reasons that sounded coherent. We wanted to work for social justice, we said, and believed that is best done in proximity to those experiencing injustice. We wanted to escape with our children from the consumerism of the suburbs that did not line up with our faith or values, we said. We wanted to get out of our comfort zone, we said, and build relationships with people from backgrounds that differed from our own. We said all of these things, but, truth be told, for me it was a matter of deciding that I really did have faith—and that faith, at that time, for me, required action. Consequences and dissenting voices be damned.

Before making this move, I held many assumptions about what goes on in under-resourced families and communities, and none of it was based on personal experience. I also held assumptions about what I could do to help the "poor" people I would be meeting and living near. I saw resources flowing one direction—from me to them. And I saw them flowing in perpetuity. I wanted to feed hungry people, but I had not thought about challenging a society that is structured in such a way that there will always be hungry people. Brazilian educator Paulo Freire calls this "false generosity," wherein I have the opportunity to express my generosity only if injustice is perpetuated.[5] That is, I can only exercise my generosity if there continue to be hungry people. Educator Stephen Brookfield says this kind of generosity "is often experienced as a patronizing attempt by the white center to empower the margins."[6] Not only did I see myself in a position to help with groceries, but I also saw myself as an empowered person willing to share my privilege. I was a master of false generosity, and I didn't even know what it was.

After nearly fifteen years here, I have developed a very different perspective. I have learned how ignorant I was about poverty. I have learned that in healthy relationships resources flow in both directions, and that resources are about far more than money. Both parties offer love, acceptance, and a commitment to learn from one another. German social psychologist Erich Fromm says that it is not the giving of material things that is most important, but rather that a person gives of "that which is alive in him; . . . of his joy, of his interest, of his understanding, of his knowledge, of his humor, of his sadness."[7]

Money is not the defining feature of any healthy friendship, regardless of how much you have. Even though a person with financial resources might help meet a financial need, the important things that are being exchanged have nothing to do with money. Sharing life, learning from one another, and laughing and crying together do not have a dollar value. I have also learned that power and privilege are not mine to give. I am no one's savior.

Most of all, I realized that the reason for many of the misunderstandings and wrong assumptions (on the part of all) is that our society is socially and geographically segregated to the point where few people have the opportunity to meet people who don't look just like them. To Freire's point, this is one way that the structures of our society perpetuate injustice, and it needs to be challenged. Since "physical proximity plays a central role in the establishment of relationships," it is easy to see why relationships across lines of race and class are rare.[8] If everyone we pass on our neighborhood streets, sit beside in math class and church, exercise alongside at the gym, and stand in line behind at the grocery store looks like us, the rather obvious result is that our friends will look like us. When we lack the firsthand knowledge that proximity would provide, we fill in the blanks with what we have overheard or seen on TV and in movies or learned from our families. I learned that much of what I used to fill in the blanks was inaccurate.

When I lived in the suburbs, I filled in the blanks about people living in poverty with the assumption that their primary (and maybe only) need was some kind of financial resource and the benefits that attach to money. If only they had more money, better education, more access to power, better health care, and so on, their problems would be solved.

But after many years in this context, my theory is that getting people these kinds of resources is only part of the solution. They are necessary but not sufficient. It is only when these resources are attached to meaningful relationships that transformation happens. And, notably, when these kinds of relationships form, transformation happens for *all* of the people in the relationship, albeit in different ways.

That money is not the primary issue was driven home to me when some of my neighbors found themselves in possession of large sums of money. During my first five years living in my urban neighborhood, three young adult friends inherited money or received a settlement of some kind. One person received $15,000 and the other two received $10,000 each. In all three cases, the people disappeared when they received the money and didn't resurface until it was all gone a few months later. All of them burned through it by buying designer clothing and purses, getting their hair and nails done, taking trips, and eating at restaurants. One of them, an eighteen-year-old girl, showed up at our door several months later pregnant and homeless and broke.

At that time, I didn't understand the choices they were making, but I do now. It's challenging to be a young person in a consumeristic society and never have the money to do what young people do. Many of the teens I know can't come up with bus fare. When I was in high school, I complained because I had to drive a station wagon to school every day, which was definitely not the image I was trying to cultivate. The teens in my neighborhood often don't have money for school clothes and shoes. They can't afford to participate in athletics, and they rarely get to eat out, something I used to take for granted. It's easy to judge people who make what we consider poor choices, but until you've walked a mile. . . .

The most important thing I learned from watching this drama unfold up close is that money solved none of their problems. None had stable housing or an education or a good credit rating or a car either before or after they had this money in hand. I began to suspect that if money didn't solve their problems, then money was not *the* problem.

However, it is *a* problem. Many of the families that I have established long-term relationships with recognize that they did not learn anything about money management when they were growing up. Since they did not learn it, they are not able to pass it along to their children, who are living in a world that is even more complex. I have seen multiple problems overlap. There is little or no money, there is limited financial literacy, there is often a belief that money will solve their problems, and there is a whole network of friends and family in the same boat.

So, while money is not the solution to all of life's problems, the lack of it—and the lack of practical wisdom about it—can make life difficult. If you throw into the mix a friend (or two) who is financially literate, lots of good things can happen. I have had the opportunity to sit down with various neighborhood friends to look at their budget or help them prioritize their bills. In the process, they have learned a few things about money. Equally important, I have learned that I should *never* complain about money. In comparison with them, I have never had a financial hardship in my life. My relationships deepened to a place where they now have a friend they can turn to when financial crises come along, and I now have friends who keep me from complaining about money. Literally.

In addition to the many things I had to learn about poverty, I also had to learn, for the first time, what it *really* means to be white. And what it means to *not* be white. I had heard about white privilege in my early thirties, but I was privileged not to have to think much more about it at the time. Having been raised in a suburb of Detroit, I had learned without realizing it far more about what it meant to be black. It meant you were not welcome in my world, that you were unsafe, that your differences went beyond skin color, that you were the ultimate Other.

In addition to growing up surrounded by people who looked just like me, I also grew up in a context where almost every house had a mother and a father, and most of the moms stayed home with their kids. There was not really diversity of any kind. I would sometimes visit my grandmother in Detroit, and, as the neighborhood turned from white to black, she would express fear and long for things to go back the way they used to be before "they" showed up. I was confused by her attitude, but at the age of seven I was not in a position to challenge her. She was nervous to go shopping on Harper Street as the stores began to put up security gates and the people started to look different from what she was used to. She sold her beautiful house with leaded glass windows and glass doorknobs and an entire apartment on the second floor in 1973 for about $6,000. Almost every home on the street turned into a drug house over the next five years. Her home was never inhabited again, and it was eventually torn down. I suppose I was taught both explicitly and implicitly that this is what happens to your neighborhood when black people move in.

In eighth grade, I started attending a conservative Christian school. It was the first time I went to school with kids who were not white, although most were. The impoverished Detroit suburb of Pontiac was near my school and a few African American students from that community attended. I remember one boy a grade ahead of me. We cheered for him in basketball and we would chat in the hallway, but the conversation never went beyond the surface. I don't think anyone in that school knew how to talk to people who were different from them. In my first and only year of Bible college, there was an African American girl and a Latina girl who were roommates, and, again, we all joked and were polite but never got around to talking beyond the surface. This was before anyone in the evangelical suburban church got around to thinking about or preaching about or facilitating reconciliation. That movement would come much later. There were some black pastors from Detroit who were trying to finish their degrees at this college, but they seemed from another world, dressed in suits and ties and in their thirties and forties.

I got married young and hung out with other people just like me. I do not recall anyone ever thinking that it should be any different than that. It was always so easy to be us. Why would we make things difficult by hanging out with people who aren't like us? This book, however, challenges us not only to think deeply about the *why*, but also to move purposely toward the *how*.

Over the past decade, I have had conversations with my friends and neighbors in St. Paul about white privilege, stereotypes, mis-understandings, and the differing ways we see the world. We have shared with one another what the world looks like through our eyes. The more we have worked through our differences, the more solid the relationships have become, and the more we have all been transformed. The closer these relationships became, the more it hurt me when these people were struggling to pay the bills, and the more my "rich white" problems became legitimized to them. I can be mad at the landlords who let the places my friends live in become slums, and they can be sad with me that my daughter is far away.

Several years back, a man from our church was laid off from his job. He and his family were surrounded by an incredible group of long-term friends who all pitched in to help pay their bills while he found another job. These are the kinds of things committed friends do for one another when they are able. The problem is that poor people tend to have poor friends, and rich people tend to have rich friends. It occurred to me that if we could mix it up a bit, there would be many opportunities for sharing of resources and growing together. But society remains segregated, socially and geographi-cally, making it unlikely that we will ever cross paths with people who are much different from us.

Although my neighborhood is now only 31 percent white (down from 82 percent in 1990), the separation remains. There is little cross-ethnic socializing, and when we first moved in, we initially met white neighbors who assumed we would share their racist per-spectives. At the same time, I have run up against an undeniable hatred of white people by black people who do not actually know any white people beyond surface or transactional relationships. They see with clarity that the work of the Civil Rights Movement is unfinished, and they mistrust white people on contact. In her memoir, *My First White Friend*, African American journalist Patri-cia Raybon says of white people, "They were so easy to hate."[9] When I hear their stories, I see that there is good reason for hatred. Most white people, however, seem completely unaware of this. In contrast, black people are very aware of ongoing, covert racism. It is another sad example of privilege that I don't have to know or care that many black people don't like me.

Due to such privilege, white people can also choose to not worry about whether the work of the Civil Rights Movement is finished. Critical race theory emerged in the 1970s as scholars, lawyers, and activists realized that the movement had stalled with the work undone. And, in some cases, say legal scholars Richard Delgado and Jean Stefancic, "the heady advances of the civil rights era . . . were being rolled back."[10] Critical race theorists questioned whether people of color were benefitting at all from the remedies put in place by the Civil Rights Movement. While the traditional view of civil rights "stresses incrementalism and step-by-step progress, critical race theory questions the very foundations of the liberal order."[11] This is the completely unexpected dichotomy I faced when I moved to the east side of St. Paul. I sustained my former relationships with people who thought equality for all had been achieved, even as I was establishing new relationships with people who saw little if any progress.

These realities made me feel an urgency to *do* something. Because we usually had a yard and house full of teens, that seemed like the place to start. A year and a half after moving here, having no idea what to expect or possibly even what I was doing, I started an organization called The Lift with the help of friends both urban and suburban. We started by working with neighborhood teens—building deeper relationships and helping them succeed in school. We also started holding an informal weekly church service, which provided a context to get to know the families of the youth in our programs.

A lot has happened since The Lift started. It became the classroom for everything I have learned since. It provided a space and a reason for a diverse group of people to be in that space. The voices of my friends from that space will be heard throughout these chapters, but I will start by sharing briefly here what I have learned in this classroom. I came here to help "the poor" and ended up making a lot of great friends who have impacted how I think, what I do, and what I believe. I have learned generosity from people who have very little but still find ways to share. I have learned how fortunate I am based merely on the circumstances of my birth. I have learned faith from friends who experience in one week the number of problems that I experience in one year. I have learned not to watch the clock obsessively and to be present with friends and neighbors, rather than always worrying about what's next. I have grown to love and be loved by people who are very different from me but who have accepted me as I am, while always challenging me to grow and see new perspectives. I came to help, and my friends schooled me in what life is really all about.

Ricky and Wesley were teenage brothers who moved in across the alley from us a couple of weeks after we moved in. They came over regularly for snacks and basketball and, later, dinners and homework help. They stayed late sometimes, sharing their life experiences with me and serving as cultural guides in my new context. Behind my back, they called me the "Happy White Lady." One night, when I was sharing one of my life experiences that contrasted greatly with theirs, Ricky said, "We shouldn't even know each other." I was struck by both the profound truth and profound sadness in his statement. We talked about that for a while. Our society is set up to almost guarantee not only that I won't be friends with Ricky, but that we won't even cross paths. The series of events that brought us together at that dining room table on that night in that neighborhood rarely happen.

Reciprocity

Those events brought me from the suburbs to the city and resulted in me building relationships with people who don't look like me and that I shouldn't even know. Reciprocity has been central to the process of creating these transforming friendships. While it may be true that one party receives financial benefits that are visible while the other receives something invisible like new knowledge or deeper faith, the larger concept of reciprocity is about the things that are not easily measured or seen. In the process of learning to see the world from a different perspective, we all see ourselves in new ways, we learn to be better people, and we are profoundly changed by love and acceptance that come from such unexpected places.

Unfortunately, the segregation that is endemic to our society ensures that these types of relationships rarely form. The most important thing I have learned from my years in this neighborhood is that while we debate public policies and throw money at poverty, we neglect the role of relationships, which I see as an essential part of the solution. Even more, this solution is not just to financial poverty, but to the poverty of our very society, in which value is determined by money.

The journey to this place of reciprocity is not one that can be clearly mapped out. It is circuitous and sometimes treacherous, and it is easy to get lost. My own journey caused me to wrestle deeply with the history of racism and segregation in our country, the effects of which we have not yet recovered from. The role of money in society, and the privilege and power that go along with it, also form an important part of my journey. Most centrally, the theme of building reciprocal relationships and friendships with people who are very different than me, including the obstacles and pitfalls, forms an important part of my story.

There is no guidebook for this journey, and there really are no experts. Little research has been done specifically on relationships that cross barriers of race and class, particularly on the benefits. In these pages, I will use my own journey toward diversity to look at the barriers to these types of relationships, and I will also explore how cross-race and cross-class relationships have impacted my diverse community of friends and myself.

In my story, white middle-class people trying to make a difference and under-resourced people, who are often seen merely as the recipients of their services and generosity, came together to form deep and reciprocal friendships. My relationships with those of different races and classes allow me to include their voices and perspectives about the impact of these relationships on them. I try to be diligent in refusing to speak for others, especially those who are not always heard. I can only tell my story; my hope is that in these chapters, my words, along with the words of my friends, will tell an inspiring story about what's possible when we step out of our own tribe into unknown territory. In the process of working for social justice, I was surprised at my own transformation as my relationships with those I came to serve deepened into authentic, reciprocal friendships. This topic also affords the opportunity to explore the continuing scourges of segregation, classism, and racism by highlighting what can happen on an individual—and ultimately societal—level when these are overcome.

Building authentic relationships of any kind takes a substantial investment of time and energy. Building them with people who experience the world far differently than you do can be even more challenging. When I first moved to the city, I wanted to get to know my neighbors, but I was driven toward longer-term goals of getting something formal started. A year or two into my life in the city, I came across this quote from Catholic priest and educator Henri Nouwen:

> More and more, the desire grows in me simply to walk around, greet people, enter their homes, sit on their doorsteps, play ball, throw water, and be known as someone who wants to live with them. It is a privilege to have the time to practice this simple ministry of presence. Still, it is not as simple as it seems. My own desire to be useful, to do something significant, or to be part of some impressive project is so strong that soon my time is taken up by meetings, conferences, study groups, and workshops that prevent me from walking the streets. It is difficult not to have plans, not to organize people around an urgent cause, and not to feel that you are working directly for social progress. But I wonder more and more if the first thing shouldn't be to know people by name, to eat and drink with them, to listen to their stories and tell your own, and to let them know with words, handshakes, and hugs that you do not simply like them, but truly love them.[12]

It is this idea that has taken root in the core of my being, planted there by Nouwen, but watered and brought to fruition by my friends on the east side. They have calmed me down, shown me what's important. At times, they have talked me off the ledge when my frenetic roots have attempted to resurface and strangle me.

I'm not going to pretend that it is easy to build these kinds of relationships. The odds are stacked against all of us. I hope that by becoming aware of what social controls and obstacles are in place to prevent people like Ricky and people like me from becoming friends, we might be able to work against these barriers, which is only possible once they are identified and named.

The People

I have had to limit the number of characters in this story in order to keep the confusion to a minimum. In addition to my friends who appear on these pages, there are many others whose stories and lives have been an inspiration to me. The main characters in my story are below, and they have all given me permission to use their real names. Several other friends make appearances throughout these pages, and those who are represented by a pseudonym are marked with an asterisk. In those cases, details may have been changed to protect their identities.

Ernest was one of the first friends I made on the east side. He was fifty-nine years old and had been out of prison for a short time. He was also a founder of The Lift and was an original board member and volunteer extraordinaire. His life story has had a major impact on our family. Ernest passed away while I was writing this book. In addition to recorded interviews with him, I also called him on my "dissertation days." I would explain what I was working on and get his ideas and input. In this way, he has left his mark all throughout these pages. Ernest's hobbies were driving around in his car being a good Samaritan and listening to jazz music, usually at the same time.

Dave is my husband of many years. He likes to say his job on the east side is "fixing toilets," as his passion is meeting physical needs in our neighborhood. He loves rock climbing, fixing stuff, and helping meet needs of any kind.

Connor is our oldest child, and when we moved to the east side, he had just had his fourteenth birthday. He manages the children and teen programs at The Lift and is a writer of fantasy novels the rest of the time. He loves board games, movies, reading, and writing.

Hadley is our daughter, and she had just turned eleven when we moved to the east side and began to lure all the neighborhood kids to our house with cookies and popsicles. She has worked at various organizations that seek to promote the common good. She is married to Kamal, who has also pursued a career in the non-profit world. Together, they lived in a converted van for over a year and visited nineteen national parks and dozens of state parks and national forests. They love to be outside doing almost anything.

Dee and her six kids were my original across-the-alley neighbors, and today we once again live near each other on the east side. She is one of the founders of The Lift, serving at various times as board member, volunteer, staff member, worship leader, and mentor to many of our students. She now has five grandchildren in her rapidly expanding family. Dee loves to sing and find ways to creatively do everything she does.

Ricky is Dee's oldest son. He has been involved at The Lift since it started when he was a teenager, and as an adult has worked on staff in various Lift programs. He is now married and runs his own small business.

Wesley is Ricky's younger brother and was also an original "Lifter." He has a passion to be a social justice leader in his community. In his spare time, Wesley reads and drums. He is the father of two young sons.

Cortez was fourteen years old when I met him. He lived with our family for about eighteen months when he was in high school. He has returned to live on the east side of St. Paul and now has a young son. As an adult, Cortez has worked in various programs at The Lift and is now employed full time as a cook. He spends his weekends performing as what he calls an "underground recording artist."

Keshia lived a few doors down from The Lift's first location. She has three adult children, and they were all in programs at The Lift as teens. She has been a good friend to me, using her experience of losing her brother to comfort me when Ernest passed away.

Keshia loves shoes and anything purple. She loves to have fun and calls herself "the quiet life of the party."

In addition to these friends, The Lift is also a main character in my story. From our start in 2005, we have grown to focus on developing the young people who come through our programs into leaders at The Lift and in our community. Our job and life skills programs for students are managed by a diverse group of young adults. More than any specific roles or jobs, we are working together to be a community. We are black, white, Hmong, Polynesian, and Hispanic. We are a community of urban and suburban, single and married, young and old, who come together to tell our stories, do life together, and work to make the world a better place. Many of us consider The Lift our church community, and our goal is to *be* the church in our community rather than merely having church services.

Up Next

In part 1, we will explore a variety of obstacles to forming relationships with people who do not look like us. These include our tribal tendencies to stereotype those from other tribes, preferring the comfort of people who look like us. Segregation, both geographic and social, is another impediment we will explore. If we don't cross paths with people from different tribes, there is no context to form a relationship.

Issues of race and class are two other obstacles that continue to challenge us individually and as a society. In some ways, we seem to be walking back whatever progress emerged from the Civil Rights Movement, and we will look at reasons why that is the case. We will also ask why Christianity does not seem to be leading the way in building bridges between tribes.

The final two obstacles we will explore are economics and freedom. Often, our tribal beliefs about these important topics are enough to keep us surrounded by people who think the same way we do.

In part 2, we will look at the opportunities we have to chart a new course toward embracing those who are different from us. Issues we will explore include the path all relationships face as they are forming and how adults can learn new ways of thinking and doing that open them up to new relational possibilities. We will finish by looking at the benefits of establishing relationships with people who do not look just like us. I will share the benefits I have experienced on this journey, as well as the benefits my friends have shared with me.

#

For nearly three-quarters of my life, I was ignorant of most of the issues I write about in this book. I was white, privileged, and surrounded by more of the same. I can't change the first two, so I had to make a conscious choice to surround myself with people who don't look just like me. I took one step in a new direction and it changed my family, my future, and myself in profound ways. This book is an invitation for others who want to be challenged—and who want our world to be better—to take one step and see where it leads.

Notes

1. Leo Tolstoy, *Pamphlets. Translated from the Russian* (Christchurch, England: Free Age, 1900), 71.

2. Elizabeth Hinson-Hasty, "The Future of the Social Gospel," *Theology Today* 66 (2009): 60–73.

3. Sherwood E. Wirt, *The Social Conscience of the Evangelical* (New York: Harper & Row, 1968).

4. Chris R. Armstrong, "Fundamentalism: Contemporary," in *Encyclopedia of Religion in America*, ed. Charles H. Lippy and Peter W. Williams, rev. ed. (Washington, DC: CQ, 2010), 887.

5. Paulo Freire, *Pedagogy of the Oppressed* (New York: Bloomsbury Academic, 2012), 44.

6. Stephen D. Brookfield, "On Malefic Generosity, Repressive Tolerance and Post-Colonial Condescension: Considerations on White

Adult Educators Racializing Adult Education Discourse," paper presented at the 44th Adult Education Research Conference (Athens, GA: University of Georgia, 2005).

7. Erich Fromm, *The Art of Loving* (New York: HarperCollins, 1956), 23.

8. James A. Vela-McConnell, *Unlikely Friends: Bridging Ties and Diverse Friendships* (Lanham, MD: Lexington, 2011), 25.

9. Patricia Raybon, *My First White Friend: Confessions on Race, Love, and Forgiveness* (New York: Penguin, 1996), 37.

10. Richard Delgado and Jean Stefancic, *Critical Race Theory: An Introduction* (New York: New York University Press, 2012), 4.

11. Delgado and Stefancic, *Critical Race Theory*, 3.

12. Henri Nouwen, *Gracias* (New York: Harper & Row, 1983), 147–48.

I

The Obstacles

1.

Tribal Patterns

Pardon him. Theodotus: he is a barbarian, and thinks that the customs of his tribe and island are the laws of nature.

—George Bernard Shaw[1]

A few years after moving to the city, I was at the grocery store with Ricky, Wesley, Jaquon,* and Cortez—four hungry black teenagers in tall tees and low-slung jeans. Boxers out. They lined up behind me in the cereal aisle and started rapping about me and my shopping cart and my Cheerios. Some of our fellow shoppers seemed to be entertained by the beats and the lyrics to this new rap song about the Happy White Lady and her groceries. I was trapped in the moment; there was no quieting them. I was laughing so hard I was crying, proud to be honored this way and only a little bit aware of how popular we had become. Around the third verse, the store manager, who happened to be a middle-aged white man, approached and asked me with great concern if I was okay. It seemed he thought he had arrived just in time to rescue me from the scary group of black teenagers that was following me. I was deflated and I told him in a marginally unfriendly way that these guys were my friends. He seemed disturbed and skeptical, but he left us to our now deenergized, deflated, desegregated shopping experience. To the guys, this was part of their normal life experience. To me, it sucked.

It sucked because it was my own life story serving as an example of tribalism and stereotypes. The message was that my friends and I didn't belong together, that there was something inherently dangerous about me as a white woman being up close with young black men. I've spoken with the guys about this many times over

25

the years. They see it differently. Ricky didn't see anything strange about the man's approach. "We should be questioned because this is the kind of people we are," he says. Being accused and questioned was such a frequent occurrence for them that this was just business as usual. Wesley said, "It wasn't nothing new; it wasn't a shock; we just laughed it off." Although it was also normal for Cortez, he told me, "You had our backs." That part was *not* normal.

Our grocery store drama showed a clear boundary between my tribe and the tribe of my friends. The store manager recognized the presence of two distinct tribes and jumped immediately to the conclusion that what he was witnessing was the beginning of tribal warfare. When tribes are consigned to separate physical spaces, operate according to different rules, speak different languages, and share a history of violence and hatred, it's no small thing to try to build meaningful reciprocal relationships. Tribal barriers can be formidable, as with the divide between Christianity and Islam. They can also be as subtle as a grocery store manager intervening in a humorous event that he has been conditioned to see as a conflict. In both cases, work is being done to maintain the tribal barrier, rather than tear it down. Ernest said it succinctly: "You don't see a lot of white people going into black folks' homes and you don't see a lot of black folks going into white people's houses. You don't see that."

Tribalism Defined

When I speak of tribes or tribalism, I am not speaking of indigenous or tribal people—that is, those who "have followed ways of life for many generations that are largely self-sufficient, and are clearly different from the mainstream and dominant society."[2] Rather, I am using the contemporary understanding of "an extended family sharing a collective identity."[3] Tribes in contemporary society tend to be differentiated either along lines of race and class or along lines of thinking and behavior. As we will see, these are often the same thing. Tribes have "markers," which clearly differentiate the insiders from the outsiders.

In my experience, it is unusual for a tribe to have both white and black or both rich and poor members who view one another as extended family members. The tribes in my churches, schools, and neighborhoods have all been homogeneous. As James Vela-McConnell, a sociologist who has researched friendships that cross lines of difference, puts it: "Our friendship patterns generally reflect the social stratification system that exists within our larger society."[4] Society agrees with Ricky's assertion that he and I shouldn't even know each other. It seems like they would even prefer we not. The only category available to describe a white woman being followed by black teens in the grocery store involves danger. In the narrative that reinforces the stereotypes, I am the innocent white woman who lives in fear of black men, who are always up to no good. I am in need of a white male savior in the frozen foods aisle who will spare me from the nefarious intentions of dangerous rapping thugs.

The tribe I grew up in was white, middle-class, conservative Christian, a tribe that had not only benefitted enormously from white privilege but had never even heard of it. My teenage friends' tribe was black, poor, and focused on survival. Our tribes are not supposed to mix—in school, in church, in neighborhoods, in life. The story I was raised with was about how *not* to have reciprocal cross-race and cross-class relationships.

As a child of the suburbs, sticking with my own tribe was the done thing, at least partially because the news from nearby Detroit was that young black men were dangerous. The murder rate was high, and I drew a picture in my head of the dark streets of Detroit filled with gangs of black people shooting each other. And stealing the purses of white ladies. Because I lacked personal contact or any source of accurate information, these streets were real to me. Decades later, some people still believe a version of this reality. Like the grocery store manager. When a person from the Happy White Lady Tribe is being followed by four people from the Dangerous Young Black Men Tribe, something bad is about to happen.

The misunderstanding between tribes works both ways. When I

was a police chaplain, I sometimes drove the chaplain car to pick up Ricky from school. I usually did it just to embarrass him. He told his friends that I was his parole officer because he said it was easier than explaining our odd reality. It was fine for him to be seen with a Happy White Lady as long as the Happy White Lady had an official reason for being around. To my tribe, Ricky is dangerous; to Ricky's tribe, I am a white do-gooder who will be tolerated as long as whatever I do doesn't cramp their style.

Why can't my tribe interact with Ricky's tribe? Why can't a middle-class white woman have a genuine friendly relationship with a black male teenager, the son of my neighbor? Why does it have to be either dangerous or hierarchical? Even on television, where boundaries tend to be pushed, I cannot find examples of authentic friendships that cross lines of *both* race and class. Early in the history of television, black people were present serving as cooks or nannies for white people, as in *Make Room for Daddy* and *Beulah*. There are shows such as *That's So Raven*, *The Cosby Show*, and *The Jeffersons* that feature middle-class black people being friends with middle-class white people. As a teen, I watched a show called *Benson*, in which the black actor Robert Guillaume played butler to a bumbling white governor but was later elected lieutenant governor. In this role, he was served by a primarily white staff. Due to its complete departure from anything in the real world, I think this show may actually have done more damage than good to my understanding of black people and race relations. There is the frequent occurrence of the "black best friend" to the central white character, as in *Ghost Whisperer* and *Ally McBeal*. But I haven't found reciprocity represented that crosses lines of race and class.

Nobel Peace Prize winner Jane Addams founded Hull House in Chicago in 1889 as part of the growing settlement movement. This movement brought together people of different backgrounds to live together, become interdependent, and work for social justice. Addams recognized that it is in the mundane activities of daily life that people from different backgrounds learn to get along with one another. She believed that time together outside of formally defined relationships would break down barriers. In my first thirty years, I never spent one day in the presence of someone from a different race or class just doing the usual things of life. I never just "hung out" with a black person or a poor person. That seems to be true for many people from my tribe, and when I asked Ernest if he hung out with any middle-class white people before he met us, he laughed long and hard. "Never, ever," he said. "I been to rich people's houses because I was selling them something or picking up something. But it was all illegal. But just to hang out having clean white fun? It never happened. I used to joke about that clean white fun." It is a rarity for people from Ernest's tribe and people from my tribe to experience what I would describe as normal, human, friendly interactions with each other. Without these shared experiences, our comfort with our own tribe is reinforced and everyone else is relegated to the category of the Other.

The Other

Sociologist Zuleyka Zevallos argues that "otherness" is "central to sociological analyses of how majority and minority identities are constructed. . . . Identities are often thought as being natural or innate—something that we are born with—but sociologists highlight that this taken-for-granted view is not true."[5] Rather, identity construction in a society is controlled by whoever is in power. If your tribe or culture is different than the tribe or culture of those with power, you are the Other.[6]

Once I started to see the world through the lens of the Other—Ernest and Ricky's tribe—I began to notice injustices. I saw things like the media's tendency to focus on white victims of violent crime and ignore black victims. This observation is frequently made by my black friends, who believe that white people simply do not see the victimization of black people as being as important as that of whites. "Our sympathies tend to be unevenly distributed," states David Livingstone Smith, a philosopher who specializes in issues of race and dehumanization. People who are near us, are related to us, or look like us (our "tribe") evoke our sympathies more readily than others. People who are different from us, says Smith, "are unlikely to spontaneously arouse the same degree of concern."[7]

Science journalist David Berreby takes this one step further and says that the tendency to classify humans is innate: "Without work, without awareness, we human beings are experts at sorting people into kinds."[8] Every group throughout history has a distinction between "us" and "others." In many societies, the name used for their own people is the same word they use for "human being."[9] Every society also sorts people into smaller divisions within tribes by everything from age to gender to family affiliation. As much as I hate to put this on paper, I have memories as a child of hearing news about children having something horrible happen to them, and I remember the strong feeling of identification with the little white girls who flashed on the screen, and much less so with the little black girls. My innate tribalism was at work.

In addition to the innate aspects of tribalism, there is the reality that tribes simply function differently on a day-to-day basis. Smith explains that "members of a tribe share a wealth of culturally transmitted beliefs, preferences, and rules of conduct."[10] My tribe of origin likes to do things on time, spend money conservatively, eat healthy food, attend church, shop at department stores, dress modestly, put kids to bed early, and prioritize school activities, to name just a few distinctives. This shared reality means that it is easier to be around people from your own tribe—

> people with a shared understanding of a common way of life, who speak the same language and adhere to the same norms and values—than it is to engage in social exchange with outsiders. Social interaction across tribal boundaries is a minefield, rife with opportunities for misunderstanding, conflict, and—at the extreme—danger.[11]

Today's tribalism encourages an "us/them" divide that exacerbates our divisions and often dehumanizes the Other. It "couples solidarity with others like yourself to aggression against those who differ."[12] It is not too great a leap from our preference to be surrounded by sameness to our dehumanization of people who are different. After all, a black person was once considered by our nation's leaders as just three-fifths of a human.[13]

The middle-class tribe I grew up in acknowledged that the tribes don't mix but offered absolutely no insight into why. Looking through the lens of my own childhood, it seemed like all this hostility emerged out of nowhere and that there was nothing that could be done to fix it. Oh, and by the way, it's mostly the black people's problem.

In my thirties, I read historian Howard Zinn's *A People's History of the United States* and sociologist James Loewen's *Lies My Teacher Told Me.*[14] These are both what might be called revisionist histories of the United States, although it's actually been shown that the history taught in my schools was a revised and inaccurate telling of history. When I read the untold stories of this nation's history, I realized how so much of the hostility between people from different backgrounds is rooted not only in the horrific realities of the past, but also in attempts to cover them up. The truth I was taught as a child was defined by those with power; the Other had no voice. If we could start our kids off with an accurate telling of the historical events that have brought us where we are today, they might arrive at adulthood more prepared to interact as tribes. (And, apart from any utilitarian justifications for an accurate telling of history, it would probably just be a good idea to tell the truth!)

Zinn writes, "In 1859, John Brown was hanged, with federal complicity, for attempting to do by small-scale violence what Lincoln would do by large-scale violence several years later—end slavery."[15] This sentence and a hundred others like it made me mad, made me weep, made me realize I'd been lied to by every single history book, class, and teacher. In 1980, when Zinn published the first edition of this book, I was just starting high school. These truths were not discovered last year. They are components of a story that it seems nobody wants to tell. We still want to celebrate Columbus and his genocidal boats and pretend the pilgrims and the Indians sat down for Thanksgiving dinner together every year. Then we want to gloss over the entire history of slavery and celebrate that everything is fine this side of the Civil Rights Movement. That was my history class.

The voices of the Other were not heard in my history lessons. I spent many Novembers in my elementary classrooms making pilgrims and Indians out of construction paper and pasting them together around a colorful table. Usually, we pasted the pilgrims on one side of the table and the Indians on the other. Somehow, deep inside, this group of ten-year-olds knew we shouldn't mix it up too much.

It is not surprising that many of us, myself included, arrived at adulthood with intertribal hostility, misunderstanding, and often hatred. People from my tribe don't understand why there is a problem because we weren't taught there was a problem and whatever problems may exist do not impact us. Because we are privileged. When tribal issues arise, we get defensive and agitated. The worldview we learned in the classroom and in life says these problems do not exist, or if they do, it is the fault of the Other.

Failure to Mix

I was helping set up a graduation open house for one of Dee's kids, and I was one of the few white people there. I sat down in the living room and attempted to introduce myself to a black woman sitting across from me. I was displaying my best Happy White Lady behavior. "I am the matriarch of this family," she said angrily to me after I told her my name. I asked her name and she ignored me. I seriously considered crawling under a piece of furniture. I needed Dee to come rescue me and tell the matriarch what a good and nice white person I was. I had no idea what was going on or what to do next. She refused to speak with me, and Dee was tied up with the helium balloons. I understand it now as mistrust of do-gooder white people, but at the time I felt wrongly treated and unfairly judged. I couldn't reconcile her attitude toward me with anything that I had done in my life. She could not apparently reconcile my presence in her niece's living room. From a distance, I can see the irony in the fact that I was upset about being unfairly judged for the color of my skin by someone who knew nothing about me. Dee and her kids had a good laugh when I told them what had happened. Looking back on this, it seems like I was part of a reality TV show that threw opposing tribes together to see what would happen.

Dee has shared with me that in elementary school, she went to a white classmate's house and found that "everything was so different it was uncomfortable. . . . I always could see differences, and differences kept me from developing relationships because I never dug deep enough to see the similarities." Even today in our community, she says she is often out of her comfort zone. The difference is that she has learned to "love being able to be thrown into something that makes me think or makes me listen or makes me wonder or question." She is describing her steps toward taking her relationships with those who are different from her to a deeper level. She acknowledges the discomfort, but she is willing to tolerate it due to the benefits of her interaction with those who are different from her.

Things have been different lately, with the regular presence of racist groups and activities on our TV screens on almost a daily basis. Dee and Wesley both speak of their frequent activity of "trying to decipher who is bigoted and who isn't," as Wesley describes it. Dee talks about her efforts to figure out who her "white allies" are. Ricky says that although racism is horrible, it has always existed, and there's a positive side to bringing it out into the open: "It uncovers the reality and forces the conversation," he says. Dee says: "In a real strong storm, all the worms come up out the ground, but they were always there." Bringing the conversation into the open is a necessary step in the right direction. It is also a hardship for people who are victims of racism. It would be much easier at times like this for Dee and her family to stay in their corner, to avoid engaging the Other.

It makes sense that people are more comfortable with others like themselves. I still feel it myself at times—the desire to seek the ease of sameness. But this tendency to stay with our own tribe can limit opportunities, especially for students. As a sophomore in high school, Tyron* was invited to be part of the International Baccalaureate (IB) program. The bottom three floors of the high school most of The Lift's students attended at the time had all the qualities of the usual urban school—gangs, violence, poor test scores, high truancy, and overcrowded classrooms. The best performing (mostly white) students were invited into the IB program, sometimes called a "school within a school," on the fourth floor. The IB students took advanced courses, had smaller class sizes, generally came from wealthier families, and tended to go on to college.

Tyron said yes to the offer and found himself in an unfamiliar cultural landscape populated by people from a different world. The dress code was entirely different, the things that made people "cool" were entirely different, and the expectations of students were foreign to Tyron. While he tried to assimilate into this new tribe, he was facing pressure from friends from his old tribe on the bottom three floors, who were accusing him of "becoming white" and of losing some of his cool factor. We begged him to hang in there, knowing what was at stake. Although Tyron was smart enough to succeed in a program like this, he lasted just a few weeks before the social stress caused him to throw in the towel and return to his own tribe. Despite spending seven hours a day in the same physical space and participating in the same classes, he was unable to find common ground. The benefits of an IB education weren't worth the social stress of trying to relate to people from different ethnic and socioeconomic backgrounds.

Of working-class youth, Sharon O'Dair—a Shakespeare scholar who grew up in a working-class neighborhood herself—points out that "a desire to read books or to succeed in school is often seen as a betrayal of the values and the integrity of the community."[16] Students may be punished for participating in learning, as it may be seen by family and friends as an act of betrayal. Stephen Brookfield, a leading scholar in adult learning theory, critical thinking, and critical theory, calls this act of participating in learning "cultural suicide." Students "risk being excluded from the culture that has defined and sustained them up to that point in their lives."

They may be looked upon "with fear and loathing, with a hostility born of incomprehension."[17]

For Tyron to succeed in the IB tribe, it would have involved him leaving behind his own tribe and assimilating into a new one (if they would even have him) that functioned according to an alien set of tribal rules. He would have been seen as betraying his origins and switching his allegiance to an opposing tribe, where no one looked like him.[18] Tyron's tribe in effect told him that he couldn't be in their black tribe if he was going to act white. The white IB tribe said he couldn't join in if he was going to act black. There was no tribal overlap that contained the best of both worlds.

In so many areas of life, from school to leisure activities to food, there seems to be the black way and the white way. These distinctions cannot be avoided, even in the most mundane aspects of life. Cortez is a black teen who lived with our family for over a year. We are vegetarians and don't keep a lot of junk food around, so he was forced into some significant dietary changes. He mourned for his "greasy meat" (his words), and I drove him crazy by reading nutritional labels with him and running a commentary on his food choices. He was eighteen years old and I had to explain to him the difference between real orange juice and orange drink (orange drink is basically orange Kool-Aid sold for a dollar in a plastic gallon jug). He loved the real orange juice so much, he was going through almost a gallon a day until I explained that his OJ habit was costing us over $200 a month. When he went with his siblings to the corner store, they made fun of him for buying juice instead of pop. They also made fun of the new vocabulary words that were popping up in his sentences. They told him he was becoming white.

In the cases of both Tyron and Cortez, their tribe was being defined purely in opposition to the dominant tribe, which resulted in a characterization of the black tribe as people who eat junk food, do poorly in school, and have a limited vocabulary. I loudly and passionately pointed this out to Cortez, and, while he agreed with me, he didn't have a solution other than for him to behave differently according to which tribe he was surrounded by. His brothers believed that by his actions, he was trying to show himself to be better than them. Wesley recognizes this reality and says he "hates" it. He says it's an example of people taking "pride in being ignorant." Ricky said this response comes out of the feeling that "the person getting out of poverty is judging them."

Legal scholars Devon Carbado and Mitu Gulati explain the double bind that black people in a white world are facing: They need to be "not too black" if they are to be accepted by white people and "black enough" in order to be accepted by black people.[19] There are landmines everywhere, as Cortez's and Tyron's experiences reveal. In Cortez's case, his siblings saw him as no longer being black enough. Tyron, on the other hand, appeared to be too black to fit into the IB world, and by staying there he would have risked not being black enough for his old friends. Referring to research on black students' assimilation onto college campuses, education expert William Tierney warns of both "cultural suicide," as defined above by Brookfield, an of "intellectual suicide," in which students who don't assimilate into the dominant culture do not succeed in the academy.[20] While Tierney argues that neither option is necessary for academic success, it is far from clear how to navigate between these two extremes.

In discussions of these tensions over the years, several of my urban neighbors have used the metaphor of crabs in a bucket. Connie was the first one. She is originally from Philadelphia, and her proximity to the ocean made this metaphor meaningful to her. She said crabbers throw their catch in a bucket. It gets full so that crabs are stacked on top of each other. The ones on the bottom will often start working their way to the top, climbing on the backs of the other crabs. When they get to the top of the heap and start reaching for the edge of the bucket, the other crabs join together to pull the crab back down and push it to the bottom of the bucket. When Cortez was eating healthy and using big words, he was not being black enough. He was reaching for the edge of the bucket, and his family and friends wanted to make sure he didn't escape. The realities of today's tribalism mean that any perceived defection to another tribe, or even a display of the rituals of another tribe, is perceived as betrayal and deserves ridicule and punishment.

Against this culture of competition and disempowerment among fellow strugglers that I have observed, activist and author Angela Davis employs the principle of "lift as we climb." We must climb, she says, "in such a way as to guarantee that all of our sisters, and indeed all of our brothers, climb with us."[21] I believe that one reason there is more pushing down than lifting going on is because when an entire tribe is disempowered, opportunities and resources begin to be seen as the payoff in a zero-sum game: "If you get out of the bucket, there is no chance I will."

There Is No *They*

It has taken me nearly fifteen years of living near and getting to know people from other tribes to begin to understand these sorts of tribal dynamics that are so alien to my own. In spite of the difficulty of understanding the world of the Other, it is a regular activity of my tribe of origin to pretend that they do. I frequently find myself saying, "There is no *they*," when in conversation with white suburban people. Generalizations about my neighbors such as "they tend to have babies without getting married" reflect the human tendency to stereotype. In this case, a particular report on single motherhood on the news may become the defining characteristic of the entire black population.

I have experienced this type of stereotyping myself as a female in a male-dominated profession. When I first started giving sermons in the 1990s, I faced criticism ("Women shouldn't preach") as well as responses such as "I always thought women couldn't preach, but you did a great job." (Thank you . . . I think?). Psychologist Derald Wing Sue would call this a microaggression based on gender, a topic we will cover in chapter 4 as it relates to race.[22] Comments like these made me realize that for some people I was representing half of the human population every time I preached. Since they did not often see women in the pulpit, their decision about whether they thought women were capable of preaching rested entirely on me. Smith says humans have a tendency toward "outgroup homogeneity bias." That is, we "perceive members of our own group as individuals, but see other groups as more or less homogeneous."[23] "If *this* woman can preach, I guess they all can," or "If this black woman is a single mom, I guess they all are." To the topic at hand, when white people use the word "they" in describing black people, they are saying that all of them are the same, even though they would not likely say that of white people.

Journalist Malcolm Gladwell provides some insight into this tendency.[24] He explains that the human brain has a limited capacity for forming and maintaining close relationships. Once we reach our connection limit, we must resort to simplified models such as stereotypes and hierarchies in order to understand the number and variety of people we are exposed to. In other words, we create a lot of *thems* to stand over against our *us*.

There is a deeper truth to the phrase "There is no they." From an evolutionary and biologic standpoint, *there really is no they*. Smith explains that there are "psychological mechanisms that lie behind ethnoracial beliefs" as opposed to beliefs about race being rooted in proven scientific biological concepts.[25] He calls the everyday assumption that each species has a specific essence that is responsible for the appearance and behavior of that species "folk-taxonomies."[26] These provide a framework for how all humans think about plants and animals. These beliefs exist in every culture that researchers in this arena have studied. The problem is that this approach is not scientifically sound. "There simply aren't any defining features—even at the genetic level—that all and only members of a species must share."[27]

Humans apply the same approach used to classify and describe races as we use to describe species. They are "presumed to be natural kinds defined by hidden essences passed down the 'bloodline' from parents to their offspring." Smith calls this presumption "scientifically vacuous but intuitively compelling."[28] When we define a specific ethnoracial group as "they," we are appealing to "folk-taxonomies" rather than science. We are saying there is a "mysterious something" that makes a person Chinese or African American or Scottish, and that it is innate.[29]

Beyond sloppy thinking, this way of categorizing the Other has massive social ramifications. Whatever definitions the majority culture applies to minorities become the basis for exclusion. The first step is, "You are a different ethnorace than I am, and therefore you are different than me in your very essence." The next step is, "Your essence makes you subhuman." Or at least, "Your essence is less than mine."

Stereotypes

The famed social psychologist Muzafer Sherif asserted that stereotypes may not emerge primarily from characteristics of the group being stereotyped, nor from the group holding the stereotype, but are more likely a product of the interaction of the groups with each other. He defined the concept of stereotype, therefore, as a *relational* category. Stereotypes emerge "when people transact with other people in the course of carrying out activities and pursuing goals within the design of living they have patterned."[30] Those stereotypes are then fostered within the group, with the result that new members (for example, children born into the group) internalize them. "In the very process of becoming an in-group member, the . . . norms prevailing in the group are internalized by the individual."[31] Thus, the lines that define the tribe of the Other are passed from generation to generation through group norms, rather than through "contact with the group against whom prejudice is directed."[32] Sherif has offered an explanation for what I observe in my neighborhood. Stereotypes potentially emerge from negative tribal interactions generations ago, are passed down, and are never overcome by new interactions *because there aren't any new interactions!* All of our friends look just like us because all of our grandparents' friends looked just like them.

Sherif's theory also explains my own family history in part. I stood in direct line to inherit prejudicial views of black people from my family, and the inheritance carried no requirement that I ever meet a black person. Sherif's claims about the formation of stereotypes ring true to me with one important caveat. As I experienced, in the case of the black/white and poor/rich interactions, there is very little interaction between the groups that can be said to be the basis for stereotypes. Rather, I suggest that in addition to family prejudice, stereotypes may also emerge from the artificial interactions portrayed in sitcoms and in movies, from media reports on black criminals, or from an extremely limited number of interactions between the groups. These limited interactions can be detrimental, sometimes resulting in a negative stereotype after just one encounter. A white friend, who had lived almost exclusively within her tribal boundaries, commented to me many years ago that black families always seem to be broken. Speaking of the men, she said, "They never stick around."

"Why do you think that might be?" I asked. "Are you saying there is an inherent flaw in African American men that causes them to abandon their families?" I explained that the ongoing difficulties in some black families were not created in a vacuum. The history of slavery that included rape, the selling off of spouses and children, and the emasculation of African men surely contributed to the social problems that exist today.

It was clear these things had never crossed her mind.

Because of culture and class differences, and because there is often little understanding or awareness of the historical realities that have led to the current realities in the black community, inter-tribe interactions begin from a place of misunderstanding and go downhill from there. How does one begin to develop a meaningful relationship with someone you have already identified as having an inherent flaw? "Let's be great friends even though you will probably abandon your family like all the other black men." It doesn't work.

Stereotypes offer simple explanations for complex problems. Over the years, volunteers at The Lift have served as mentors for our students. A frequent occurrence is that the adult mentor makes an appointment with the student and the student doesn't show up. Some volunteers get so frustrated by this behavior that they quit volunteering. The stereotype that emerges from these interactions is usually along the lines of "black people never show up on time." I have been part of these conversations, and I have had the opportunity to explain to a volunteer that the student who stood him up got stuck at school with no transportation and no phone. I've responded to a mentor's disappointment about a no-show that the student's mom needed him to babysit his siblings so she could pick up some hours at work. On the cultural level, I have found that an appointment to a black teen (and likely any teen) means something different than it means to a white adult. Stereotypes such as "they don't show up" are the easy way out.

Stereotypes are a major barrier in trying to bridge the divide between races and classes and work toward reciprocal relationships. My experience indicates that it is normal and socially acceptable for middle-class white people to speak of poor black people as a "they" who can all be lumped together and defined by whatever adjective emerged from today's news or yesterday's sit-com, but rarely can this be demonstrated from substantive personal experience. Living in a suburb of Detroit, I arrived in adulthood believing that black men were dangerous, based on the news and on the attitudes of family members. Then I met a whole bunch of actual young black men who were not dangerous. Dee's sons and their friends gathered around the basketball hoop in our backyard on a daily basis and laughed, ate cookies, sweated buckets, and were not, in fact, scary.

Sherif conducted research that shows that stereotypes and attitudes can be altered when two opposing groups are presented with a problem or goal that must be dealt with, but that neither group can solve on its own. Sherif calls this a "superordinate goal," as its solution transcends the tribal tendencies of the groups and forces them to work together for the common good.[33] Stereotypes were significantly overcome as groups worked together on several superordinate goals over time. Jane Addams said that people learn to get along with each other in the daily activities of life; a superordinate goal provides a reason for people from different tribes to engage together in various activities.

Sherif's research has also shown that prejudicial attitudes can be reduced when people of diverse backgrounds are forced to interact, but when they return to their own tribe, the former prejudices return. Given the issues of social and geographic segregation, it is hard to imagine a situation arising naturally in which black and white, rich and poor, would have the opportunity to identify and work toward a superordinate goal together, and then stick together long enough afterwards for the new attitudes to take root. Creating such opportunities is precisely what The Lift community is trying to do in our neighborhood. Over time, we have had enough shared life experiences that a new tribal reality has begun to form. We have monthly cookouts in our neighborhood, we plan fundraisers, we share the responsibility of putting together an informal weekly church service, and we create events at which students in our neighborhood learn important life skills. We have at least begun to create a tribal "us-ness" that is helping us to acknowledge and work through the things that would normally keep us in our own tribe.

Caught Sorting

When I look back over my years in this context, I see embarrassing evidence of my own sorting activities. When I met Dee, my first thought was that she was black and I was white. This may be accurate, but why was my first thought not that we are both women, or both mothers? Why the infantile tendency to sort by color? It bothers me that that's where I went first. Especially because over the past twenty years, many theorists have come to the conclusion that racial categories cannot be justified scientifically.[34] Categorizing Dee by race was a sort based on comfort, rooted in my limited life experience with the Other. Although Dee and I could be united by our role as mothers, somewhere deep inside me, I was more comfortable putting her into a different box than myself.

Another example: Dee and I were taking a class taught by a middle-aged bald man, whom I initially thought was white. His skin and features were generic, and that's where I placed him without much thought. After a few meetings, he said something that made me think he was black. I asked Dee if she thought he was white or black. She did not hesitate: he was black. For a few weeks, I had seen him as white (a member of my tribe). Now I had new information that he was black (not a member of my tribe). Absolutely nothing changed about him, but I dumped him in the Other bucket. I felt myself do it. The best explanation I can come up with is that when I thought he was white, I believed (without being conscious of it) that we shared a common perspective of the world and that we understood one other. After I found out he was black, I was not so sure either of those things was true. I didn't think less of him; I just thought Other of him. I didn't *choose* how to feel about him regardless of which category he was in. It just happened. Whatever the thing is that seeks out the comfort of sameness made me realize that I had initially put him in the wrong bucket. Even after a decade of spending a lot of time in community with black people, I still needed to be clear on everyone's label, and I was apparently still more comfortable with people from my tribe of origin.

Philosopher George Yancy would describe my thoughts in this regard as an example of the "white gaze" on "black bodies."[35] The sight of a black person arouses suspicion in whites due to a historical narrative that assumes black people are up to no good. While I may claim that there was no value judgment attached to my recognition of my teacher as black, Yancy would reject my claim to neutrality. By my whiteness and social power and privilege, I have been conditioned on "what to expect of a black body (or nonwhite body), how dangerous and unruly it is, how unlawful, criminal, and hypersexual it is."[36] These were not my thoughts at the time, but after fifteen years of watching the white gaze on my black friends in places like restaurants, retail stores, suburban neighborhoods, gas stations, and movie theaters, I am willing to concede the point to Yancy. Regardless of my conscious thoughts, I put my teacher into the tribe of the Other.

This sorting by tribe leads to a divide between people that prevents understanding the behaviors and attitudes of opposing tribes. Sociologist Richard Sennett explains that even Aristotle, in the fourth century BCE, articulated the problems inherent in such sorting: "Tribalism . . . involves thinking you know what other people are like without knowing them; lacking direct experience of others, you fall back on fearful fantasies."[37] Aristotle's insights were prescient. Because of media portrayals, it is reasonable to think that white (or rich) people believe they know what black (or poor) people are like without actually knowing any, and the response is fear, which is a major barrier to forming any kind of relationship. Young black males in my neighborhood love to capitalize on white people's fear of them in an effort to gain social control for their own tribe, as when a group of young black men walk down the middle of the road and refuse to get out of the way of cars. When I bounced this explanation off the guys, they agreed. "You take power where you can get it," says Wesley. It makes you feel "powerful in the moment," says Cortez.

Waiting for a group of kids to get out of the road really pissed me off at first, but my growing realization of the disempowerment of these young men has given me patience until they decide to yield the right of way. One time, when Keshia was in the car with me, she rolled down the window and screamed at them to get out of the way (something I would never do when I'm driving alone). They casually glanced back at us and slowly made their way to the side of the road. "You are at our mercy," they seemed to be saying.

Ricky and his friends have admitted that as teens they would "play" with white people in our neighborhood at times, especially middle-class white people who stood out because of their clothing, vehicle, or look of sheer terror as they walked down Payne Avenue. The guys would start posturing in the way that the media presents them. They put their hoods up, assumed a look of defiance, walked three abreast on the sidewalk, and took great pleasure in seeing the power their tribe had to frighten the Other. I have watched white people who see any black man approaching from far enough away cross to the other side of the street to avoid contact. In these situations, white people don't know that a game is being played, and as teens Ricky and his friends were either unaware or unconcerned that their game was likely to reinforce negative stereotypes of black teens as dangerous and scary. Cortez admits he was proud of his ability to scare people as a teen. Even today, he dresses in what he calls "intimidating ways" when riding the bus to avoid being bothered. He knows he will be stereotyped, but he has decided as an adult that he has the power to reject the stereotype while utilizing the power of it when needed.

#

There are many reasons why we stick with our own tribes and end up with friends who look just like us. In the next chapter, we will look at one of the major obstacles to forming relationships that cross lines of race and class. Our history of geographic and social segregation has limited the opportunities to engage with people who do not look just like us.

Notes

1. George Bernard Shaw, "Caesar and Cleopatra," in *Three Plays for Puritans: The Devil's Disciple, Caesar and Cleopatra, & Captain Brassbound's Conversion* (London: Grant Richards, 1901), 121.

2. Stephen Corry, *Tribal People for Tomorrow's World* (Alcester, UK: Freeman, 2011), Kindle loc. 342.

3. Darrell Fasching and Dell deChant, *Comparative Religious Ethics: A Narrative Approach* (Oxford: Blackwell, 2001), 84.

4. James A. Vela-McConnell, *Unlikely Friends: Bridging Ties and Diverse Friendships* (Lanham, MD: Lexington, 2011), 22.

5. Zuleyka Zevallos, "What Is Otherness?" in *The Other Sociologist* (blog), October 14, 2011, https://tinyurl.com/y37mjacw.

6. Fasching and deChant use the phrase "the stranger who is wholly other" to capture the absolute separation between the self and the Other. See Fasching and deChant, *Comparative Religious Ethics*, 20.

7. David Livingstone Smith, *Less Than Human: Why We Demean, Enslave, and Exterminate Others* (New York: St. Martin's, 2011), 51.

8. David Berreby, *Us & Them: The Science of Identity* (Chicago: University of Chicago Press, 2008), 94.

9. Berreby, *Us & Them*, 125.

10. Berreby, *Us & Them*, 196–97.

11. Berreby, *Us & Them*, 197.

12. Richard Sennett, *Together: The Rituals, Pleasures and Politics of*

Cooperation (New Haven, CT: Yale University Press, 2012), 3.

13. Michelle Alexander, *The New Jim Crow: Mass Incarceration in the Age of Colorblindness*, rev. ed. (New York: New Press, 2010), 26.

14. Howard Zinn, *A People's History of the United States: 1492 to Present* (New York: HarperCollins, 2003); James Loewen, *Lies My Teacher Told Me: Everything Your American History Textbook Got Wrong* (New York: Touchstone, 1995).

15. Zinn, *A People's History*, 171.

16. Sharon O'Dair, "Class Matters: Symbolic Boundaries and Cultural Exclusion," in *This Fine Place So Far from Home: Voices of Academics from the Working Class*, ed. C. L. Barney Dews and Carolyn Leste Law (Philadelphia: Temple University Press, 1995), 202.

17. Stephen D. Brookfield, *The Skillful Teacher: On Technique, Trust, and Responsiveness in the Classroom* (San Francisco: Jossey-Bass, 2006), 84.

18. Brookfield, *The Skillful Teacher*, 85.

19. Devon Carbado and Mitu Gulati, *Acting White? Rethinking Race in "Post-Racial" America* (New York: Oxford University Press, 2013), 4.

20. William G. Tierney, "Models of Minority College Going and Retention: Cultural Integrity vs. Cultural Suicide," *The Journal of Negro Education* 68, no. 1 (1999): 83.

21. Angela Y. Davis, *Women, Culture & Politics* (New York: Vintage, 1990), 5.

22. Derald Wing Sue, *Microaggressions in Everyday Life: Race, Gender and Sexual Orientation* (Hoboken, NJ: John Wiley, 2010).

23. Smith, *Less Than Human*, 51.

24. Malcolm Gladwell, *The Tipping Point* (New York: Little, Brown, 2006).

25. Smith, *Less Than Human*, 186–87.

26. Smith, *Less Than Human*, 187.

27. Smith, *Less Than Human*, 188.

28. Smith, *Less Than Human*, 192.

29. Smith, *Less Than Human*, 208.

30. Muzafer Sherif, *In Common Predicament* (Boston: Houghton Mifflin, 1966), 2.

31. Muzafer Sherif, *Social Interaction: Process and Products* (Chicago: Aldine, 1967), 448.

32. Sherif, *Social Interaction*, 242.

33. Sherif, *Social Interaction*, 183.

34. Smith, *Less Than Human.*

35. George Yancy, *Black Bodies, White Gazes: The Continuing Significance of Race* (Lanham, MD: Rowan & Littlefield, 2008), xv.

36. Yancy, *Black Bodies*, 3.

37. Sennett, *Together*, 4.

2.

Tribal Land

The great tragedy of segregation isn't so much that we see less of each other but that in separating from each other we see less of God.
—Tullian Tchividjian[1]

For the first two years that I lived in my urban neighborhood, I felt the need to explain to anyone who would listen why I lived in this "bad" neighborhood. I was a snob. It was okay to live here as long as (1) it was my choice and (2) I could leave whenever I wanted. I needed to be sure people didn't think I was uneducated or working-class or down on my luck—in the wrong kind of tribe. I could say I *chose* to live here to help the poor and be noble, as opposed to simply saying I live here and risk the possibility of being incorrectly categorized as a loser.

Although I have stopped explaining, the fact that I felt the need to do it for so long is one piece of evidence that segregation is about more than your street address. It associates you with a specific tribe—rich or poor, educated or uneducated, empowered or disempowered. I needed to make sure people knew that regardless of where I lived, I was in the rich, educated, empowered category. Then I could use my choice to live among poor, uneducated, disempowered people as evidence of my innate goodness. It provided a great opportunity for people to tell me how wonderful I am.

This fear of being labeled as part of the wrong tribe because I lived in the wrong neighborhood was deeply rooted in the context I grew up in. Keeping up with the Joneses was a reality. It was important in the neighborhood I grew up in that the right kind of people moved in (people who looked like us) and that our cars and yards all sent the message that we had our act together. It was not unusual to have dinner-table discussions about the neighbor whose grass was turning brown, the ones who were getting a divorce, or the ones who had just moved in driving a rusty car. There was judgment toward single parents and even toward families in which the wife and mother had to (or chose to) work outside the home. The social boundaries of our neighborhood tribe did not extend far in any direction.

Segregation is traditionally defined as the geographic separation of people who are racially or socioeconomically different from each other. In the United States, segregation has been primarily about keeping black people out of white neighborhoods, which means black people are also kept out of white schools, businesses, community centers, and shopping centers.

From my life in the suburbs and then in the city, I have three observations about segregation. First, despite changes in the laws that restricted where black people could live, the suburbs are still segregated. This may put some people on the defense, but the white middle-class tribe has marked out its territory, and they not very open to sharing their space with other tribes. All of the suburbs that I have lived in would be considered segregated, as they were nearly 100 percent white and 100 percent middle class.

Second, many of the white people in the city are moving away, or trying to move away, from diversity. It is fairly common to hear white people in my urban neighborhood lamenting the decline of the neighborhood as "those people" move in. In 1990, my neighborhood was 82 percent white. Today, it is 36 percent Asian or Pacific Islander, 31 percent white, 14 percent Hispanic, 13 percent black, and 6 percent two or more races.[2] This is not a trend most of my white neighbors are happy with.

Third, even with growing diversity, the people in my neighborhood still generally live socially segregated lives, regardless of who their next-door neighbors are. If they lack the resources to isolate themselves from other tribes geographically, they settle for social segregation. Most of the gatherings I see taking place in the backyards in my neighborhood are homogeneous. "It is the separation of groups, and the socially constructed boundaries between different groups, that allows for the emergence of prejudice and social distance," says sociologist James Vela-McConnell.[3] We will look at both the geographic and social segregation between tribes.

Geographic Segregation

When my husband and I had been married for a few years and were looking for a larger home in a first-ring suburb of Detroit, our realtor and family members warned us that the area we were looking in had a lot of black families moving in, which in the Detroit area was a guarantee that property values would be plummeting and that we would have black neighbors if we moved there. And this was in the late 1980s! There is no other way to say it than that metropolitan Detroit was just a flat-out racist place. When I went to a Detroit parade or department store as a child, I recall my grandmother clutching her purse more tightly. When any black person showed up in our neighborhood, church, school, or really anywhere, it was a major topic of conversation, due to the rarity of the occasion. Other than my grandmother, no one in my family made explicitly racist statements, but the event-like nature occasioned by the appearance of a black person sent the message that this was abnormal. It was abnormal to even *see* a black person and out of the question to think of living near one.

Why is it such a radical choice to live in a diverse neighborhood? What happened in our history that would make friends and family question my sanity for buying a home in a neighborhood where I would have black neighbors? Segregation is merely a social construct; it is not embedded in the nature of existence in order to ensure safety and well-being. According to sociologists Douglas Massey and Nancy Denton, immediately after the Civil War, blacks and whites were not residentially segregated, although blacks were disadvantaged in other ways.[4] At the end of the nineteenth century, the US Supreme Court upheld segregation and proclaimed "separate but equal" as constitutional in their ruling in *Plessy v. Ferguson*.[5] The groundwork was laid for blacks and whites to live in isolation from one another.

Jumping ahead to the middle of the twentieth century, Massey and Denton point to various strategies used by whites to ensure the maintenance of the "color line." The color line refers to geographic racial segregation that began after the Civil War when slaves were freed and there was an effort to draw lines around where black people were allowed to live and, more importantly, where they were not allowed to live. Despite the supposed eradication of the color line, de facto segregation is still in place.

In the first half of the twentieth century, neighborhood improvement associations throughout the country lobbied for zoning restrictions, boycotted real estate agents with black clientele, bought property from black owners, and offered cash to black renters if they would leave the neighborhood in question. Neighborhood residents agreed to restrictive covenants, which prevented them from selling or renting to blacks, or even allowing them to occupy their property. When these efforts were declared unenforceable by the Supreme Court in 1948, they were merely driven underground. On the rare occasions when blacks were successful at integrating a neighborhood, it resulted in whites fleeing and property values plummeting. According to Massey and Denton, "the ghetto constantly followed the black middle class as it sought to escape from the poverty, blight, and misery of the black slum."[6]

Nowhere is this more true than in the city of Detroit, where my early perspectives on race were shaped. In 2019, the city was 79.7 percent black with a median income of $26,200, whereas in Oakland Township, where I spent most of my childhood, the population in 2015 was 85.1 percent white and 3 percent black with a median income of $126,200.[7] The drive from Detroit to Oakland Township takes about thirty minutes, but in that short trip you leave one world behind and enter an entirely different one.

My own experience aligns with Massey and Denton's assertion that the passage of time and improvements in the socioeconomic status of blacks have brought little or no change to the geographic segregation of blacks and whites. Writing in 1993, they affirmed that "there is little evidence of substantial change in the status quo of segregation."[8] This is the case in both the North and the South and regardless of income level. Of all races, it is only blacks who experience this pattern of hypersegregation that appears to be impervious to socioeconomic or other influences. "No group in the history of the United States has ever experienced the sustained high level of residential segregation that has been imposed on blacks in large American cities for the past fifty years."[9]

A few years ago, I watched a story of desegregation take place right in front of me. One of our students, Malik,* moved with his family to the suburbs for his freshman year of high school. He was in a school that was primarily middle class and 74 percent white, with an 88 percent graduation rate. He learned that in this new context, he could get good grades and still be cool. He earned all As and Bs in both semesters. When he moved back to the city the following year, he was surrounded by his old set of friends and his old set of values, and his grades dropped to Ds and Fs. He started getting locked up regularly for petty crimes. Malik is a smart kid living by a set of rules that guarantee failure in the larger community. When he was forced into a different set of rules, he was perfectly able to comply. He also told me that he had access to far more resources in the suburban school to help him academically. There is nothing magical about the suburban school that made Malik succeed there while he failed in the urban school. The major reason there were more resources to help Malik succeed in the suburbs is that there was more money allocated toward his education than there had been in his urban high school.

Many states rely on property taxes to fund local education. According to *The Journal of Blacks in Higher Education*, this means that "expenditures per pupil in many thousands of inner-city, predominately black public schools are substantially less than expenditures at mostly white suburban public schools."[10] Studies show a $3,000 to $5,000 per student spending gap between urban and suburban schools. This is especially discouraging as research on four major cities and their surrounding suburbs found that the urban schools employed more security officers than they did counselors or social workers, while the opposite was true in suburban schools.[11] The already great disparity in per-student spending is exacerbated by the ways the urban schools are sometimes forced to allocate their limited resources.

Like Malik, I moved outside of the geographical area that was largely populated by people who looked like me. I am a product of desegregation by my own choice. It has become (mostly) normal and (mostly) comfortable now to be in meetings or groups in which I am in the minority as a white person. That was not always the case. About two years after I arrived in this neighborhood, I went to a local barbershop where a woman rented a chair to do hair braiding. I showed up at 9:00 a.m. and sat in the chair getting my hair done for over ten hours. The shop served primarily black men, and throughout the day I was surrounded by a stream of men arriving for haircuts with their wives, girlfriends, and children in tow. It was chaotic and noisy and intimidating for me. I felt out of place even though I was mostly ignored. After the owner left for the day, the men decided to pull out a TV and watch videos of dog fights. As a vegetarian committed to nonviolence, this was bad news. I spent two hours in the chair directly in front of the TV with my eyes closed, listening to the dog fights and the men cheering them on. This was a far cry from my suburban salon experience, which usually involved a relaxing spa-like environment, quiet music, and no children. I have had a couple of similar hair-related experiences, and they still make me long for my old "normal."

Malik's experience and my own are oddities. This kind of integration rarely happens with the students I work with or the adults I know. There is so much working in favor of segregation. In 2013, an application for smartphones called "Ghetto Tracker" was released. The app was promoted as a resource "to help people identify safe areas in unfamiliar cities." The app was accused of being a "racist, classist app for helping the rich to avoid the poor."[12] This image was helped along by the photo it featured of a smiling white family alongside text promising to show them which neighborhoods are ghetto. In response to criticism, "Ghetto Tracker" was renamed "Good Part of Town." The developers removed all use of the term "ghetto" and replaced the smiling white family with an ethnically diverse family. However, critics say the very idea of the app assumes that poor areas should be "categorically avoided" and that "every person who lives in an area with comparatively high crime or poverty is a criminal, or that these areas are devoid of culture or positivity."[13]

Residential segregation ensures that these beliefs will not be overcome. Black people and white people will not associate with one another and create a shared history or work together to build a shared future. People from different worlds will not learn what the other has to offer. Misunderstandings, stereotypes, and fear of the Other will continue to be the norm.

This is especially tragic as the schools where children spend the majority of their time, and where stereotypes could presumably be overcome, continue to be segregated, situated as they are in neighborhoods that are largely segregated. The hope of *Brown v. Board of Education*, the landmark Supreme Court case in which the policy of separate but equal schools for black and white students was found to be unconstitutional, was that creating schools where black and white students learned together "would weaken hateful stereotypes and promote interracial understanding among the young—and in time among society at large."[14] So says history professor James Patterson, who goes on to admit that "the complicated issues that *Brown* tried to resolve in 1954 still torment Americans a half a century later."[15]

Current statistics back up his claim. Despite increasing diversity in the United States, in the public schools, there is little contact between students who do not look like each other. According to the Urban Institute, "America's public schools are highly segregated by race and income."[16] In every state but two (New Mexico and Hawaii), "the average white student attends a school that is majority white."[17] In states with little diversity, this is not surprising. However, it holds true even in states such as California and New York, where the population is increasingly diverse.

Even when a school manages to be desegregated, social segregation becomes an obstacle. With so little physical contact, people tend to avoid social interaction as well. We will now explore the realities of social segregation.

Social Segregation

I didn't realize it at the time, but when my family moved to the east side and met Wesley and Ricky, they never had a thought about us having cookouts together or socializing in any way. Wesley expected that we would be "stand-offish and scared of the possibilities of being taken advantage of and robbed" in our new context. Ricky assumed from his past experiences with white people that we were better off than them and that that would be a barrier. It didn't matter that our yards were on the opposite sides of the same alley; we were still in different worlds, from their perspective.

A year later when we met Cortez, he admits, "I was intimidated by you guys." He assumed we held certain stereotypes and that we had come to help them. "It's usually the white person helping the black person out, and that's all I had ever seen before I met you. I didn't think that white people would want to associate with black people. I thought you guys would be more scared." Today at twenty-eight, Cortez realizes that our relationship actually taught him to not be intimidated by white people. He says, "You didn't take shit from me, so I had to be completely transparent with you. You could see right through." Because we had a relationship in which he was known, and it was safe, his perspective on white people changed. He knows not all white people are the same, but he assumes a more open stance toward them at this stage of his life.

In 1944, Gunnar Myrdal, a Swedish economist whose work later influenced the ruling in *Brown v. Board of Education*, stated that segregation "exerts its influence in an indirect and impersonal way: because Negro people do not live near white people, they cannot . . . associate with each other in the many activities founded on common neighborhoods."[18] According to Vela-McConnell, our workplaces, schools, and churches "are more socially integrated today than in the past." Because of this, "we like to imagine we live in a world in which there is egalitarianism and greater parity in status."[19] He cautions that we are deluding ourselves. Even here in my neighborhood, where black and white people *do* live near one another, they still do not generally work together to build a common neighborhood. I have heard more explicitly racist statements from my white neighbors in the city than I ever did from my suburban neighbors. We need something more than geographic integration.

According to Massey and Denton, segregation "created the structural conditions for the emergence of an oppositional culture."[20] This culture often devalues education, work, and marriage and encourages attitudes and behaviors that work against success in the larger (white) economy. It creates peer pressure to *not* succeed in school, as in Tyron's story in chapter 1. It has also resulted in the emergence of black English, "which has become progressively more distant from Standard American English."[21] This often puts its speakers at a disadvantage in school and work. When white middle-class people observe the behaviors and artifacts of this oppositional culture, they often do not have a context to understand the significance of them, and thus the already great social distance is increased.

I witness this oppositional culture every day in my neighborhood related to language use. Our students use phrases such as *she don't* and *he ain't* and *they is* as a matter of course. I used to try to correct these grammatical errors; it's an annoying hobby of mine to tell people how to speak (and spell and punctuate) correctly. What I did not initially realize is that there is another aspect to this issue of speech and language that is important, especially as it relates to social segregation. My friends are actually speaking a recognized dialect called Ebonics or African American Vernacular English. The Linguistic Society of America has recognized Ebonics as a dialect of the English language.[22] Although it has been characterized as merely "slang," "mutant," "lazy," or "broken" by speakers of standard English, the dialect has West African and Caribbean Creole roots and follows consistent patterns, such as pronouncing the "th" sound as "t" or "f," dropping final consonants, or using an invariant "be": *They be goin to do their maf homework.* So it is not so much that the students don't know about "proper" English as that they are not interested in speaking it. Thus, in a social situation involving black people and white people, there may be both a legitimate language barrier in place and an unwillingness by Ebonics speakers to conform to the dominant culture.

In one way, this can be seen as an activity similar to the one mentioned in chapter 1, in which students defiantly walk down the middle of the street blocking traffic. The urban school culture defines rebellious activity and academic failure as cool, and the limited interaction with the larger world, due to geographic and social segregation, means that other perspectives are not represented. In the IB program, for example, *which is in the same building where failure is believed to be cool*, there is an entirely different set of values in operation, which increases social distance and leads to very different outcomes.

My experience with St. Paul students and opposition mirrors research in Birmingham, England, and in South Texas. Social scientist Paul Willis found that the working-class boys he studied in Birmingham intentionally embraced the oppositional ideas of their class as they transitioned from secondary school to manual labor. He asserts that "working class lads come to take a hand in their own damnation."[23] Their oppositional stance basically ensured their oppression. My own neighborhood students share this skepticism about the value of mental over physical work, as well as their acceptance of filling their expected role in an unjust system.

Far from Birmingham, ethnographer Douglas Foley found that Mexican American students in South Texas also held mental work in low esteem. He asserts that this attitude is actually inculcated by teachers who convinced them that "they were dumb about books and learning Standard English. Years of failure had taught them to publicly reject, but privately internalize, the criticism of teachers."[24]

Whether the blame belongs on the students for their complicity in their own damnation or on the intentional actions of teachers, the results are the same. In over ten years working with teens at The Lift, we have had just two students graduate from college. Many others have started but not made it past the first year. In contrast, my son and all of his friends graduated from a suburban high school that clearly had a destination in mind for their students that did not involve manual labor. Among his group of nine friends, all graduated from college in four years. My daughter and her seven high school friends also all graduated in four years. I'm proud of my kids, and they are definitely smart, but the reason that they went to college and graduated in four years and Ricky, Wesley, and so many others did not is not because they are smarter.

These realities serve to broaden the already wide chasm between us. Beyond lacking a shared history—geographically or educationally, we are also lacking a basic understanding of one another's reality. Our limited experience with each other literally means we do not know how to interpret what would be obvious to those from the other tribe.

Wesley has a humorous description of how he viewed my family when we arrived in St. Paul and moved in across the alley from his family. He said we were the perfect family of happy white people, with two parents, two perfect children (a boy and a girl), a cute little dog, and two cars. We fit perfectly into the sitcom mold that had formed us in his mind. Nothing about how we lived was familiar to him, so he had to come up with a new script. Wesley and his friends decided my husband Dave must be a hit man of some kind. They decided this because Dave worked at home for a software company. This type of work was unfamiliar to the teens, and they surmised that, since we seemed to have so much money and Dave was at home most of the time, the plot in our sitcom must be that Dave was involved in some sort of secretive, very lucrative work. Cortez admits they hid in the bushes and staked out our house to see what was *really* going on. The guys' limited experience with my world caused them to incorrectly interpret things that other middle-class tribespeople would see as normal.

At The Lift, we have noticed that in our program for elementary-age children, the kids don't seem to care who looks like them. They eat and play games together, and I have never heard a racist word or any of the tribal behavior so common among adults. This starts to change in high school. Our teen program is made up of a majority of black students. As a rule, any white or Hispanic students who attended the elementary program disappear soon after graduating to the teen program.

Spelman College president Beverly Daniel Tatum has written

about this type of social segregation among students in her best-selling book, *Why Are All the Black Kids Sitting Together in the Cafeteria?*[25] She explains that as a society, we do not have the necessary skills and knowledge to talk about racial differences. Another issue pulling young people apart, according to Tatum, is that nonwhite youth, by virtue of their Otherness, tend to explore their racial identity development at a much younger age, often out of necessity. White youth are often not aware that they have a racial identity and since they are the majority, they are privileged to not have to think about it.

In an attempt to overcome these barriers, The Lift is intentional about hiring a staff that crosses lines of diversity at our job skills program at the Plaza Theater, which we've been running since 2013. In addition to a diverse staff, we also serve a clientele that includes individuals and groups from urban and suburban contexts, many different ethnic backgrounds, and people with various physical and mental disabilities. It's been interesting to observe how so many social differences pile in together in our tiny two-screen theater. When it comes to customer service, the differences become clear. When serving popcorn, some staff members tend to ask, "Would you like butter on that?" while others say, "Is there butter?" Some say, "You're welcome" when a customer thanks them; others say, "No problem." "Whatchuwant?" instead of "What would you like?" is another notable difference.

Staff members point out that the differences in speech cut across urban/suburban lines as well as ethnic differences. Depending on who the customer is, these word choices sometimes work and sometimes don't. Our white, middle-aged operations manager continues to slap his forehead about what he sometimes sees as lapses in good customer service. The staff have a good-natured phrase they use when he gets frustrated. "He be red!" they say.

Unfortunately, there are limited contexts that bring such a diverse group of people together. This means limited information and resources flow between tribes. I was once at a social event that included some very wealthy people. In a conversation with one business owner about what I do for a living, I went into an explanation of the problems our students face at home and in school.

I explained that there were so many factors contributing to the achievement gap that it was nearly impossible to know where to begin. There are problems at school, such as overcrowded classrooms, outdated or nonexistent textbooks, and very few black teachers for the kids to look up to as role models. The problems at home include the lack of a computer, a printer, school supplies, space to do homework, and parental support. Kids miss the bus and the family has no car to drive them. Some kids miss school to babysit younger siblings when mom has to work. I explained all this, and this man was aghast. "Nobody knows this," he almost yelled. "People need to know this."

The people who live it every day know it. Many of the people who are in a position to help with some of these barriers to education do not know it, because they live in an entirely different world, their kids attend private or wealthy suburban schools, and in our segregated world, there are simply no contact points where this story can be seen or heard. It makes little difference whether we are discussing geographic or social segregation; the tribes find a way to carry on as though the other tribe does not exist.

I was in my thirties before I decided to forgo my inherited privilege of pretending other tribes did not exist. I decided I wanted my own and my children's view of the world expanded to include the perspective of the Other, and so we made the move from the suburbs to the city. Some of my friends and family did not see the value in this decision. It's not just that people do not know *how* to desegregate our world; it's that most do not even *want* to desegregate it. My own past experiences working in a pizza restaurant, law firm, consulting firm, brokerage office, and college admissions office have not put me in the path of any diversity initiatives. Efforts to diversify the churches I've attended or worked in have been largely unsuccessful. According to sociologists Michael Emerson and Christian Smith, "The structure of religion in America is conducive to freeing groups from the direct control of other groups, but not to addressing the fundamental divisions that exist in our current racialized society."[26] Their surveys of white Christians revealed an understanding of racism as a purely individual issue (to be dealt with on an individual basis) with little or no understanding of the racist structures in our society. We will look more in-depth at this issue in chapter 5.

I've also seen few efforts toward what I see as the very important work of diversifying our personal lives. I've heard white ministers and church board members lament the lack of diversity in their programs, but they don't have any diversity in their personal lives! They want black people in the choir, but not around their dining room table. It seems like people want to avoid diversity on a personal level, while embracing it for appearances or for business reasons.

#

Geographic and social segregation contribute to the lack of understanding and the presence of stereotypes between tribes. If we don't live near or socialize with people who look different than us, the tribal boundaries will continue to be enforced. Those boundaries are also enforced by the usually unspoken barrier of class, to which we now turn.

Notes

1. Tullian Tchividjian, *Unfashionable: Making a Difference in the World by Being Different* (Colorado Springs, CO: Multnomah, 2009), 100.

2. Minnesota Compass, "Planning District 5: Payne-Phalen Neighborhood," https://tinyurl.com/y5t4fe9t.

3. James A. Vela-McConnell, *Unlikely Friends: Bridging Ties and Diverse Friendships* (Lanham, MD: Lexington, 2011), 29.

4. Douglas S. Massey and Nancy A. Denton, *American Apartheid: Segregation and the Making of the Underclass* (Cambridge, MA: Harvard University Press, 1993).

5. Ronald Takaki, *A Different Mirror: A History of Multicultural America* (Boston: Little, Brown, 1993).

6. Massey and Denton, *American Apartheid*, 39.

7. Statistical Atlas, "Overview of Detroit, Michigan," https://tinyurl.com/y6q6ayk4; "Overview of the Oakland Charter

Township, Oakland County, Michigan," https://tinyurl.com/y2cc3rqn.

8. Massey and Denton, *American Apartheid*, 81.

9. Massey and Denton, *American Apartheid*, 2.

10. "The Persisting Myth That Black and White Schools Are Equally Funded," *The Journal of Blacks in Higher Education* 22 (1998): 17–20.

11. Matt Barnum, "Exclusive Data: City Schools vs. Suburban Schools, See Where Security Officers Outnumber the Counselors," *The 74*, March 7, 2017, https://tinyurl.com/y34p79eb.

12. Lydia O'Connor, "'Ghetto Tracker,' App That Helps Rich Avoid Poor, Is as Bad as It Sounds," *The Huffington Post*, September 4, 2013, https://tinyurl.com/y5zatv93.

13. O'Connor, "'Ghetto Tracker.'"

14. James T. Patterson, *Brown v. Board of Education: A Civil Rights Milestone and Its Troubled Legacy* (New York: Oxford University Press, 2001), xviii.

15. Patterson, *Brown v. Board of Education*, xiv.

16. Reed Jordan, "America's Public Schools Remain Highly Segregated," *Urban Wire* (blog), Urban Institute, August 26, 2014, https://tinyurl.com/yygsdk9z.

17. Reed Jordan, "America's Public Schools."

18. Gunnar Myrdal, *An American Dilemma: The Negro Problem and Modern Democracy* (New York: Harper), quoted in Massey and Denton, *American Apartheid*, 3.

19. Vela-McConnell, *Unlikely Friends*, 59.

20. Massey and Denton, *American Apartheid*, 8.

21. Massey and Denton, *American Apartheid*, 13.

22. John R. Rickford, "What Is Ebonics (African American English)?" Linguistic Society of America, https://tinyurl.com/y3ge2e3l.

23. Paul Willis, *Learning to Labor: How Working Class Kids Get Working Class Jobs* (Farnborough, England: Saxon, 1977), 3.

24. Douglas E. Foley, *Learning Capitalist Culture: Deep in the Heart of Tejas* (Philadelphia: University of Pennsylvania Press, 1990), 89.

25. Beverly Daniel Tatum, *Why Are All the Black Kids Sitting Together in the Cafeteria? And Other Conversations about Race* (New York: Basic), 2003.

26. Michael O. Emerson and Christian Smith, *Divided by Faith: Evangelical Religion and the Problem of Race in America* (New York: Oxford University Press, 2000), 18.

3.

Tribal Customs

> Over time, this growing tendency of like marrying like will only reinforce clustering and geographic sorting along class lines, giving the emerging map of social, economic, and cultural segregation even greater permanence.
>
> —Richard Florida[1]

When I was growing up, we had an etiquette book in the house that my sister regularly consulted and schooled me on. I learned the rules for weddings, proper apparel, gift giving, elevators, silverware, and other important topics. When using an elevator, I learned, you let everyone off before you attempt to get on. I had a very hard time keeping the rule that you are not to stare at people, and I was confused by the fact that although bodily noises in public are rude, my four brothers seemed not to know this. Apparently, they were not consulting my sister and her book on some topics. In addition to the many enlightening rules in this book, I learned from my family what "RSVP" meant, that you never ask for a gift, that there is a correct way to answer the telephone, that rock and roll is suspect, and that art museums are cool places. I learned the hard way not to ask older women their age.

Despite this effective schooling on issues of middle-class behavior, I didn't know I was learning rules of class, and I rarely thought about social class in my pre-urban life, other than the frequent references to the "middle class," which I apparently was a part of. It was a throwaway category, as almost everyone in my life was also middle class. Upper-class and lower-class people were out there somewhere, but I didn't have to deal with them. After I moved into a diverse neighborhood among people who would be labeled as "lower class," I began to recognize how wide the gap is between classes—perhaps wider than between races. I was surprised by the stark contrast between my own and my new neighbors' attitudes and activities related to education, marriage, parenting, financial management, the arts, and pretty much everything else. As I gained an understanding of class differences, I became much more aware of the judgmental language and attitudes I had carried. This judgment was often around modes of dress (too tight, too loud, too short) or types of cars (too flashy, too expensive, too ghetto). True to tribal behavior, these things are not seen as mere differences; they are seen as evidence of inferior taste.

Class Defined

So I knew I was middle class, and I knew that meant there was something above me and something below me. I had no idea that society meted out power to people based on their current place in this hierarchy. I also didn't know it was possible to move among the levels. But class is a fluid category, closely related to status and power in society. According to the *Concise Encyclopedia of Pragmatics*, class and status "are central concepts in attempts to describe and explain social inequality and divisions arising from industrialization, capitalism, and democracy spanning two centuries."[2] For Karl Marx, class was primarily about a person's relationship to the means of production. The proletariat were workers exploited by the capitalist bourgeoisie, who claimed ownership of the surplus value created by the workers.

Sociologist Max Weber expanded on Marx's definition and argued that status and power were on equal footing with class. Class became about more than the relationship to the means of production. People could band together in "status groupings" along political, religious, or ethnic lines, thus upsetting Marx's clear delineations between the workers and owners.[3] They could also gain individual status through their accomplishments. People in politics could gain power regardless of their wealth or status.

Both Marx and Weber saw society in terms of constantly conflicting human needs and interests. Certain members of society were privileged to own property and excluded others from using or benefitting from that property. The excluded members owned only their own labor and were forced to sell it for a wage they had little control over. Thus, the classes were always in competition with one another. In contrast, sociologist Emile Durkheim's approach to class, which is called *structuralism,* led to an understanding of class as a category as opposed to a social relationship: "By measuring income levels or classifying people into occupations, one can determine social class."[4] In this understanding, "class order represents relationships that are potentially, if not actually, a harmonious and rational social division of labor" that serves the social good.[5]

In a nutshell, Marx and Weber saw class as a constant conflict between groups with opposing interests, while Durkheim and his followers saw class as a neutral system of categorization based merely on externals. Life would be much easier if classes could be neutral categories that people fit into based on their jobs. However, I believe Marx and Weber had it right when they saw class and conflict as bedfellows. The average CEO earns 380 times the *average* worker's, and at a handful of companies, they earn over 1,000 times as much.[6] It would be hard to argue that there is not conflict inherent in a system that produces such numbers.

There is an ongoing dialogue in academia about the nature of classes. "Are classes a scientific construct invented by people or do they exist in reality?" asks Pierre Bourdieu, a French sociologist whose writing focused on power dynamics in a society.[7] That is, are they invented by people with power, or are they an essential part of how humans are defined? For my purposes, the important question is not so much whether they are constructed by humans or part of their very essence, but rather what impact their presumed existence has on society. Bourdieu insists that a class only exists if someone "with a reasonable chance of being taken seriously" as a member of that group asserts its existence.[8] And, unfortunately, people within the lower classes are generally not taken seriously. Those with power may use it to define the structure of society in ways that legitimize their power, as though it were part of the very nature of reality. My discussion of class in this chapter assumes its existence as a social, if not ontological, reality and will focus on ritual and relational distinctions between people of differing classes. In chapter 7, I will explore in more depth the role of economics in class distinctions.

The Intersection of Race and Class

There is an ongoing debate about whether race or class is the major point of division in society today. Legal scholars Richard Delgado and Jean Stefancic explain the controversy as between those who assert that racism is the means by which white people assume priority, and those who blame a "culture of poverty" that includes crime, unemployment, lack of education, and broken families as the reason minorities lack material advantages.[9] It comes down to who you blame for the problem. Those who see class as the reason for social division tend to blame the poor for lacking resources, which is why they are lower class. Those who see race as the reason see ongoing racism perpetuating division.

The distinctions of class and race go hand in hand. According to sociologist Richard Sennett, "Economic inequalities translate in everyday experience as social distance."[10] Since a disproportionate percentage of black families live below the poverty line, whatever social distance already exists due to segregation or racism is increased. For these reasons, it is impossible to speak of class without issues of race being present and vice versa. Nevertheless, it is worthwhile to explore the two issues separately, as the two cannot be entirely conflated.

The distinction between race and class is further confused by the fact that my own story of crossing lines of race and class conflates these issues. That is, my story includes mostly middle-class white people and under-resourced black people—and rarely middle-class black people and under-resourced white people. Because of this admittedly narrow account, the decision to include a story under the category of class rather than race is purely subjective, but I generally include stories here that involve economic considerations, and whose central point extends beyond what can be adequately explained merely by an examination of racial issues.

The specific impact of class on the type of reciprocal relationship I am studying can be described in the broad tribal categories of *relational* distinctions of class and *ritual* distinctions of class. Relational distinctions are about the different ways individuals in different classes relate socially to others in their tribe, as well as to those from other tribes. Ritual distinctions, on the other hand, relate to tribal behaviors that identify ingroup and outgroup members.

You can often recognize relational distinctions by differing uses of the English language in social situations: What topics do we favor, and how formal or casual is our vocabulary? Ritual distinctions can often be seen in aesthetics: How much attention does our wardrobe or hairstyle attract when we are among members of other tribes? Let's explore each of these distinctions of class—*relational* and *ritual*—in turn.

Relational Distinctions of Class

I learned fairly quickly that the usual middle-class social ice-breaker, "What do you do for a living?" was not appropriate in my new context. I asked this question a few times and received a sort of mumbled nonresponse, followed by the person I had asked changing the subject or wandering away from me. I began to notice that no one was asking me that question. In my old neighborhood, this question came right after "Hello." While middle-class people tend to closely identify with their vocation, the same cannot be said of those living in poverty. Many of my neighbors are unemployed or working at low-wage menial jobs that they are not anxious to claim as part of their identity. I learned that starting the conversation around topics of children and family is a better approach in this context, but not until I had erred by starting off with questions of livelihood a few times.

I also learned that asking, "Where do you live?" right after meeting someone set me apart as an outsider. This is another rather formulaic launch into middle-class conversations. In my current context, it is properly asked, "Where do you *stay*?" Although it seems such a small thing, it is a marker that reveals whether you belong. Asking this question properly has the power to designate me as a cultural insider. Ernest told me that when someone asked, "Where do you live?" his first thought was "What do you mean 'Where do I live?' I live everywhere!" The question made no sense to him. He also cautioned that trying too hard to be an insider can backfire. There is a correct way, he said, to ask, "Where do you stay?" His explanation seems to indicate that articulating too clearly makes the person sound like a fake.

There are many examples of these types of semantic differences, and I find myself codeswitching as I move between environments. When I'm in the suburbs, I say, "Wait a minute" to mean a short period of time. When I'm in the city, I say, "It's going to be a minute" to mean a long period of time. These semantic distinctions add to the list of challenges of getting to know someone who doesn't look like us.

As described in chapter 2, my black friends engage in another form of codeswitching around the use of Ebonics and standard English. At home, students engage in speech patterns that are not acceptable in school. Despite research that shows that students speaking nonstandard English are "transferring in the detailed grammar patterns of their home language,"[11] they are still usually required to follow the rules of standard English if they want to succeed in school. And this ability to codeswitch is even more critical in the job market. Ebonics may have been recognized as a legitimate vernacular dialect, but it is also seen as lacking prestige by middle-class employers. It puts young people of color at a distinct disadvantage in the context of a job interview. Saying, "I ain't got no problem working the weekends," while clearly communicating the point, will likely cause a middle-class employer concern as he ponders this candidate's ability to communicate with customers. In this situation, there are several levels of evaluation going on, and the interviewee is likely unaware of some of them.

It can be a brave thing for a person to reach across lines of race and class and engage someone who is different from themselves. When that engagement is challenged by differing ideas of what constitutes an appropriate opening question or by the use of a different form of the English language, the attempt to connect is often aborted.

For some of these reasons, Lift events in our neighborhood often end up segregated, a form of microsocial segregation, if you will. If black people stake out the living room, white people stake out the patio, or vice versa. On the surface, this may appear to be an issue of race, but it is at least equally, and perhaps more so, an issue of class. Wesley explains that it's "easier to associate with what you're used to." Conversations are more fluid when "you don't have to go out of your way to explain yourself." I observed this phenomenon when I was on the deck at a cookout, talking to other white middle-class parents who have children in college. We were talking about their classes and activities, and when they would be coming home for a visit. I noticed that Jaleesa* and a few other black neighbors were sitting in the screened-in porch. I went in to join their conversation, the topic of which was how all the temp jobs they had recently been getting calls for required them to have a car, which they did not have. These topics are worlds apart, and it drove home to me again how difficult it can be to develop relationships across the many barriers that exist.

Sociologist Erving Goffman helps further explain this social phenomenon. He argues that people claim social value for themselves by their conduct in social situations. He explains the devastating "loss of face" that can occur when social situations are presented in which a participant does not know how to demonstrate expected and appropriate behavior.[12] When my friends from different backgrounds are out of their comfort zone, they often become awkward and very nervous, which seems to lead them to seek out a "safer" conversation where they can save face. This highlights the difficulty of moving beyond niceties to genuine relationships of the sort that can be transformative: we cannot even attend a neighborhood cookout without fear of losing face. Goffman notes that even a middle- or upper-class black person may avoid "certain face-to-face contacts with whites in order to protect the self-evaluation projected by his clothes and manner."[13]

Many times over the past decade, I have found myself the only white person among a crowd of black people. Even after many years, I still need a translator to understand what is going on at times. The cultural references, slang, and idioms are different. I've used the online *Urban Dictionary* once I get home to try to figure out what I was confused about. I kept hearing the word "swag" all the time but couldn't figure out what it meant by the context. During a trip to Valleyfair, a local amusement park, Ricky pointed out a person walking by and said something along the lines of "That's some crazy-looking swag." When I asked what that meant, the kids all laughed at me. I looked it up on *Urban Dictionary*, and I still didn't understand it! It is apparently the "most used word in the whole fucking universe," and if you have it, you wear your hat sideways.[14] I recently posed the question about swag again, and the kids rolled their eyes and told me it's just about your clothing and "look." Cortez says, "It's the way you carry yourself and talk smooth."

I have learned to be comfortable when I'm the minority, but I can tell at times that my presence makes other people nervous. It's like they aren't sure who invited someone from the opposing tribe. My dress and language can still sometimes make me stand out. Dee has joked that she must have a dictionary on hand sometimes to understand what I am saying. I consult the *Urban Dictionary* and Dee consults Webster, as we each try to figure out what's going on. In this diverse context I now live and work in, I've realized how valuable the former can be. It's a great tool for people like me who are committed to engaging people who are not just like them.

Erving Goffman uses a metaphor of the stage and performance to examine human interaction. Social life, he says, consists of performances by which people try to move up the social ladder—or at least try not to move down it. To do this, they must learn the proper lines (preferably delivered in standard English) and obtain the "proper sign-equipment."[15] Since the most important sign-equipment in contemporary society are symbols of wealth, such as cars, houses, and designer clothing, and since a high percentage of black people continue to be mired in poverty, Massey and Denton's assertion that blacks have formed an oppositional culture that has different status symbols and value assignations makes sense. It also takes black people and white people further along on divergent paths.

Ritual Distinctions of Class

Ancient tribes had rituals that defined their social interactions and served as markers for who was in the tribe and who was not. One example I've experienced is the rituals surrounding the Christmas holiday. In the world I came from, most gifts were put under the tree late on Christmas Eve, and they were all opened in the morning, with one person at a time opening a gift so that everyone could see it. Most of my St. Paul friends have very different rituals. Often the gifts don't get wrapped at all but are just given to the recipient sometime before Christmas. Many families open all gifts on Christmas Eve. Some of those who wait until Christmas morning have a mad dash to the tree, in which everyone dives into the gifts and opens them all at the same time. Cortez has a simple explanation: "Black people don't like holding onto things." He tells the story of one of his brothers stealing one of his Christmas presents from under the tree when they were children. He denied it at the time but admitted it ten years later. Cortez grew up with the fear that "anything nice is going to be taken," so you grab your presents while you still can.

Hair rituals also play a major role in the contemporary tribal class divide. For starters, almost every white middle-class person who comes into our neighborhood to volunteer has an odd obsession to ask about and touch black people's hair. It's crazy how often it happens. It results in awkward encounters, and it clearly identifies outgroup members—basically white people who keep bringing up hair! In this situation, culturally competent white people just don't do this. They know the rules. I have learned the vocabulary, ritual, and set of rules around hair in this tribe. These rules are very different from any rules in the tribe I grew up in. Of note, a "perm" in my tribe of origin was meant to make your hair curly. In my neighborhood, a perm is meant to straighten the hair. It took me longer than it should have to recognize this semantic difference.

Hair is central in my community in a way that it never was in my middle-class world. There are several stores in my neighborhood filled with row after row of wigs and panels of human and synthetic hair. Some of these panels cost over $100, and at least two are required for the hairstyle (called a weave), not including the hairstylist's fee. And it has to be redone every two to three months. And almost everyone regularly has one. People who live as much as 300 percent below the poverty line have this as a major budgeting priority. Some of our teenage girls end up in tears when their weave is falling apart or sections of their glued-on hair are coming off and they have no money to get it fixed. It is often impossible for them to wear their hair natural, as the chemicals or extreme stress from braids and weaves have created bald spots on their head.

I decided to get a hairstyle called microbraids after I had lived here for a couple of years. This involved having extra hair woven in with my natural hair to make hundreds of tiny braids all over my head. It took more than ten hours to get it done. Of note here is a point related to the section on time below: I learned that regardless of how long someone told me it would take them to do my hair, it would take at least twice that long! I missed a wedding ceremony before I understood this reality. It's also very painful, which no one bothered to mention. I couldn't sleep for the first few nights, and I had to carry around a spray can of oil to keep my scalp from cracking open. No joke. I was experiencing a ritual that most of my black female friends had experienced many times, and they were excited that I was joining their club. I boarded an airplane wearing my microbraids, and a black woman I had never met came up and thanked me for having that hairstyle because now I could understand what it's like. A couple of years ago, I had my hair dreadlocked, and I now have weekly conversations with strangers with dreads, mostly black men, about our hairstyles.

A few points about cultural appropriation are in order here. White people have been accused of stealing cultural signs and symbols from black people and appropriating them in ways that suit them and do not necessarily respect the origins of the signs and symbols. One of the areas of discussion around appropriation is about hairstyles. I have dreads, which are basically matted ropes of hair, achieved and maintained by doing not much of anything besides leaving them mostly alone (and sometimes rolling them).

I've had a few hairstyles over the past several years that clearly come from a culture other than my own. It was a friend from the east side who talked me into getting microbraids the first time, and my neighbor did my hair in her living room. I sat all day and into the evening with her and various friends who stopped by, taking turns doing sections of my hair. It was a communal event, and I can't say that I have ever had an experience like it. There was no clock-watching (except by me), and it was obvious that I was participating in a ritual that was an ordinary one in the lives of the women I met. They seemed very interested in this Happy White Lady who wanted to participate in this ritual with them.

After years of trying various kinds of weaves, I landed with my current dreadlocks, which I've worn for several years. According to journalist Emanuella Grinberg, "Historians and anthropologists have found evidence of the 'do in ancient Egypt, Germanic tribes, Vikings, Pacific Islanders, early Christians, the Aborigines and the New Guineans as well as the Somali, the Galla, the Maasai, the Ashanti and the Fulani tribes of Africa."[16] Nevertheless, white people with dreads have been publicly accused of cultural appropriation over the past few years, with the claim being that white people have stolen this hairstyle from black people, who claim it as part of their culture.

This debate on cultural appropriation is taking place at the popular level, with researchers and academics almost universally acknowledging that there is no way to use history to prove any one culture's claim on the hairstyle.[17] Writer and dreadwearer Jamia Wilson is fine with anyone wearing dreads, but explains that "if you're going to take on something that does have sacred and historic significance and an unequal history of power dynamics it's important to honor that history. Be an ally by knowing your stuff and being respectful and acknowledging where it comes from."[18]

When I had my hair braided or dreaded, I did not have a thought about cultural appropriation. That criticism showed up in the media a few years later. I was simply participating in rituals that were unique to my new context. I have never had a single person question my hairstyle. It has emerged from my values, my chosen lifestyle, my friends, and my changing tastes. Cortez says my hair-style actually creates "common ground" and laughs off the idea that I am appropriating black culture. Dee, who also has dread-locks, says, "I know you. I know you're not appropriating any-thing. We both locked our hair because it's easier!"

Returning to the point on hair as it relates to class, Wilson also says, "Hairstyles are not innocuous. There are gendered and racial-ized connotations and stereotypes attached to them."[19] A friend of mine who is a member of a country club in St. Paul said I would never be allowed to join with my hair dreaded. Although I am an educated white middle-class person, I apparently have low-class hair.

Another important category of rituals in my neighborhood involves food. Holiday events in our neighborhood involve expen-sive dishes served in quantities enough for an army. When we first started having Thanksgiving dinners with a group of neighbors, I tried so hard to tell people living at or over the edge of poverty that they didn't need to bring anything. They ignored me and showed up with huge quantities of food! Apparently, no social event can be had without macaroni and cheese. It is a point of pride, as well as an expectation, that if we are going to celebrate together, certain foods must be included. Families will live on noodles for a week to make sure they can afford the holiday dinner.

Conversely, the day-to-day meal rituals I grew up with (prayer before the meal, everyone eating together around the table, TV off) are mostly unheard of in my current context. Most kids who have lived with us had no experience of sitting around the dinner table discussing the events of the day. Their big social meals were reserved for holidays; most other days found the family eating in the living room in front of the TV. They thought I was weird (and probably annoying) when I initiated our game of "Best Thing/ Worst Thing" in which everyone shares those aspects of their day at our dinner table. It's a chance to reflect on how our day went and share the highlights with the family. One teen told me that until he ate at my house, no one had ever asked him about his day. Cortez said, "It was hard for me to answer because I had never thought about how my day was or how I was doing. It was kind of scary because I didn't know the answer." Now, he says, this ritual is something he wants to do with his own kids.

A great place to observe further ritual differences between classes is at a movie theater. My culture says that when you go to a movie, you sit still, you shut up, you don't text, and you don't answer your phone. When I go to the movies with my neighbors of any age, many of these things happen throughout the movie. It's not because they are socially inferior; it's because their tribe has different rules than mine. I have a tendency to compartmentalize, so when I am at a movie, I don't want to be distracted by the real world. I don't want someone's text or phone conversation to draw me out of my movie-watching experience. I don't want people bugging me. My friends' culture seems to operate more holistically. Texting, getting up for snacks, talking back to the screen, and discussing the plot makes moviegoing an interactive experience.

I went to see the movie *Precious: Based on the Novel "Push" by Sapphire* with a bunch of black neighborhood teens and a couple of their moms. I had already seen the movie once, and it made me cry with its themes of abuse, incest, brokenness, and hopelessness. I had a very different experience this time around. I was surprised when one of the moms laughed during what I experienced as the most hopeless scene in the movie. The teens talked back to the characters they disagreed with, such as the mother of the main character, and expressed support to the teens they identified with. The theater was in the suburbs, and there was a diverse population in attendance. It felt like in addition to the one on the screen, we had a potential real-life drama in the theater. None of the white people made a sound, but I saw sideways glances. I was torn between asking my friends to be quiet and defending them. I saw the potential for stereotypes about uptight suburbanites and rude city people to be further entrenched. "It's okay to accept that we're different," says Dee. But, at least on this occasion, watching the differences play out in real life was very uncomfortable for me. It is somewhat ironic that I was watching a movie about the suffering of a black urban teen and wanted to tell the black urban teens I was with how they should respond.

Sociologist Pierre Bourdieu asserts that the "most intolerable thing for those who regard themselves as the possessors of legitimate culture is the sacrilegious reuniting of tastes which taste dictates shall be separated."[20] Humans have an aversion to different lifestyles, and with the aforementioned oppositional culture that has emerged in some black communities, the divide between rich and poor culture has grown. According to Bourdieu, cultural preferences are products of one's upbringing and education, yet another strike against shared life experiences ever emerging from within our segregated and stratified society. It is this closed-mindedness toward what is different that Bourdieu names as the "strongest barrier between the classes."[21] Fashion and time are two other areas where I have seen this sort of barrier in action.

When I first met Cortez, he frequently wore a too-large powder blue velour FUBU sweat suit with some fancy embroidery on it and some heavy bling around his neck, usually involving large shiny dollar signs. I used to joke with the boys that if my son Connor showed up at his suburban high school wearing an outfit like that, it would be the event of the season as people tried to figure out what was going on. The color, the fabric, the style, the size, the bling. All of it would have been called into question. Was he in costume for a play? Was it a joke? On Cortez at his urban high school, the outfit was just business as usual.

When we first moved to our neighborhood, the fashion for young men was to wear white tall tees, which hung down nearly to the knee, jeans that were several sizes too big and were often belted below the hips, and perfectly white (and often expensive) tennis shoes. Among Connor's suburban friends, narrow jeans, Converse high-tops, and graphic tees were the thing. His friends also removed all the tags from their clothing, while teens in my neighborhood would then, and still do, leave tags and stickers on clothing as a fashion statement.

Beliefs about, managing, and the use of time are probably the most significant differences I had to learn about and navigate. Due to years of messaging in my culture about the need to be "on time" for everything, this one took me a while to learn. The first instance of running into this difference was when Dee invited me to her daughter's birthday party. The party was on a Sunday evening from 6:00 to 8:00. We are middle class, so we arrived at 6:00 and found we were the only ones there. Dee was still cooking and getting the house ready. We took a seat on the porch and waited. Extended family members began to show up between 7:30 and 8:00—the time we expected to be going home. Later, Wesley and Ricky explained to me that I didn't understand CPT—or Colored People Time.

I understand it now. When we started The Lift, we had a twelve-passenger van that I used to pick up the kids and bring them to our building. If I spoke to them at noon on a Saturday and told them I would pick them up at 4:30, I would show up at 4:30, call their phone, and get no answer. I would go to the door and find out they were taking a shower or had gone to the store. This was not a once-in-a-while occurrence; it was a constant norm. If I told them we were going roller-skating or bowling in a week, the day would come, and they would have no recollection of the previously announced plans. A neighbor kept missing her doctor appointments, and I found out she didn't have a calendar. I printed one for her, and we wrote her appointments on it and stuck it to her refrigerator with magnets. She still missed her next appointment, however, because she forgot to look at the calendar.

This view of time is a major class distinction. In my middle-class tribe, time is to be managed, and the focus is on the future; in the tribe of my neighbors, the focus is on the present. This initially drove me crazy, but I have learned to relax. I had no choice. I wasn't doing anything but harming myself physically by stressing about a situation that repeated itself every day and was out of my control. I remember driving the van with my heart pounding because I knew, once again, we would be late for whatever we were doing. I began to realize there were more important things going on in the lives of my students, and that I was missing out on the chance to engage on these other topics because I was constantly worrying about what time it was and irritated when people were late. It wasn't helping anyone, and we still weren't on time.

As I began to relax about this a little bit, I realized that the students were more open to listening to me because I was not coming across as such a judgmental bitch. Over the years, many of the students *have* learned that the world of jobs and school does not run on CPT. The idea of time as a social construct had never occurred to me. In my culture, time is an absolute, and starting and ending times are to be honored at all costs. Over the past decade, I have lost my tendency to obsess or worry about time. I didn't realize the world wouldn't end if a meeting started a little late or went a little long. This is just one of the gifts of reciprocity I will discuss in chapter 10.

Differences in seemingly minor things such as vocabulary, movie theater etiquette, and hairstyles make up one part of the class divide. Although they may seem insignificant, they create awkward interactions and lead to misunderstandings. They define who is in and who is out. The deeper issue related to class is about the power differential between classes. From my experience, it is the awkward interactions in movie theaters or misunderstandings about hair that create social distance, and without a context to bridge that distance, misunderstanding and judgment will continue, and the power structure will not be challenged. This is a heavy burden to be borne by a trip to the movies.

Class and Power

Brazilian educator Paulo Freire provides additional insight into the divide between classes. He argues that the oppressors (the rich) believe it is their right to *have*, and that they *have* because of their own effort. Those who do not have enough are "incompetent and lazy" as well as ungrateful for the sometime generosity shown by their oppressors.[22] As a result, the oppressors must keep an eye on the oppressed, whom they view as potential enemies. This is not a recipe for building harmonious cross-class relationships. It is also a theme that appears frequently in our political discourse. According to journalist Evan Popp, this is because "the very notion that government should help those less fortunate came under attack in the 1980s by a renewed right wing intent on destroying social safety-nets. President Ronald Reagan's 'pull yourself up by your bootstraps' revolution changed the political and public mindset toward poverty."[23] Moving ahead a few decades, we actually see both political parties either ignoring or maligning the poor.[24]

Outside of politics, this class divide is exacerbated by attempts by resourced people to "save the poor" or "liberate the oppressed." These efforts are often misguided, as the rich do not invite the participation of the poor and oppressed in their liberation goal, with the result that the oppressed are "treated as objects which must be saved from a burning building" and "transformed into masses which can be manipulated."[25] This brings to mind Freire's false generosity, in which generosity becomes a tool to ensure that the oppressed remain so. Those who dispense this sort of generosity, says Freire, "become desperate at the slightest threat to its source."[26]

I have had many conversations over the years that exemplify this attitude. In conversation with a white middle-class person, I will mention that I live in the city and work with at-risk kids and families. In many cases, the person launches into a diatribe about the problems with welfare and how people cheat the system, and they share their proposals about how the situation should be fixed. This despite the person not knowing a single poor person. They almost never ask for *my* opinion about the problems or possible solutions, despite the fact that I just told them I have lived in this context for years. However they formed their opinions, they didn't want me messing with them. Sennett defines the French word *ressentiment* as "the feeling of ordinary people that the elite does not know much about their own problems first-hand, even though presuming to speak on their behalf."[27] We need an English word for that!

For middle-class people, it goes beyond merely recognizing difference. There is usually a judgment attached. Sociologist Herbert Gans says that the poor "are inevitably charged with the failure to adhere to one or more mainstream values by their behavior."[28] He offers the example of the label "welfare recipient," which refers specifically to economic dependency, but also tends to implicitly refer to a lack of family values: "failing to get married, being sexually promiscuous, raising school dropouts and delinquent youngsters, as well as giving birth to another generation of unmarried mothers who will turn welfare dependence into a permanent state."[29] The people using these labels (often politicians) are people who have power in society. Placing these labels on disempowered people further silences their voices.

Whenever I am in meetings that are about topics such as how to fight poverty or homelessness, I suggest that it would be helpful to have a person who has lived through these difficulties as part of the conversation early on. It is either ignorance or arrogance that makes people think they are doing good by attempting to solve the problems of others without seeking the input of those others. When I bring this up, everyone in the meeting nods their head and agrees that we need that input, but it has been my experience that most of the planning takes place without that voice present, although sometimes a token poor black person is brought in at the end once all of the decisions are made.

#

Although classism and racism are intertwined, judgments related to class seem to be more about whose way of life is better or who has better taste. There exists the hope that people from the lower class might become educated and formulate an acceptable aesthetic that allows them to be accepted into the middle class. There is also the assumption that that is everyone's goal. Racism, on the other hand, is a whole different story. The judgment is about *who* a person is rather than merely how they live. I believe it is the biggest barrier to building relationships across tribal lines, and we will now turn to it.

Notes

1. Richard Florida, *Who's Your City? How the Creative Economy Is Making Where to Live the Most Important Decision of Your Life* (New York: Basic, 2009), 285–86.

2. D. F. Brown, "Social Class and Status," in *Concise Encyclopedia of Pragmatics,* ed. J. L. Mey (Oxford: Elsevier, 2006), 952.

3. Brown, "Social Class and Status," 953.

4. Brown, "Social Class and Status," 954.

5. Jake Ryan and Charles Sackrey, *Strangers in Paradise: Academics from the Working Class* (Boston: South End, 1984), 106.

6. Jennifer Liberto, "CEO Pay Is 380 Times Average Worker's—AFL-CIO," *CNN Money,* April 19, 2012, https://tinyurl.com/yyljzdje.

7. Pierre Bourdieu, "What Makes a Social Class? On the Theoretical and Practical Existence of Groups," *Berkeley Journal of Sociology* 32 (1987): 2.

8. Bourdieu, "What Makes a Social Class?," 15.

9. Richard Delgado and Jean Stefancic, *Critical Race Theory: An Introduction* (New York: New York University Press, 2012).

10. Richard Sennett, *Together: The Rituals, Pleasures and Politics of Cooperation* (New Haven, CT: Yale University Press, 2012), 7.

11. Rebecca S. Wheeler and Rachel Swords, *Code-Switching: Teaching Standard English in Urban Classrooms* (Urbana, IL: National Council of Teachers of English, 2006), 11.

12. Erving Goffman, *Interaction Ritual: Essays in Face-to-Face Behavior* (Chicago: Aldine, 1967), 10.

13. Goffman, *Interaction Ritual*, 15.

14. "Swag," *Urban Dictionary,* submitted by jonnypage on July 20, 2012, accessed July 30, 2016, https://tinyurl.com/y3xqmv4j.

15. Erving Goffman, *The Presentation of Self in Everyday Life* (Garden City, NY: Doubleday, 1959), 36.

16. Emanuella Grinberg, "Dear White People with Dreadlocks: Some Things to Consider," *CNN,* April 1, 2016, https://tinyurl.com/yyj-gauuv.

17. See, for example: Bert Ashe, *Twisted: My Dreadlock Chronicles*

(Evanston, IL: Agate Bolden, 2015); Sede Alonge, "Why the Fuss Over a White Woman Having a Black Hairstyle?," *Guardian*, July 24, 2015, https://tinyurl.com/y6aoxsgl.

18. Grinberg, "Dear White People."

19. Grinberg, "Dear White People."

20. Bourdieu, *Distinction: A Social Critique of the Judgment of Taste*, trans. Richard Nice (Cambridge, MA: Harvard University Press, 1984), 56.

21. Bourdieu, *Distinction*, 56.

22. Paulo Freire, *Pedagogy of the Oppressed* (New York: Bloomsbury Academic, 2012), 59.

23. Evan Popp, "Why Politicians from Both Parties Ignore the Poor," *The Progressive*, July 10, 2017, https://tinyurl.com/y2n3bkb3.

24. Popp, "Why Politicians."

25. Freire, *Pedagogy of the Oppressed*, 65.

26. Freire, *Pedagogy of the Oppressed*, 49.

27. Sennett, *Together*, 49.

28. Herbert J. Gans, *The War against the Poor: The Underclass and Antipoverty Policy* (New York: Basic, 1995), 16.

29. Gans, *War against the Poor*, 18.

4.

Tribal Hostilities

> I have a dream that one day little black boys and girls will be holding hands with little white boys and girls.
> —Rev. Dr. Martin Luther King Jr.[1]

The first summer we lived in St. Paul, I was invited to a backyard party for a candidate for local political office. I had never been to an event of this kind and I saw this as a chance to learn more about my neighborhood, so I bravely showed up alone. I was very surprised to find a house and yard full of white people. I hadn't yet figured out the social segregation thing. I met the homeowner in the kitchen; she was very friendly, describing herself as a life-long east side resident. More white people showed up, including the candidate. He gave a short talk on his priorities and opened up for questions. I was barely listening as I pondered the racial demographics of the event. There was exactly one black person present. The discussion caught my attention when I realized there was a lively exchange going on about the need for more hockey rinks for the neighborhood kids. Did these people not know that right down the street, there were kids without enough food in the house and who had no mattresses? Almost none of the families I had met in the neighborhood so far could afford to buy a pair of skates, let alone the rest of the equipment required by the sport. And did Hmong people play hockey? I didn't know.

I raised my hand: "I don't think the attendance at this event is very representative of the diversity of our neighborhood. What are you doing to reach out to the many people in this community who are not white and who are living below the poverty line?" The candidate had no chance to respond as the formerly friendly homeowner angrily stated, *"They* were invited! If *they* would quit partying all night and sleeping all day, then maybe *they* could show up to events like this." After I mentioned that her response was racist, several people started talking at once (none of them on my side). The voice I zoned in on was the sole black man in attendance, who was defending the statement of the white homeowner, and who clearly did not identify with our many African American neighbors living below the poverty line. The homeowner pointed to him as evidence that she was not racist. I told her that if her non-white neighbors knew this is how she felt about them, it was not surprising they stayed home. Then I left.

This nice little conversation between me and my new neighbor revealed an instance of *individual* racism. She believed that black people were inferior because (according to her) *they* party all day and sleep all night. *Structural* racism is the more insidious brand, as it involves the many institutions that keep society functioning, including government, police, courts, school systems, universities, and corporations. Built into the structure of social institutions are barriers to black people achieving at the same level as white people. I will discuss structural and individual racism separately, but in reality they are two sides of the same coin.

Structural Racism

Richard Delgado and Jean Stefancic argue that racism is "the usual way society does business, the common, everyday experience of people in this country."[2] It is the ordinariness of racism that makes it difficult to address. Legal scholar and civil rights activist Michelle Alexander says the success of people such as Barack Obama and Oprah Winfrey contributes to the assumption of color-blindness. If *they* can make it in the United States, it is believed, we must not be a racist society. This is the theory of black exceptionalism, which has been a core pillar of white supremacy for over a hundred years. Black exceptionalism says "race no longer matters." If a black person is not making it in society, it is thought, there is something wrong with that particular black person. "Black success stories," says Alexander, "lend credence to the notion that anyone, no matter how poor or how black you may be, can make it to the top, if only you try hard enough."[3]

I wish it were so. One of the main things I have learned over the past decade, and one that I think I least express, is the reality that I have benefitted by living in a society built on the backs of others. Obsessing about this can lead me to unproductive shame and guilt. Pretending it isn't so is just putting my head in the sand. I think I don't talk about it very much because I don't know what to do about it. My husband discovered in his ancestry research that my family on my dad's side bequeathed slaves to their heirs in 1813. What does one do with this information? Dee is my very good friend, and the fact that I am more educated than she is, have better insurance than she does, and own a house while she does not is not because I work harder than she does. It's because I was born on a hill built by my ancestors, and she was born in a hole dug by them. I can continue to work against my own racism, but I feel largely powerless to address the issue of structural racism effectively. It's an all-encompassing problem that goes back to the very birth of this country.

Alexander argues that US history reveals a series of mechanisms of social control of black people. First it was slavery, then it was Jim Crow laws, and today it is the mass incarceration of black men. America has a redesigned caste system, she says, one that perfectly disguises racism. She casts the so-called "War on Drugs," which began in the 1980s, as a war on black men, pointing to stiffer penalties for using crack (a "black" drug) than cocaine (a "white" drug), and stiffer sentences for black convicts for the same crimes.[4]

The prison population has exploded in the past three decades, increasing from 300,000 Americans to over two million today, with drug convictions of nonwhites making up the majority of the increase. According to author and activist Angela Davis, black women are one of the fastest-growing groups of prisoners, adding weight to the argument that structural racism is at the root of this problem.[5] This mass incarceration of people of color is legitimized by the common belief that those who are struggling in society chose this fate for themselves, rather than being the victims of structural racism. This belief can be justified "only to the extent that the plight of those locked up and locked out is understood to be their choice, not their birthright."[6] In other words, we can't blame structural racism for the high percentage of black men in prison. We will take the easy way out and blame the black men for making poor choices.

Davis attributes the swelling of the prison population to the fact that imprisonment is seen as "the response of first resort to far too many of the social problems that burden people who are ensconced in poverty."[7] It's easier to put people in jail than deal with their needs, whether those are jobs, housing, drug treatment, or other forms of social support. She points to the effect that the high incarceration rates in the black population have on official unemployment rates. Excluding imprisoned men from these statistics "assumes that the vast numbers of people in prison have really disappeared and thus have no legitimate claim to jobs. . . . Mass incarceration is not a solution to unemployment."[8] And employment rates that ignore this issue are not telling the whole story.

The stark racial disparities between the percentages of whites and blacks who are imprisoned "cannot be explained by rates of drug crime."[9] Studies show that people of all racial backgrounds both use and sell drugs at very similar rates. But, according to Alexander, research has revealed that in some states, black men facing drug charges are admitted to prison at rates up to fifty times greater than white men. The United States "imprisons a larger percentage of its black population than South Africa did at the height of apartheid."[10] There are few, if any, ways to interpret these realities as anything but examples of structural racism. Building meaningful relationships across these structures of inequality can sometimes seem impossible.

Until I moved to the city, I did not personally know anyone in jail or prison. Since moving here, I have visited multiple teens and young men in the juvenile detention center or jail. Cortez, the young man who lived with my family, was expected to follow in the footsteps of his three older brothers, who had all been to jail before the age of twenty-one. These young men feel profiled, singled out, and judged on first sight. They are not even surprised when they are arrested, whether or not they've done anything to warrant it. If they have done something to warrant it, structural racism ensures that there will be no effort to look beyond individual behavior and ask what the larger society has contributed to the young man's choices. The judicial system is not asking how we can create a society in which young black men have opportunities and role models that would help them make better choices. The system is never implicated. The belief seems to be that there is something inherently wrong with young black men that causes so many of them to become criminals.

Shortly after my neighbor Lemar* turned eighteen, he was picked up by the police for theft and locked up in the county jail. When he got out a few weeks later, he said he wouldn't mind going back because at least there he knew he would have a place to sleep every night and three meals a day. Structural racism explains not only the likelihood of his future incarceration, but also why it seems like a good option to him. The schools he attended ensured he would not have the opportunities my kids did in their suburban school. The neighborhoods he grew up in offered opportunities for trouble on every corner, including gangs always looking for new recruits. The police he interacted with from a young age had no doubt that his future included time in prison. He could not afford to go to college, and while my children were getting individual attention from their school counselors for things like college and scholarship applications and test scores, he was assigned to a counselor who was responsible for so many students that only a select few got the attention they needed. Today, when Lemar walks into a store to apply for a job, the owner is as likely to think he is there to rob it.

This is what structural racism looks like up close. Philosopher George Yancy says that our "anti-black racist world" tells a black person, "You are a *problem*, a sub-person, worthless and inconsequential, inferior, criminal, suspicious, and *something* to be feared and dreaded."[11] And this reality didn't spring up overnight. Generation after generation of organizational and institutional racism has created an insidious and invisible norm. No one questions why it should be like this for Lemar. It *should* be like this because it has *always* been like this.

Today, Lemar is twenty-nine years old and he's been locked up three more times in the past decade. He is currently unemployed and has recently moved back in with his mom, bringing with him a girlfriend and her two children. He is taking an online class to try to create more opportunities, but he vacillates between hopelessness and continuing to fight for a better life.

Structural racism is at its worst when power enters the equation. My whole life, I have been taught to view the police as friendly and helpful. Officer Bob visited my kindergarten class in his shiny uniform and gave us candy. I knew that Officer Bob would always be there if I were in trouble. I assumed that most people saw the police in this positive light. Who doesn't love Officer Bob? For starters, my black neighbors. They have had very different experiences with the police than I've had. My negative experiences have only been when I've been pulled over for speeding, and since I really was speeding, I couldn't really blame it on the officer. And since I could afford to pay the fine, the whole event barely registered.

So I was surprised one afternoon when I was picking students up in our twelve-passenger van and taking them to our Lift tutoring program. All of a sudden, everyone in the van ducked down and starting yelling. They explained that a police car was next to us, and they didn't want to be seen. Due to Cortez's brothers' many run-ins with the cops, he always thought they were looking for him. This became our routine. I would see a police car, then I would watch in my rearview mirror as all the students hunched over. They weren't hiding because they had committed a crime; they just operated out of the assumption that all contact with the police was bad.

And who can blame them? The stories of police shootings of black men, often unarmed, show up in the news on a regular basis. After the *Guardian* launched an effort to count all people killed by police in 2016, they reported, "Black males aged 15–34 were nine times more likely than other Americans to be killed by law enforcement officers last year. . . . They were also killed at four times the rate of young white men."[12]

Rarely do our black neighbors bother to call the police to report crimes. "They aren't going to believe me" or "It's not going to do any good anyway," they say. After Ricky got his driver's license at the age of twenty, he was pulled over and asked what he was doing driving in the neighborhood (where he lived). One time, he and his passengers were told to get out of the vehicle so the cops could search it. This is not a search that Ricky was required by law to submit to, as it was not based on anything the officer observed, but they knew that if they said no, the cops would take them in to the station on some charge or another. They submitted to the inconvenience of the search and were finally allowed to go after nothing was found. This is routine for young black men.

After two rapes in our neighborhood that were said to be committed by a young black male wearing a hoodie and baggy jeans, all the young black men were being stopped and questioned about the rape (since at the time, they all wore hoodies and baggy jeans). One was slammed up against a tree and questioned. In an effort to try to mediate the problem, I took Ricky to the monthly community police meeting. He didn't want to go, so I sort of dragged him. I told him he could help his friends by telling the story of how they were all were being treated. This meeting is attended by police, community members, county legal staff, city council members and their staff, and neighborhood business owners, most of whom are white. When the topic of the rapes came up, Ricky bravely described the experience he and his friends were having of being stopped and harassed.

The advice of the county attorney was that he and his friends should "stop wearing hoodies and baggy jeans."

Rather than solving the problem at its source—police officers who were profiling young black men and treating them all as guilty—he wanted to solve the problem by telling these teens to stop wearing hoodies in subzero winter temperatures and, apparently, start dressing more like him. Ricky left this meeting feeling "hopeless." Yancy calls the hoodie "a piece of racialized attire that apparently signifies black criminality." It is the black man "covering his head and face because of the crime he is always already about to commit as opposed to keeping dry because it is raining or keeping warm because it is so cold."[13]

As a white person, I have had limited experience being judged and mistrusted by people who know nothing about me other than my outward appearance. It is a reality my black friends face on a regular basis. One time, I took the guys to Target, and we shopped through the music and electronics section. For the first time in my life, I was followed by store security. It was obvious and I was angry; the guys thought it was no big deal. They said they were always followed when they shopped, and they were able to laugh about it. How is it not profiling when store security shows up to follow a group of black teens who just walked in the door?

I believe one of the most significant barriers to the formation of relationships across lines of race is that racism is alive and well but not acknowledged by many white people, who really do believe that we've been doing just fine since the Civil Rights Movement. Even those who admit to isolated instances of individual racism seem not to understand what structural racism is and how it impacts our society. This is white privilege in action. It is invisible to them and it was invisible to me for most of my life. It didn't touch me except in ways that were beneficial. Since so many benefit from structural racism, and since they mostly hold the power, there is little motivation to enter the conversation, and many reasons to avoid it.

I find that the existence of white privilege is denied by white people I interact with more often than the existence of racism. But, as race and gender theorist Paula Rothenberg says, "White privilege is the other side of racism."[14] Antiracism activist Peggy McIntosh describes it as "an invisible package of unearned assets which I can count on cashing in each day . . . an invisible weightless knapsack of special provisions, maps, passports, codebooks, visas, clothes, tools and blank checks."[15] She also says white people are meant to remain oblivious to these privileges. Once you learn about the unearned privileges you have that keep other people down, a moral response is required. If we can remain oblivious, we don't have to respond.

Relationships are powerful here, because when I get tired of the conversation (and I frequently do), I have my friend Dee beside me, or sometimes in front of me, dragging me along to places that used to be easy to avoid. McIntosh brings clarity to the many, many privileges I have that Dee does not have, just by virtue of our different skin. I can move anywhere I want, and my neighbors will accept me. I can choose to structure my life so that I rarely have to interact with people from a different race. I can go shopping alone and not be followed by security. Most of the time, I have been able to protect Connor and Hadley from people who don't like them, while Dee cannot do the same for Ricky and Wesley. I can speak to a group of powerful men without my race being judged. When I am pulled over by the police, I can be sure it is not because of my race. I can easily buy a birthday or graduation card that features people of my race. I can buy "flesh-colored" bandages that match my skin.[16] The list goes on. I literally never have to think about race if I don't want to. The world has carved out a place of safety and privilege for me, but not for Dee.

My tribe of origin has a tendency to look at the *effects* of structural racism (single-parent families, drugs, poverty) and see them as the *cause* of social problems rather than looking at structural racism as the cause. This type of pronouncement is yet another example of white privilege: voicing strong opinions about issues about which we know very little—and still being heard. Because of this particular pronouncement, we treat these symptoms rather than addressing the core issue of racism.

An example is increasing the penalties for drug use, as outlined by Alexander, as though mass incarceration of black men actually addresses the problem. Davis calls this "believing in the magic of imprisonment."[17] The result is that people who are victims of structural racism next become victims of judgment based on the deleterious effects of living under these structures. It's kind of like breaking the legs of an athlete and then punishing her for poor performance on the field. The first step toward relieving these kinds of symptoms is to dismantle structural racism (stop breaking legs); the next is to resource programs that actually strengthen black communities and begin to undo the damage of generations of structural racism.

Seattle writer Ijeoma Oluo uses strong language when addressing this issue. She ups the ante, referring to structural racism as white supremacy. She writes:

> White supremacy is in our workplace, our school system, our government and our prisons. It is in our books and movies and television. White supremacy has been woven into the fabric of our nation from the moment that white settlers decided that their claim to land was more important than the lives of indigenous people. This is not a new problem. This is America.[18]

For white people like me, this language is disturbing. White people like me need to listen. Oluo goes on to point out that the resurgence of racism in the twenty-first century is rooted in past promises that "poor and working-class whites would always get more than everyone else—that they deserved more than everyone else." When that belief is called into question by current economic realities, "the anger of being cheated out of their just rewards is easily funneled into racist hate."[19]

The relationship between structural racism and individual racism can be confusing. It is hard for some people to see structural racism, but easier to accept, since it doesn't require an acknowledgment of any personal views, behavior, or complicity. Individual racism, on the other hand, can be quite easy to see, but very hard to accept, since no one wants to admit to being a racist. Nevertheless, we persist on the topic.

Individual Racism

Several years ago, I was in a suburban Target store with my twelve-year-old daughter Hadley and Dee's eight-year-old daughter Ansaya. We ended up in a crowded aisle where several shopping carts were pointed in both directions. It was jammed up and people were having a hard time getting through. I was pushing a cart, and the girls were somewhere behind me. I turned around to see where they were, and I watched a woman ram her cart into Ansaya a few feet behind where I was standing and say, "Get out of the way, little black girl." I was just close enough to hear this evil sentence, and I turned on her and told her exactly what I thought of her racist comments. She said she wasn't being racist, but that I needed to "control that kid." I had turned around in time to watch the whole thing unfold, and what actually happened was that Hadley and Ansaya were slowly and patiently trying to make their way through a crowded aisle. Hadley benefitted from her privilege; Ansaya was the victim of racist remarks and physical violence by a woman who thought she was an unattended black girl.

Thirteen years later, Ansaya still remembers feeling hurt and sad, and she looks back on it as a dehumanizing experience. I remember feeling a murderous rage. Ansaya and Hadley's experience exemplifies the subtleties of both hidden racism and white privilege. The woman claimed her comments had nothing to do with Ansaya's color, but Ansaya, Hadley, and I, and everyone else in that aisle, knew differently.

When blatant racist words and actions are in the open, they can be confronted. Until recent events, it has been rare to find anything very explicit to confront. One unintended consequence of the Civil Rights Movement was to drive these words and actions underground, where they continued to have devastating effects on society, but left little to explicitly address. Sociologists Joe Feagin, Hernan Vera, and Pinar Batur say it this way:

> White racism is an open secret in America and most white people sense its presence at some level but fail to acknowledge its effects on people of color or their role in it. In everyday life, the majority of whites engage in a routine of acknowledgement, pretense and denial.[20]

The open secret is not so secret anymore. In 2016, former president Jimmy Carter told a group of faith leaders that the United States is experiencing a "resurgence of racism."[21] This was before the events of Charlottesville, the controversy surrounding the kneeling of NFL players during the national anthem, and the reemergence of the Ku Klux Klan and other white supremacist groups.

Still, the idea that racism is a thing of the past persists in some circles. Feagin, Vera, and Batur argue that the prevalent belief that the importance of race is declining "cannot be reconciled with the empirical reality of racial discrimination."[22] Further, racism results in little exposure of whites to black culture, leading to "ingrained antiblack beliefs."[23] In most contexts, these beliefs are difficult or impossible to overcome, as they are both ingrained and kept secret.

To black people or to those who have been sensitized to the realities of racism, it is not hard to recognize racism when you see it, regardless of whether anyone admits to it or not (and really, they rarely do, even when confronted head-on with evidence of racist words and actions). I have had unique opportunities to observe racism and stereotyping up close. Some friends of ours in a St. Paul suburb were giving their washer and dryer to one of our neighbors. While they were out of town, I took some guys over and used their garage code to pick up the appliances. The guys I took were all young black men. We went into the house through the garage and the guys carried the appliances out to our truck. When we came outside, we realized that there were three sets of neighbors standing out on their lawns watching us.

Maybe they would have been watching even if the guys had been white, but all of us had the feeling that the tribe was gathering to defend their turf. I called out that I was a friend and that I was picking up an appliance donation. They all continued to stare as we drove off down the street. If we had stopped and talked to them, they would have told us they were merely keeping an eye on their friends' house while they were out of town. I am sure they would have admitted to no more than that.

Like our experience in the grocery store, my friends experienced this incident differently than I did. I felt it as a deeply important moment showing the brokenness of our society, and even all of humanity. For Wesley and Ricky, it was business as usual. "To me it just is what it is," Wesley said when we talked about it later. Ricky said, "I'm like a resident alien in this world, and you just start to accept it." Cortez's first thought was, "I didn't care because

I was with you." Later, he realized they were "automatically going to judge us until they seen a white person."

I lived most of my life unaware of my privilege, and a long way away from being impacted by racism. I am saddened and angered as I observe racism in action and see its impact, especially on kids. When Dee's son Kahlil was fifteen years old, he said the hardest thing about his life was the feeling he gets when people see him and are immediately afraid of him. Keshia tells the story of moving to Minnesota from Chicago. She and her three kids spent their first month here in a family shelter in a first-ring suburb of St. Paul. Three families from the shelter walked to a local recreation center up the road. She says that when the group walked into the pool area, they realized they were the only black people there, and every person was staring at them. "They looked at us real bad, real nasty," she says. Coming from a Chicago neighborhood that was 100 percent African American, Keshia says her kids had never been in a situation where they were in the minority. When they moved, they were looking forward to living around cultures different than their own. She didn't want to only be around people who looked just like her. She said she felt "hurt and embarrassment" from this experience at the rec center. It is a moment that has stuck with her for nearly fifteen years.

The New Racism

Like many good liberal white people, I always saw myself as a kind and caring white woman who was against all forms of prejudice (a Happy White Lady, if you will). Over a period of fifteen years, I have had to confront my own experience of white privilege and complicity in the current reality of black Americans. While living in the suburbs, I could keep these realities at arm's length, study them in school, and speak out against them without really understanding them. What my geographic move forced me to do was to get up close to the hidden aspects of racism that continue to define the relationship between white and black Americans in the twenty-first century.

I had never even heard the term "white privilege" until I was in my early thirties and watched an educational video of a group conversation about race, called *The Color of Fear*.[24] It was eye-opening both because I wondered how I had lived so long without ever hearing about white privilege, and also because the video illustrated the meaning and impact of privilege in a powerful way. It didn't give me any kind of an out. I thought I was attending a meeting to engage in a theoretical or philosophical conversation about equality, but when they showed this video, I had the wind knocked out of me by the raw pain being shared by people of color who stared racism in the face every day. They forced me to acknowledge the crappy and very concrete realities of racism and white privilege. I often forget movies a few days after I see them. Although this documentary lacks the dazzling production qualities of other films, the words, faces, and even clothing of those in the video are still etched in my mind.

Racism looks different in each generation. Even today, when many deny it even exists, some new insidious forms of it have been named, and some new concepts have emerged in an attempt to explain racism in the twenty-first century. We will take a look at microaggressions, aversive racism, and white epistemology.

Early on in my journey of learning about racism, I was sitting in a food court in a shopping mall with a friend. Two black women walked by and out of the corner of my eye, I saw my friend bend over and pick up the strap of her purse that was sitting at her feet. I called her out, and she denied that her actions had anything to do with the black women. I didn't realize at the time that I had just witnessed a microaggression. Old-fashioned racism that involves "conscious and intentional racial hatred and bigotry" has been replaced by a less obvious and therefore more insidious brand.[25] In the 1970s, Richard Delgado, along with other scholars, began to develop an area of scholarship and activism called Critical Race Theory (CRT). This movement "questions the very foundations of the liberal order," not being content with incremental progress. Adherents are intent on "studying and transforming the relationship among race, racism, and power."[26] One of the areas of study within CRT is the prevalence of these microaggressions.

The term "microaggression" has been coined to refer to subtle racism that may include "insults delivered through dismissive looks, gestures and tones toward people of color; often automatic or unconscious."[27] Along with Jean Stefancic, Delgado defines a microaggression as a "stunning small encounter with racism, usually unnoticed by members of the majority race."[28] In my childhood, there was some overt racism in my family, but more often I observed these kinds of microaggressions. Relatives would exchange judgmental looks about a black person in need of assistance or assume every black woman was a single mom. I recall locking our car doors when passing black people in my grandmother's neighborhood in Detroit. These observations obviously shaped my racial development growing up.

Today, my black friends come alive when we talk about their experience of microaggressions. Ernest described watching women hold their purse tighter when they saw him or refusing to respond when he greeted them. He told of waiting to get served in restaurants when others who arrived after him had already been served. Cortez has noticed white people moving quickly to put distance between themselves and him. Ricky and Wesley say they notice things like white drivers locking their doors when they see them, but they say it doesn't bother them. Wesley sees it as just another symptom of the much larger problem, and he thinks getting caught up in these small things takes the focus off the bigger issues.

Knowing the regular occurrence of these types of events, I am not surprised that many black people are looking more to avoid white people than to befriend them. Despite this, people like Ernest and Dee have continued to open themselves up to diversity, which requires the skill of quickly determining which kind of white person they are dealing with.

I had never heard the phrase "aversive racism," although once I found out what it was, I knew I had clearly seen it in action many times. I shared previously that when I met Dee across the alley in 2003, my primary thought was that she was black, rather than a female or a mom. While that was a key piece of the narrative running through my head, it took a long time for me to actually talk about race in any way with her. Dee is an activist, and she first brought up the topic while we were talking about unfair treatment Ricky had received in school. Once Dee started the conversation, it grew into a rich dialogue and I learned more from Dee about race and racism than I ever could have in a book or class.

I had been engaging in aversive racism with Dee. This is a term used to describe the tension that white people feel about engaging in open and honest conversations about race for fear that they will appear racist or even realize they are racist. The option of avoiding these conversations is another example of white privilege, putting black people in the position of being the only ones who will raise racial issues, which psychologists Derald Wing Sue and Madonna Constantine say results in the likelihood they will be accused of being hypersensitive.[29] In our community, we have conversations about race, which are often difficult and awkward. White people who are able to engage more honestly in these conversations seem to be making an attempt to own their privilege and lean into the pain of their own complicity. This topic is a minefield, and white people often use their privilege to avoid it altogether, as I did with Dee in the beginning of our relationship.

I have had many white people quietly ask me if it's okay to say "black" or if they should only use the term "African American." While I understand why this uncertainty may make people hesitant to bring up questions of race, it is a problem that is solved with minimal effort. White privilege often means people don't even bother to invest that level of effort. I have also watched white people try to describe a black person in a context where black people are present. People are hesitant to describe the person as "black," for fear it will be seen as racist. While it may sound ridiculous since skin color is a major part of a person's physical description, it shows how far white people will go to avoid discussing anything related to race, to the point of not wanting to say the word "black" when they are around black people.

I received a gift from Dee when she took the risk of starting a conversation on race with me. If she had not done that, my aversive racism could possibly have prevented most of what has happened to me for the past fifteen years from ever happening at all.

"Epistemology" is a very long word that refers to the branch of philosophy that explores theories of knowledge. It asks questions such as "What counts as knowledge?" and "How are beliefs justified?" I am a white epistemologist, which means, among other things, that I live in my head and relentlessly pursue rationality. I want things to make sense. Maybe you can see how we are about to get into trouble here. The question that emerges regarding epistemology is "Who gets to decide what counts as knowledge?" Who decides what is a belief, an opinion, a fact? The answer to these questions in the United States is, as a rule, white people. As a white epistemologist, I believe that the way I determine issues of knowing is the right way. Sometimes without realizing it, I impose my brand of rationality on others around me.

One area where I have noticed my tendency to name what is rational and what is irrational is in the context of death and funerals. These important events are handled among my diverse neighbors in ways that do not always make sense to me. We moved into our house the day after our Hmong neighbor's wife died. There was an endless stream of visitors literally twenty-four hours each day for nearly a month. I learned that traditional Hmong beliefs require rituals and a constant presence with the body of the deceased in order to guide their soul back to their placenta rather than having it roam free for eternity. My first thought upon learning this was that I was being awakened several times each night due to a ridiculous superstition.

When I attended my first black funeral when a friend's father died, I was amazed to see that the family members, most of whom were struggling financially, were all wearing new suits and dresses, and they were also throwing themselves on the body of the deceased and laying their children on top of him in the casket. At another funeral, everyone was wearing a matching T-shirt with the face of the deceased printed on it. I found out this is a common practice. These funerals were a far cry from the quiet and solemn versions I had been to in my suburban world. I remember thinking it was all ridiculous.

And it *was* all ridiculous from a white epistemological perspective. Educator Doug Paxton, who specializes in leadership and social/racial justice, explains the role of white epistemology in Western society today. The way we know something and the way we define right and wrong are defined by white people. This exacerbates the reality of racism in ways that are immeasurable and often unnoticed. Paxton lists "individualism, competition, positivism, rationality, logic and objectivity; scientism and dualism" as components of the "European American system of knowing."[30] These are very different values than I find at work in my neighborhood, where I have found that people think more communally and value their feelings in a way that is empowering. In any social system, even one as informal as mine, decisions and plans have to be made and the question becomes, "Whose values will guide our decision-making?"

Although the term "white epistemology" has likely never been uttered in my neighborhood, I believe it defines the subtext of many of our processes and conversations. For a few years, the program staff at The Lift included one black person, Dee, and three white people. Most of our tensions can be traced to fundamental assumptions about what is true about the world. While all of us are friends and no one has been accused of being racist, I believe there are underlying misunderstandings that can be traced to white epistemology. Planning a youth event has sometimes been stressful because our white staff (including me) has clear opinions about how things *should* be done. These opinions include things like how far ahead plans should be made when we are taking students to an amusement park, how quickly emails should be answered, and even how rigid the boundaries are about who is to be included in the event. (Can staff bring their younger children along?) Dee holds a much more relaxed view about these things, and it continues to be a struggle for me to remember that there is nothing really at stake and that I should probably just relax. Now that Dee is on the board of directors of The Lift, she has taken up the important role of keeping the faith when finances get tough, which is most of the time.

Admitting (and Resisting) Racism

The ultimate statement of white privilege is that racism does not exist anymore, the evidence being that I as a white person have not seen it. White privilege and segregation afforded me the opportunity for the first three decades of my life to ignore the fact that racism still exists and continues to have deleterious effects on the lives of African Americans. Even today, I want to exercise my white privilege by thinking and saying things, "Can't we all just get along?" Based on my own experience, I do think there is much to be gained by moving beyond the narrative that all whites are racist and all blacks are victims. This narrative has not brought us very far toward equality, and it seems to have done little to end racism. However, I also recognize that my privilege is still leading the way in these (mostly) internal dialogues. I'm not in the best position to decide who's racist or to evaluate the potential benefits of moving toward healing relationships. However, I am in a position to recognize my own privilege, acknowledge all I've gained from generations of racial violence and inequity, and commit to do what I can toward the goal of equality.

I have run into a danger in playing the role of the "enlightened white person." Trying to engage in dialogue with white people who don't see things the way I do can lead to "exhorting in an officious and tiresome way," according to the European-American Collaborative Challenging Whiteness (ECCW), a group of educators devoted to exploring white consciousness.[31] These behaviors, they demonstrate, can actually impede progress. They can perpetuate white privilege, cause us to view ourselves as superior, or shut down meaningful conversation. In an effort to persuade, we alienate. The desire to be right, the desire to bring about change, and the desire to have meaningful relationships can all come into conflict in these situations. If I prove my rightness, I risk alienating white friends. If I keep silent, I allow a racist attitude to go unchecked. There sometimes seems to be no way to win.

The ECCW recommends a practice called "critical humility" in efforts to have meaningful conversations about race with other white people.[32] Critical humility involves having "genuine care and compassion for the other person and ourselves, remembering we have something to learn." As we strive to act in ways that challenge racism, "we also strive to remember that even as we challenge white privilege, we are still immersed in it."[33] Taking an attitude of inquiry is one way to move toward an attitude of critical humility.

After more than a decade, I am not always able to be critically humble. I still find myself in frequent and frustrating conversations with white people, trying to explain the ongoing existence and effects of racism. My daughter Hadley ran into this problem in her suburban high school. At the age of sixteen, she felt the burden of trying to enlighten her privileged white friends to the reality that black people are still the victims of racism. One friend told her it was a "nonissue" these days. Slavery is over, she said, and we all need to just move on.

It is very difficult to address these attitudes *effectively*—but if not addressed, they present a significant barrier to the formation of substantive relationships between black people and white people. If the first stages of the relationship require a black person to defend the idea that racism still exists, the relationship is over before it even starts. This is exacerbated by the fact that the question of racism is not just about today, and it is not just about individual attitudes. It is embedded in our nation's history of injustice and the systems and structures that arose from it and still guide our daily lives. Sociologist Michael Eric Dyson states:

> The denial of our racial past, in some measure, means that we are forever doomed to a battle over just how bad things are in our racial present. If we can't agree—and, really, tell the truth—about the history of race, we can't tell the truth about the politics of race.[34]

In addition to admitting our racial past, however, we must acknowledge the racist realities that black people continue to face on a daily basis. It is my experience that unless white people affirm the existence of racism and are active against it, they will not succeed in creating a reciprocal relationship with those who see their lives very much defined by individual and structural racism. They will continue to live in a world where all their friends look just like them.

#

We will next tackle the topic of tribalism in the church. Those who attend church will not be surprised to learn that churches have not made much progress at diversifying their congregations. We will look at why this is and explore some possible steps forward.

Notes

1. Martin Luther King Jr., "I Have a Dream," speech presented at the March on Washington for Jobs and Freedom (Washington, DC: Lincoln Memorial, August 28, 1963).

2. Richard Delgado and Jean Stefancic, *Critical Race Theory: An Introduction* (New York: New York University Press, 2012), 7.

3. Michelle Alexander, *The New Jim Crow: Mass Incarceration in the Age of Colorblindness*, rev. ed. (New York: New Press, 2010), 248.

4. Alexander, *The New Jim Crow*.

5. Angela Y. Davis, "Masked Racism: Reflections on the Prison Industrial Complex," *Colorlines* 1, no. 11 (September 10, 1998): https://tinyurl.com/yy8adng2.

6. Alexander, *The New Jim Crow*, 248.

7. Davis, "Masked Racism."

8. Davis, "Masked Racism."

9. Alexander, *The New Jim Crow*, 7.

10. Alexander, *The New Jim Crow*, 6.

11. George Yancy, "Trayvon Martin: When Effortless Grace Is Sacrificed on the Altar of the Image," in *Pursuing Trayvon Martin: Historical Contexts and Contemporary Manifestations of Racial Dynamics*, ed. George Yancy and Janine Jones (Lanham, MD: Lexington, 2013), 238.

12. Jon Swaine and Ciara McCarthy, "Young Black Men Again Faced

Highest Rate of US Police Killings in 2016," *Guardian*, January 8, 2017, https://tinyurl.com/y56cueoe.

13. Yancy, "Trayvon Martin," 245.

14. Paula S. Rothenberg, "Introduction," in *White Privilege: Essential Readings on the Other Side of Racism*, ed. Paula S. Rothenberg (New York: Worth, 2008), 1.

15. Peggy McIntosh, "White Privilege: Unpacking the Invisible Knapsack," in Rothenberg, *White Privilege*, 123.

16. Peggy McIntosh, "White Privilege," 124–25.

17. Davis, "Masked Racism."

18. Ijeoma Oluo, "So You Want to Fight White Supremacy," *The Establishment*, August 14, 2017, https://tinyurl.com/y3by4e7y.

19. Oluo, "So You Want to Fight."

20. Joe R. Feagin, Hernan Vera, and Pinar Batur, *White Racism*, 2nd ed. (New York: Routledge, 2001), 89.

21. "Jimmy Carter: The U.S. is Seeing a 'Resurgence of Racism,'" CBS News, September 15, 2016, https://tinyurl.com/yxqbqwtd.

22. Feagin, Vera, and Batur, *White Racism*, 13–14.

23. Feagin, Vera, and Batur, *White Racism*, 35.

24. *The Color of Fear*, directed by Lee Mun Wah (Berkeley, CA: Stir-Fry Seminars, 1994), 90 min.

25. Derald Wing Sue and Madonna G. Constantine, "Racial Microaggressions as Instigators of Difficult Dialogues on Race: Implications for Student Affairs Educators and Students," *College Student Affairs Journal* 26, no. 2 (2007): 139.

26. Delgado and Stefancic, *Critical Race Theory*, 3.

27. Sue and Constantine, "Racial Microaggressions," 137.

28. Delgado and Stefancic, *Critical Race Theory*, 167.

29. Sue and Constantine, "Racial Microaggressions," 136, 139.

30. Doug Paxton, "Transforming White Consciousness," in *Handbook of Race and Adult Education: A Resource for Dialogue on Racism*, ed. Vanessa Sheared, Juanita Johnson-Bailey, Scipio A. J. Collin III, Elizabeth Peterson, and Stephen D. Brookfield (San Francisco: Jossey-Bass, 2010), 123.

31. European-American Collaborative Challenging Whiteness, "White on White: Developing Capacity to Communicate about Race with Critical Humility," in Sheared et al., *Handbook on Race*, 146.

32. ECCW, "White on White," 145.

33. ECCW, "White on White," 155.

34. Michael Eric Dyson, "We Must Stop Denying Our Racism," *Newsday*, January 1, 2003, https://tinyurl.com/yxdnjzxw.

as "Jiminy Cricket" and "cheese and crackers," which were presumed to be stand-ins for taking the Lord's name in vain. People who used these words were also wrong, unchristian, and bad. My church was trying to avoid syncretizing with the world around it, but their extreme approach actually forced them to judge rather than love the world, while looking both ridiculous and crazy at the same time.

During our annual family vacations to northern Michigan in the late 1970s, we became friends with another family in a campsite close by. They had kids the same age as us and enjoyed the same water sports as we did. They were not from a Christian background, but after we had spent a few years getting to know each other, one of their daughters decided she wanted to be a Christian. My older brother, who was attending Bible college at the time, talked a lot about Jesus, and his words impacted her. As a senior in high school, she applied to and was accepted to a midwestern conservative Christian college. When she received her acceptance packet, there was a form she was supposed to sign and send back agreeing that during holidays and summer breaks from college, she would not associate with non-Christian people. They did not want her to be around people who thought differently than she did, so that her faith would not be compromised. Unfortunately for Stacy,* this included her entire family. She ended up at a state university, and her family ended up thinking less of Christianity.

While our society is very much a place where all our friends look just like us, the church has actually taken it a step further and created a place where not only do our friends *look* just like us, but they also *think* just like us. In the face of the overwhelming scriptural mandate that Christians are called to be change agents in a broken world, bring reconciliation, and draw people to Christ through a radically compelling love, evangelical Christians instead live in fear of being soiled by the world they are called to transform. In attempting to avoid syncretizing with immorality, they instead syncretize with the judgmental Pharisees, the only people in the gospels that Jesus got really pissed off with.

Gandhi has been quoted as saying, "I like your Christ. I do not like your Christians." There is a great deal of controversy over whether Gandhi actually said this, but regardless, I've heard this same thought from another source. Hadley came home with her future husband Kamal during her senior year of college. He was raised in an eastern religion and had not had much exposure to Christians or Christianity. After time with our family and our community, he was talking about issues of faith with Hadley and me. He said, "My dad always said that *real* Christians are awesome, but he also said I would probably never meet one." How disappointing, but also motivating. Kamal's dad knew that the message of Christianity is radical and transformational. He saw the message as compelling, but he had not met many people actually living out that message. In some ways, he showed a greater understanding of Christianity than many Christians do. The church has forgotten its radical mandate to reconcile, heal, love, and be awesome.

What is the syncretism operating in the church today? It's the combination of racism with a lack of repentance, and classism combined with the pursuit of the American Dream. I have already explored the many facets of racism and classism, and I do not want to belabor the same points. However, there are specific issues related to these sins that must be addressed within the evangelical church.

Jesus and Race

Some friends of mine were members of an all-white church that hired a black associate pastor. One Sunday a black family showed up to visit, and the usher who greeted them at the door excitedly told them they needed to meet the (black) associate pastor. It's a rare Sunday morning that finds a black Christian and a white Christian standing in the church doorway together and the first thought of the white Christian is to offload the black family to someone from his own tribe. The family never came back, and the associate pastor lasted less than a year.

There was no overt racism happening here. There was no name-calling or lack of kindness. There was merely an enormous tribal divide. There was a white Christian who literally did not know how to make a connection with black Christians. This story is a microcosm of the evangelical church. Sunday mornings at eleven are a great time to witness Western tribalism up close. Martin Luther King Jr. famously identified this time as the most segregated hour of the week.[2]

In an op-ed in the *Los Angeles Times*, religious history professor Randall Balmer explains:

> In the 19th and early 20th centuries, evangelicals took the part of those on the margins of society—women, the poor, workers, people of color. The 2016 election, coupled with the religious right's anemic response to racism and white supremacy, suggests that this once proud and noble tradition is morally bankrupt.[3]

Regardless of whether you agree with this analysis, the fact that a major newspaper is publishing an op-ed by a respected academic calling the evangelical church out for being racist is not a good sign.

Sociologists Michael Emerson and Christian Smith, writing from *within* the evangelical community, conclude that "white Evangelicalism likely does more to perpetuate the racialized society than reduce it."[4] This is because the church is attempting "to solve the race problem without shaking the foundations upon which racialization is built."[5]

How did the evangelical church go from being champions of the poor and disenfranchised in the early twentieth century, as Balmer gives it credit for, to being accused of racism by Christians and non-Christians alike in the early twenty-first century? In between these two poles, the church fell down in its mission of reconciliation. Theological ethicist H. Richard Niebuhr lamented in 1929:

> The color line has been drawn so incisively by the church itself that its proclamation of the gospel of the brotherhood of Jew and Greek, of bond and free, of white and black has sometimes the sad sound of irony, and sometimes falls upon the ear as unconscious hypocrisy—but sometimes there is in it the bitter cry of repentance.[6]

In the mid-twentieth century, we see the church's lack of engagement during the Civil Rights Movement. Theologian and social activist Ron Sider explains, "It is common knowledge that during the civil rights movement, when mainline Protestants and Jews joined African Americans in their historic struggle for freedom and equality, evangelical leaders were almost entirely absent."[7]

And here we are nearly a century after Niebuhr's prophetic vision, and a half-century after the Civil Rights Movement, and we are not seeing much repentance. We are not seeing a church actively pursuing racial justice. We are actually seeing the opposite. Both secular and Christian pollsters have unfortunately found that white evangelicals are "even more racist than their pagan friends."[8] In 2005, a Gallup survey attempted to more thoroughly define the problem by asking people if they would object to having a black neighbor. They found that 17 percent of Baptists and evangelicals would object to having a black neighbor. They were "among the most likely groups to object to black neighbors," surpassed only by the Southern Baptists, where one in five objected.[9]

On an individual basis, any given evangelical may argue against these indictments. "I'm not racist," we all cry. "I have no problem with black neighbors," we argue. Still, the data persist in making the broader point about structural racism in the church.

This is a complex issue with multiple tentacles in history and in present-day realities. The church is functioning in a broken world and is faced on a daily basis with challenges that have the potential to tear the world apart and take the church with it. We are confronted with questions about law enforcement's treatment of black people, whether black lives matter, the resurgence of white supremacy, and how we deal with the icons of the confederacy, among others.

In hopeful moments, I like to think that Christianity has the answer to these tribal divides that continue to plague us. I like to think that faith has the power to heal. In the New Testament book of Revelation, a future is described in which those who are worshipping God come "from every nation, from all tribes and peoples and languages" (Rev 7:9). In 1997, activist and minister Eugene Rivers wrote of the church, "There is no other quarter in this society that has the institutional, moral or spiritual capacity to bring this country back together again."[10] Over twenty years later, I am still hoping to witness the church fulfilling this calling.

What the church needs in order to begin to fulfill this calling is reconciliation. Unfortunately, the church's efforts at reconciliation have been less than robust. Allan Boesak and Curtiss DeYoung are pioneers in the work of reconciliation. Boesak worked with South Africa's antiapartheid movement to overthrow the unjust regime. DeYoung has written and spoken extensively on the topic. They assert that "interracial churches tend to cater to the predilection of whites" and are mostly led by white ministers.[11] Further, "reconciliation is often understood today as assimilation, appeasement, a passive peace, a unity without cost, and maintaining power with only cosmetic changes."[12] Dee's son Ricky agrees: "The black people don't have a voice in these efforts at reconciliation."

It will take more than cosmetic changes undertaken by white people. It is not a matter of merely adding some persons of color, but rather fundamentally "transforming the central identity from white (and male) to a truly inclusive human identity."[13] Ricky adds, "Until the church starts being radical and understanding the true calling to follow Jesus, they are not going to realize the importance of racial reconciliation." Those in the church with power must trust and follow the lead of those who have been oppressed. "Reconciliation occurs between equals," say Boesak and DeYoung.[14]

This sort of reconciliation has the power to come against racism. Activist and minister Eugene Rivers adds the warning that reconciliation "divorced from a commitment to truth and justice is a sham," and he goes on to say that much of what pass for attempts at reconciliation are a lot of "feels good" and "sounds good" without a lot of substance.[15]

I believe one reason for the lack of engagement of so many churches around issues of race is that these issues have been politicized. But racial reconciliation is not a political issue. Loving and welcoming people who are different from you is also not a political issue. These are deeply spiritual issues. They are biblical issues. Reconciliation in the midst of brokenness and sin points to a different way, to redemption, to hope and healing. It is at the center of the gospel, and it has the power to make the good news real to people like Kamal's father.

But we can't be reconciled while also being racist. And we can't just quietly disavow racism; we have to repent. There is no way to get around this reality. It must be named. The white evangelical church, in ways big and small, actively and passively participates in the sin of racism. While doing this, the church publicly pursues reconciliation in various ways that do not get to the bottom of the issue. Instead of merely looking for black people to sit on our boards and drive buses around the inner city to pick up black kids for Sunday school, we need to pursue truth and justice in more substantive ways that actually address the injustices of the past.

South Africa found itself in great need of reconciliation at the end of apartheid. Almost fifty years of extreme geographic and social segregation, housing and employment discrimination, subjugation, and violence against the majority black population had left them decimated. From 1961 through 1994, 3.5 million people experienced forced removals from their land, which was then sold to white farmers, and they were deposited into so-called "homelands" (Bantustans, for the Bantu people) where conditions were dire and hopeless.

Apartheid began to be dismantled in 1991, and a new constitution was put in place in 1994. However, getting rid of apartheid did not rid the country of apartheid's horrible effects. Black people had lost their property, their livelihood, their family members. White people had benefitted greatly under apartheid's unjust laws. To say reconciliation was needed was a vast understatement. The new government formed the Truth and Reconciliation Commission in 1995, which worked to heal the wounds of the country. Although it was not a perfect process, and there is still healing left to do, there are lessons we can learn from them.

Black Anglican clergyman and social rights activist Desmond Tutu, who led the Commission, has been often criticized for his calls for forgiveness. He led the country in naming the sins of apartheid, he led the perpetrators in repentance, and he led the victims in forgiving. Both the repentance and the forgiveness were taken seriously, as part of a spiritual process guided by the Holy Spirit:

> I believe that I certainly stand under the pressure of God's Holy Spirit to say that when that confession of wrongdoing is made, those of us who have been wronged must say, "We forgive you," and then together we may move to the reconstruction of our land. The confession is not cheaply made and the response is not cheaply made.[16]

What Rivers would say, I believe, is that the church in the United States is dealing cheaply with reconciliation, and that's a problem. Boesak and DeYoung talk about white people's desire to "engage in reconciliation on their own terms. They want people of color to come to them in places where they [the white people] feel comfortable and in control."[17] Boesak and DeYoung warn they cannot simply move from segregated church to multicultural reconciled church without an active process of reconciliation. And this will be painful, and it will cost something more than hugs.

It will cost humility, an acknowledgment of white privilege, and the time that it takes to engage in intentional and intimate relationships with people who are different from you, "where you are transformed by the other person's reality."[18] This may sound easy, but it is very difficult to let go of the privilege that has likely been invisible to you and actually enter into the pain that racism has brought and continues to bring to individuals and communities.

What if the white evangelical church said, "This country has a racist history and it has a racist present. Not only will we not be part of it, but we will name it, repent of it, and actively work for its end. We will ask for forgiveness and seek true reconciliation between black people and white people by the power of the Holy Spirit"? *What if?*

In his letter to the Colossians, the apostle Paul tells us, "Here there is not Greek and Jew, circumcised and uncircumcised, barbarian, Scythian, slave, free; but Christ is all, and in all" (Col 3:11). Paul is telling the church that there are no tribal differences that should divide people. All of the contrasting pairs he lists point to social realities that kept people divided in the first century. He is giving the early church a radical command to model something different than the social norms of the time. He is challenging his people to build relationships across lines of difference—to have friends who do not look like them or think like them. To reach across the color line and the political aisle in the name of Jesus.

We've looked at the presence of racism in the church. We turn now to classism, which is the other side of the coin.

Jesus and Class

A friend of mine works at a firm specializing in church architecture and design. A while back he arrived early at a wealthy suburban church for a meeting and waited in the plush lobby. The church was interviewing firms to potentially help with the design and construction of a new addition to their building. He was there to learn about the finer details. As he waited, a distraught woman came into the building and approached the vast mahogany reception desk. In broken English and through her tears, she requested to see a certain staff person. The receptionist coolly and professionally informed her that the person was in a meeting and not available. The woman became more distraught and continued to plead to see the staff person, attempting to tell her what she needed. She was told repeatedly that the person was not available but would call her if she were to leave a phone number. Finally, the woman left a number and fled. Soon after, my friend was ushered into his meeting to discuss the potential design of their new $9 million *community outreach* facility.

Obviously, we are lacking important details that might help us understand the situation better. But regardless, this story represents a trend in Christianity to fashion our spaces and practices after the ethic of the business community, where time is money and people who are hurting take too much of both. What, I am asking myself, could this staff person possibly have been doing that was more important than ministering to the needs of someone who was clearly in pain? How did the receptionist's training prepare her to deal pastorally with the hurting? Behind how many walls do we in full-time ministry hide to protect ourselves so that we can "get our work done" without being interrupted by the needs of humanity? When did serving people in need begin to be viewed as a hassle in ministry, rather than as one of the most important roles of a minister? And finally, how does a $9 million facility benefit the community if those on staff are unwilling to embrace the community, along with its needs, with their time and presence?

In this section, we are specifically talking about the topic of class from a socioeconomic perspective. How is the church doing at creating a community where rich and poor people worship together and do life together? This question insists that we look at how the church and church people use their resources.

Unfortunately, the church often fails to use its resources in ways that reflect the priorities of Jesus. It doesn't look any better on the individual level. Christians tend to carry consumer debt at approximately the same levels as non-Christians. And despite radically growing incomes, the percentage of income given to charity by Christians is going down. In 1969, Christians gave 3.2 percent of their income to charity; in 2004, the percentage had decreased to 2.5 percent, where it stands today.

The combined income of Christians in the United States is estimated to be $10 trillion, while around the world three billion people live on less than two dollars per day. Because of this poverty, over thirty thousand children around the world will die of starvation and easily preventable diseases *today alone*. Every month, the "silent tsunami" of poverty claims the lives of nearly one million children. At this very moment, children are dying from lack of iodine, from lack of clean water, from lack of food.[19] Where is the church in these statistics? Where are the church people? If this reality is not an opportunity for the church's radical mandate to go into action on both a corporate and individual level, then what is? The Bible is not unclear in its commands to feed the hungry and care for those in need.

In some ways, evangelical Christians' views on poverty are even more alarming than their views on race, especially when you realize that poverty rates among black Americans stand at 27.4

percent while the rate is 9.9 percent for white people. Over 45 percent of black children under the age of six live in poverty, while 14.5 percent of white children in that age group live in poverty.[20] Because of this, when Christians say something judgmental about those living in poverty, they are usually doubling down on their racist views.

Beyond these sobering statistics is the reality that, more than any other demographic, white evangelicals blame poverty on the poor. In 2017, the *Washington Post* reported on their research with the Kaiser Family Foundation that found that "religion is a significant predictor of how Americans perceive poverty."[21] White evangelical Christians are more likely than non-Christians to blame poverty on a lack of effort on the part of the poor. And they are not just a little more likely; they are *a lot* more likely. "Compared to those with no religion, the odds of white evangelicals saying a lack of effort causes poverty were 3.2 to 1."[22] Of white evangelicals polled, over half blamed poverty on a lack of effort. Americans who are atheists or have no religious affiliation were twice as likely as white evangelicals to blame poverty on difficult circumstances.

It would be bad enough to find this syncretism nipping at the *edges* of our faith and our churches. But it has penetrated to the core of our value system and lifestyle choices. Theologian Michael Horton says that Gallup and Barna "hand us survey after survey demonstrating that evangelical Christians are as likely to embrace lifestyles" that are antithetical to the gospel as the world in general.[23] There is little difference, in practice, between pursuing the American Dream and following Jesus. There is a cost to the consumerism attached to the American Dream. There is a cost to the church of pews full of Christians struggling with debt while judging poor people. And the cost is more than financial. It is our very identity as followers of Jesus that is at stake.

So we have a problem here. I won't walk into a white evangelical church with my struggling neighbors, knowing that half the people there think my friends have major shortcomings. White evangelicals are not going to pursue reconciliation by attending urban churches if most of them think the people there are living the results of their own poor choices. If over half of evangelicals blame the person, and if black people are overrepresented among the poor, there seems little hope for reconciliation. What Christians are basically saying is that it's black people's fault that so many of them are poor, that something is morally wrong with them. This is far afield from the good news of the gospel for all people.

Albert Mohler, the president of Southern Baptist Theological Seminary, told the *Washington Post*:

> There's a strong Christian impulse to understand poverty as deeply rooted in morality—often, as the Bible makes clear, in unwillingness to work, in bad financial decisions or in broken family structures. The Christian worldview is saying that all poverty is due to sin, though that doesn't necessarily mean the sin of the person in poverty. In the Garden of Eden, there would have been no poverty. In a fallen world, there is poverty.[24]

Mohler seems to have the ability to look beyond individual causes for poverty and at least hint at structural problems. Christians who blame poverty on the poor point to verses in the book of Proverbs that emphasize personal responsibility and hard work. Those who blame poverty on the social structures that emerged through the political and social shortcomings of our history emphasize the prophets who called on Israel to care for those among them in need, and of course the words of Jesus throughout the gospels.

As I mentioned, everyone who attended the church I grew up in was white. Almost all were middle class. The Dillard* family was the exception. Mrs. Dillard came with her three kids, but we never saw Mr. Dillard. Their daughter Missy was my age, and they had two younger sons. The only things I personally noticed were that the kids didn't smell good, and their clothes were pretty raggedy. There were whispers that they did not have indoor plumbing at home. I didn't understand what that meant until a rumor spread that the family just got its first toilet. In my sheltered life, I didn't know it was possible to live without a toilet in the house. I caught my mom rifling through my clothes one time, and I found out she was looking for things to give to Missy, which both upset and baffled me. As an elementary student, I didn't fully understand what was going on, but from my perspective today, I definitely saw Missy as the Other even then. She was someone to be helped. She was not my equal, and her family suffered in comparison to the other families in the church. There was definitely something wrong with them.

It is amazing to me, looking back on a church I have not attended since I was seventeen years old, how much I remember about the people who attended who had "problems." Mrs. Jones* was divorced. The Harlows* *had* to get married. The Johnsons'* daughter was not very smart. The Websters'* daughters wore two-piece bathing suits. But I digress from our discussion of class! When I was in high school, the church bus started picking up teens from subsidized housing, and we all knew they were poor and not good enough to be our friends. It didn't even have to be said. Missy and the bus kids may have looked like me in some ways, but they didn't *really*.

When you know Jesus, you know that he didn't view people from the perspective of their shortcomings. He cared without judgment for the sick and the lame and the poor and the blind. I didn't know about this aspect of Jesus despite many years in church, but just because I missed the message for thirty years doesn't mean it isn't there. At the very beginning of Jesus's earthly ministry, he quoted Isaiah, saying, "The Spirit of the Lord is upon me, because he has anointed me to proclaim good news to the poor. He has sent me to proclaim liberty to the captives and recovering of sight to the blind, to set at liberty those who are oppressed, to proclaim the year of the Lord's favor" (Luke 4:18–19). These words are a clear command to the followers of Jesus to prioritize those in need, those without money, those without indoor plumbing. Those who sit beneath the middle class in the hierarchy of our classist syncretism.

When he left this earth, Jesus told his followers to serve others as they had seen him serving. Saint Teresa of Ávila captured this idea:

Christ has no body on earth but yours, no hands but yours, no feet but yours. Yours are the eyes through which Christ's compassion for the world is to look out; yours are the feet with which He is to go about doing good; and yours are the hands with which He is to bless us now.[25]

It seems like there would be very little for evangelical Christians to object to in these words. However, these activities have also been politicized and are often seen as the province of "liberals." This results in an enormous amount of cognitive dissonance for some in the conservative church, because they have been forced to make political decisions about things that are simply moral, ethical, and biblical—things that should be apolitical. They have also been taught that being liberal is bad and unchristian.

If we take politics out of it, I do not believe most evangelical Christians would argue that we should not make an effort to meet the basic needs of poor people in any and every way we can. United Methodist pastor John Pavlovitz hits the church hard:

> Christianity was a movement from the street. It was an organic *yeast in the dough*, formed in the gathering of the rejected and the marginalized and the poor—led by a homeless, itinerant street preacher and the motley assortment of fishermen, prostitutes, and ex-tax collectors who found affinity in his invitation to love radically and to shun power relentlessly. Without buildings or lobbyists or national boycotts or political position, it became exactly what it was designed to be: an interdependent community that resembled Jesus. It was the visibly different people who tangibly altered the places they traveled in life-giving ways.[26]

Jesus was homeless through his three years of earthly ministry. I wonder how well he would fare today if he stopped by a suburban church asking for a meal without an appointment.

These thoughts on the brokenness of the church make me weep as I type them. I think of German theologian Jürgen Moltmann's profound thoughts on the meaning for all of humanity of the suffering of Christ on the cross. These sufferings are "the sufferings of the poor and weak, which Jesus shares in his own body and in his own soul, in solidarity with them."[27] Beyond that, Moltmann writes elsewhere, "What Christ, the incarnate God, did in time, God, the heavenly Father, does and must do in eternity."[28] The eternal God is suffering on behalf of his creation, while a large percentage of people who claim to follow him believe the suffering people are only getting what they deserve.

Sider says, "The church should consist of communities of loving defiance. Instead, it consists largely of comfortable clubs of conformity."[29] He argues that Christians uncritically participate in an unjust world despite the clear biblical mandate to do otherwise, offering as an example the reality that 200 million US citizens consume enough food "to feed over one billion people in the poor countries" and that "people in the United States spend between $30 and $50 billion each year on diets . . . to reduce their caloric intake." The amount that we spend on golf on an annual basis could provide basic necessities for those in developing countries: "health, education, family planning, and clean water."[30]

Speaking prophetically to fellow Christians, Sider says, "Millions of people die unnecessarily every year because rich folk like you and me have ignored the Bible's clear teaching that God measures the integrity of our faith by how we respond to the poor."[31]

The Cost of Syncretism

The impact of syncretism on the evangelical church is not small. I was raised under its spell, and it's been a long journey out. We are called to make a difference with this radical love of Jesus, modeling a new humanity. Not only are we not doing that; we are actually exacerbating the racist and classist divides by displaying a divided church. One problem with a divided church is that we are called to minister in a society that is increasingly divided, especially in recent times. A divided church cannot bring healing to society until it is itself healed. And a divided church does not draw people in; it often repels them.

Social psychologist Erich Fromm says that European-North American history, in spite of the church, is a history of conquest, pride, greed; our highest values are to be stronger than others, to be victorious, to conquer others and exploit them.[32] "In spite of the church," he says! The church has not had a moderating impact on humanity's base desire for power and exploitation. There is a high cost to this syncretism of ours. We cannot both exploit and befriend those who are different from us.

The statistics and stories above tell of one kind of impact. The voice of Kamal's father tells of another. What if the evangelical church was so generous and loving and welcoming of the Other that their efforts began to have a major impact on the scourges of racism and classism, to the point where people began to take notice? I would love it if Kamal's dad regularly met *real* Christians.

British theologian Lesslie Newbigin says that the call of the church is to "challenge the reigning plausibility structure" rather than being co-opted by it.[33] In the areas of racism and classism, the church has been thoroughly co-opted. Girls wearing snow pants is the least of our worries.

#

Money is another obstacle to developing relationships with people who do not look like us, both inside and outside the church. The divergence of beliefs about the meaning of money, the purpose of money, and how it should be properly used are the cause for a variety of misunderstandings. I believe it is one of the most significant reasons we stay within our own tribes, and we will take a look at why in the next chapter.

Notes

1. Hélder Câmara (1909–99) was an archbishop of the Roman Catholic Church in Brazil from 1964 to 1985.

2. Martin Luther King Jr., interview by Ned Brooks, *Meet the Press*, NBC, April 17, 1960; the same idea is eloquently restated by Otis (last name omitted) in Michael O. Emerson and Christian Smith, *Divided by Faith: Evangelical Religion and the Problem of Race in America* (New York: Oxford University Press, 2000), 71.

3. Randall Balmer, "Under Trump, Evangelicals Show Their True

Racist Colors," *Los Angeles Times*, August 23, 2017, https://tinyurl.com/y3aruwfk.

4. Emerson and Smith, *Divided by Faith*, 170.

5. Emerson and Smith, *Divided by Faith*, 132.

6. H. Richard Niebuhr, *The Social Sources of Denominationalism* (Hamden, CT: Shoe String, 1954), 263.

7. Ronald J. Sider, *The Scandal of the Evangelical Conscience: Why Are Christians Living Just Like the Rest of the World?* (Grand Rapids: Baker, 2005), 25.

8. Sider, *Scandal*, 12.

9. Sider, *Scandal*, 24–25.

10. Eugene Rivers, "The Responsibility of Evangelical Intellectuals in the Age of White Supremacy," in *The Gospel in Black and White: Theological Resources for Racial Reconciliation*, ed. Dennis L. Okholm (Downers Grove, IL: InterVarsity, 1997), 21.

11. Allan Aubrey Boesak and Curtiss Paul DeYoung, *Radical Reconciliation: Beyond Political Pietism and Christian Quietism* (Maryknoll, NY: Orbis, 2012), 79.

12. Boesak and DeYoung, *Radical Reconciliation*, 11.

13. Boesak and DeYoung, *Radical Reconciliation*, 23.

14. Boesak and DeYoung, *Radical Reconciliation*, 20.

15. Rivers, "Responsibility of Evangelical Intellectuals," 14.

16. Desmond Tutu, *God Is Not a Christian* (New York: HarperOne, 2011), 29.

17. Boesak and DeYoung, *Radical Reconciliation*, 88.

18. Boesak and DeYoung, *Radical Reconciliation*, 88.

19. Statistics shared by Ron Sider in a workshop in Chicago in February 2005. Further statistics are available in his *Rich Christians in an Age of Hunger* (Dallas: Word, 1997). See also Mike Holmes, "What Would Happen If the Church Tithed?" *Relevant*, March 8, 2016, https://tinyurl.com/y4dkc7xh.

20. Economic Policy Institute, "Poverty," *The State of Working America*, https://tinyurl.com/y2y56db3.

21. Julie Zauzmer, "Christians Are More Likely to Blame Poverty on

Lack of Effort," *Washington Post*, August 3, 2017, https://tinyurl.com/y8boc9xv.

22. Zauzmer, "Christians."

23. Michael Horton, "Beyond Culture Wars," *Modern Reformation*, May–June 1993, 3.

24. Zauzmer, "Christians."

25. Attributed to Saint Teresa of Ávila (1515–82), although it does not appear in any of her volumes.

26. John Pavlovitz: "Rescuing Jesus from American Evangelicals," *johnpavlovitz.com*, August 28, 2017, https://tinyurl.com/yyj-gaana.

27. Jürgen Moltmann, *The Spirit of Life: A Universal Affirmation by Jürgen Moltmann*, trans. Margaret Kohl (Minneapolis: Fortress, 1992), 130.

28. Jürgen Moltmann, *The Trinity and the Kingdom*, trans. Margaret Kohl (Minneapolis: Fortress, 1993), 31.

29. Ronald J. Sider, *Rich Christians in an Age of Hunger: Moving from Affluence to Generosity* (Dallas, TX: Word, 1997), 210.

30. Sider, *Rich Christians*, 9–14.

31. Sider, *Rich Christians*, xvi.

32. Erich Fromm, *To Have or to Be* (New York: Continuum, 1976), 116.

33. Lesslie Newbigin, *The Gospel in a Pluralist Society* (Grand Rapids: Eerdmans, 1989), 96.

6.

Tribal Fortunes

This planet has—or rather had—a problem, which was this: most of the people living on it were unhappy for pretty much of the time. Many solutions were suggested for this problem, but most of these were largely concerned with the movement of small green pieces of paper, which was odd because on the whole it wasn't the small green pieces of paper that were unhappy.

—Douglas Adams[1]

I almost cracked up mentally in the summer of 2011. The wealthy parents of my daughter's college friend invited our family to spend the weekend at their summer home, which happened to be a mansion on the ocean. After eight years in the city, we were fully acclimated to our under-resourced urban environment. We had a new normal. And what we found when we arrived at the summer home was not even in the same solar system as the east side of St. Paul. Walls of windows facing the blue ocean, room after perfectly clean room, each tastefully and subtly decorated. And empty. Three stories, two kitchens, multiple staircases, a game room. And did I mention the monogrammed bath towels that weighed more than some of my furniture? It was both beautiful and depressing. It was just *so much*. So much stuff and so much extra. At the end of our visit, we flew back to the solar system in which St. Paul is located, which admittedly looked a little different. I wasn't sure if I felt angry or jealous. Or both.

The day after we got home, we had our weekly staff meeting at The Lift. These typically start with everyone checking in. Dee shared that her landlord had not been paying his mortgage, even though she had been paying her rent, and that she had received a notice that the house was in foreclosure. She also told us that her power would be turned off in two days, as she was struggling financially, with five children still at home and only a part-time job.

I experienced something akin to the bends, which divers get when they surface too quickly. It wasn't healthy for me to move so quickly between such radically different environments. Symptoms of the bends can include anything from a rash to paralysis to death. At that moment, I felt closer to the death end of things. I walked around that week trying to figure out how these two families were part of the same country. It wasn't just that one was rich and one was poor—that's obvious. It was like they lived in different worlds, and they were so unaware of the existence and lifestyle of the other that they may as well have. They knew it as a truism that there are rich and poor people in our country, but they didn't know it as a reality. Their day-to-day lives were worlds apart. The wealthy people had so much money they didn't know what to do with it. They owned three large homes and between them had enough bedrooms for family members to have six apiece. Dee had so little money at the time that she didn't know what to do, and she lived with five children in a soon-to-be-foreclosed rental with two bedrooms, one bathroom, and an attic, that was about to be without gas and electricity. She was out of options in this free country.

My years here have taught me that even if we can eradicate racism and classism, the biggest barrier will still remain—and it is the barrier of all things financial. Money is a real problem. Karl Marx declared:

> Money is the universal, self-established *value* of all things. It has, therefore, robbed the whole world—both the world of men and nature—of its specific value. Money is the estranged essence of man's work and man's existence, and this alien essence dominates him, and he worships it.[2]

The contrast of the mansion on the ocean and Dee's eviction makes it clear that contemporary Western society now exists in spheres that cannot be Venn-diagrammed. There is no overlap, except that we all worship money, if Marx is correct. Any attempt to build a more just society seems destined to fail, rooted as we all are in this worship of money.

In thinking about barriers to reciprocal relationships, I initially thought of this barrier as being purely about economics. While money is the obvious artifact of this unique society, more thought has convinced me that money is, among other things, a token that determines which sphere you inhabit in our society: the one made up of free and empowered people who live in a world of options, or the one filled with unfree and disempowered people offered only the illusion of freedom. We'll tackle money in this chapter and freedom in the next.

Money Rules

I grew up in a middle-class family with very clear rules about money. First, you should always try to get more of it while staying within the law. Bills and debts should be paid on time, money should be kept in a bank, you shouldn't live on credit, and some of your money should be saved. Today I don't spend my time trying to get more of it, but other than that, these are the rules I still live by. They are the rules of the middle class. Along with philosopher Friedrich Engels, Marx famously proclaimed, "The history of all hitherto existing society is the history of class struggles."[3] This becomes apparent when comparing my middle-class rules about money with the rules my urban friends grew up with.

Dee says that in her family the rule was that "when money came, it got spent." There was never enough, no one had a bank account, and there were no savings. She describes the arrival of money as bringing happiness that lasted as long as the money did, which wasn't long.

Speaking of his childhood, Ernest said, "Money was to make sure you had something to eat. And that's about it." As a teen, his goal was to get money to get high. The older he got, he said, the more he worried about getting money so that he wouldn't have to sleep outside. When I asked him whether he had ever heard of a savings account as a child, he rolled his eyes and said, "No, dear." Later, when he was making money in ways that would eventually land him in prison, he was making a lot, but he said he never spent it. He saved it under his living room rug as a guarantee against hard times that he was sure would be coming. In his concern about the future, Ernest stood in contrast to many of my neighbors, whose money doesn't even make it under the rug, let alone to the bank.

Representing the younger generation, Wesley says that money is "always easy to spend and hard to save." He describes buying things he doesn't need just because he can. It's a way to feel like his standard of living is being raised. Ricky describes money as something he's always watched come and go. Since the money isn't going to last, he says, "Spend it!" Cortez's father told him to save money, but he never told him how that was done.

One way I would describe my own experience with money compared with my friends' here is that for me, money is about "later," whether that's retirement, hardship, or when it's time to buy a car. For my friends, money is about "now." And that makes sense, since the money is not going to stay around long.

Writer Lee Stringer, who grew up poor, says of those living in poverty:

> Money is a thing that is for all effects and purposes already spent before it is earned. Successful handling of it is measured, not in years, or future generations, but in making it to the next payday. The sweat of their brows comes to be understood as a means of funding the moment, rather than as a way to finance the future. Thus if they do happen to get a little ahead, the extra cash doesn't go into a savings account, but to buy a new flat screen TV.[4]

These conflicting money rules add further explanation to the difficulties in forming relationships across differences.

In the introduction, I mentioned that a few of our teens and young adults had inherited relatively large sums of money and spent it very quickly. After Jasmin,* the pregnant eighteen-year-old, came back to us broke and homeless, I had a chance to talk to her about what happened to the $10,000 she had received after the death of her grandfather. She had spent it on clothing, purses, eating out, hairstyles, and acrylic nails, among other purchases that don't retain their value. She was ashamed, but she also had a fairly good justification. She knew that friends and family would be circling, trying to get a piece of it. She believed the best way to protect herself and her money was to get rid of it as soon as possible. Her approach was proven partially right when she had a call from a family member a little while later saying that they needed some of the money back as the uncle had not taken into account the inheritance tax on the estate. They were calling all of the recipients, trying to get enough returned to pay the tax.

Researchers Anuj Shah, Sendhil Mullainathan, and Eldar Shafir have shown that the desperate economic situations of people in poverty cause them to make unwise financial decisions affecting the long term. They focus on the short term for survival reasons. "Resource scarcity," they say, "creates its own mindset, changing how people look at problems and make decisions."[5] If a person has plenty of money, she will buy groceries without giving it much thought. If a person is lacking in financial resources, she may focus to an extreme degree on buying groceries, and thereby neglect other problems, such as paying the rent. She may focus on putting gas in the car, but not on routine maintenance of the car. When a crisis hits in the midst of these daily survival needs, I have seen everything go out the window. I had a friend bail a relative out of jail using rent money that was due the next week. The needs of today, whatever they are, often trump the needs of next week.

But desperate economic conditions and the need to survive are not the only causes of unwise financial decisions. In one of our discussions about money, Wesley describes money as "a system that you have to learn. You have to learn how to speak and walk and talk money. If you don't come from money," he says, "you don't know money." Taking Wesley's views into account, it's the combination of resource scarcity and financial illiteracy that leads to decisions of instant gratification.

Malik* is a perfect example. One of our volunteers regularly hired this high school student on weekends to help him with projects at his house. He always offered him the option of getting paid ten dollars per hour right away or getting paid fifteen dollars per hour if he would wait on getting paid until he had enough saved for something like driver's training. In every case, Malik chose to take the lesser amount and get it right away. After a few months, we pointed out to him that he would have made an additional $400 if he had agreed to defer the payment. It didn't matter to him. He wanted to go out with his friends, and he wanted to get minutes for his mobile phone, and there was no way he was waiting for that money, no matter how much extra it would be. He was desperately caught up in a rush to get it and spend it. His needs were immediate, and other options for meeting them were not on his radar.

Lenora* was a thirty-year-old single mom with zero college credits but several thousand dollars in student loans that she was in default on. She explained to me that a few times she had registered for community college courses and was granted student loans to cover tuition and living expenses. Since loans are disbursed the third week of school, she attended class a few times those first weeks, and then once the loans had been disbursed, she dropped out. A couple of days later a check for thousands of dollars would arrive made out to her. It's the portion of the student loan that is allocated for living expenses. She cashed the check and spent the money, ignoring the student loan bills that showed up six months later. Eventually, Lenora couldn't get any more student loans, but the system is slow enough to allow Lenora, and others like her, to get into serious financial trouble after only a couple of semesters. This practice is widespread. One young man getting out of prison said that he was immediately enrolling in college. I was excited about this decision until I realized he wasn't actually planning to attend; he just needed some quick money.

Cortez was one of the other young people who came into a relatively large sum of money—nearly $15,000. He was twenty-one years old, and before he received the money he was living couch to couch and job to job and didn't really have a plan for his life. I explained to him the long-term benefits of making the money that he would be receiving work for him. I said, "You have two choices: one, you can live on your usual $5,000 of annual income and go on a shopping spree with this $15,000, or two, you can use the $15,000 to attend a training program to be a mechanic. In option two, you will only have your $5,000 in income this year, but next year, when you have a skill, you may be able to make $25,000, and that amount will only go up every year after that." He understood what I was saying and agreed it was a good idea, but that pile of money was just too tempting. He *knew* he was choosing a short-term gain over long-term stability, and he did it anyway. Today, he remembers thinking that he had never had money that was all his own. "All of this is mine," he thought. "No one can tell me anything."

He bought a cheap car that died after a few months and spent the rest on whatever fun thing was right in front of him. He visited bars, casinos, clubs, hotels, and upscale restaurants. "I felt good having money," he said. He wanted to believe it could buy him the life he'd been looking for; what it actually did was enable him to consume for a short period of time. He says he's glad he did it, while sheepishly admitting that after his spree, he ended up living with six people in a one-bedroom apartment, sleeping on the floor on cushions he pulled off the sofa every evening.

Cortez felt like he purchased some freedom with his $15,000, but it could be argued that his behavior was self-injurious. Social theorist Herbert Marcuse describes those who unwittingly buy into "false needs" that lead to their demise, all the while thinking they are making decisions in their own best interests.[6] Society told Cortez that consuming would make him happy, that he *needed* to make those purchases, and he obliged. Conversely, social scientist Paul Willis describes working-class schoolboys in England as believing they are gaining power by rebelling against the institution of the school "to defeat its main perceived purpose: to make you 'work.'"[7] Thus, those on the margins of society can lose either by giving in to the message of consumerism or by rebelling against the value of working hard in school, all the while believing they are winning.

In addition to these external forces that impact decision-making, some of my friends also battle internal forces. In the 1960s, Stanford researcher Michael Mischel conducted the infamous "Stanford Marshmallow Experiment," measuring the ability of four-year-olds to delay gratification. Children were given one marsh-mallow and told that if they didn't eat it until the researcher came back into the room, they would receive a second marshmallow. Future research on the same students upon graduation from high school revealed that those who ate the marshmallow right away were "more troubled, stubborn and indecisive, mistrustful, less self-confident" than the children who did not eat the marshmallow right away, and "still unable to delay immediate gratification." In addition, those who were able to delay eating the marshmallow for twenty minutes had SAT scores 210 points higher than those who could wait only one minute.[8]

Ricky will attest to our many conversations about the impor-tance of looking more than five minutes into the future when making decisions. He was interning at one of The Lift's youth programs, where we offered students involved in our token econ-omy the opportunity to win a new iPad. If they attended the pro-gram every week or had only excused absences, they would be entered into a drawing for the iPad at the end of one semester. Every student declared their intention to be in that drawing. One week later, over half the students did not show up and did not call in with an excuse for their absence. I asked one of the moms about this, and she said, "Oh, he's not thinking that far into the future." Cortez agrees, "If it's not instant, it doesn't exist." He explains that the kids are not making a conscious choice between the iPad and whatever they choose to do that night. Rather, they don't have a plan, and when they are presented with something immediate, they choose "what's in front of their face." The iPad, for all intents and purposes, does not exist.

This combination of a lack of resources, social pressure to con-sume, and financial illiteracy has long-term effects on youth that go far beyond the inability to secure basic resources in adulthood. Healthy relationships, success in school and work, and physical health are all tied to the issue of delayed gratification, meaning that the financial divide between the rich and poor has the potential to impact every single area of life, creating further division.

The Predators

The cost for people in my neighborhood to consume is far greater than the cost to consume in the suburbs. My neighbors who are poor have actually become the target of a system that preys on both their unspoken desires and the hopelessness they live with. A predator is "one who, for personal profit, takes advantage of another by unfair, albeit technically legal, means," and the east side has a lot of them.[9]

There is a large rent-to-own store in the center of our neighborhood where, with no down payment, people can walk out with brand new furniture and appliances. There is a biweekly or monthly rental charge, with the idea that once the item is paid off, the item belongs to them. There are problems with this business model from the standpoint of the consumer, however. First, as soon as one payment is missed, the store comes and repossesses whatever is being rented, regardless of how much money has already been paid. Second, if a person were actually to make all of their payments, they would have paid two to three times more for the item than anyone with good credit would pay to buy it at a big-box store. But poor people rarely have credit cards that allow them to enter into negotiations at a store where the prices must be competitive. The rent-to-own website and store promotions claim that everyone is preapproved (as long as they have a source of income and two references).

Back in the 1980s, Ernest rented a console TV (the kind where the fake-wood box around the set is as big and heavy as a car) at a cost of almost $100 per month. He fell on hard times, missed one payment, and they showed up to take the TV away, despite the fact that he had already paid hundreds of dollars for it. Dee had the same experience when she was first married with a living room full of rented furniture. The business model seems to rely on a high percentage of defaults, enabling the store to rent out the same item multiple times.

There's more. In January of every year, a dancing Uncle Sam and the Statue of Liberty show up on a busy corner on the east side, luring people into a tax preparation business to have their taxes done. These costumed characters offer immediate filing and "Refund Anticipation Loans" (RALs). RALs are short-term loans made against a taxpayer's expected refund. The costs for RALs equal about 10 percent of a taxpayer's refund. At Jackson Hewitt, a tax preparation business, "73 percent of its customers make less than $29,000 per year . . . and 70 percent of its customers are sold RALs and other high-cost bank products."[10] The result is that some of my neighbors living far below the poverty line end up paying these businesses almost as much as I pay an actual CPA to file my family's tax return. The loans against their tax returns enable my neighbors to pocket their refund a month earlier than they otherwise would have, but that extra month comes at a high price.

Payday loans are even more troubling, as they are available all year long. These are "extremely high-interest, short-term loans offered to cash-strapped consumers."[11] Consumer law expert Creola Johnson offers as an example the story of a woman who borrowed $300 and was charged a $90 interest fee. The loan was to be paid off by her next payday. The actual annual interest rate on this loan amounts to 780 percent, due to how the interest is calculated and collected. Like most of these loans, if you can't pay off the entire loan on the due date, the lender will debit your bank account a late fee every two weeks. In the case of the woman with the $300 loan, she was charged a total of $1,800 in interest over the next ten months, on top of the original loan. After managing to pay that interest, she still owed the lender the original $300. Thus, consumers are caught "in a vicious cycle of indebtedness."[12] Normally these interest rates would be illegal, but lenders are able to charge rates that exceed state law by taking advantage of loopholes in federal banking laws. One of these loopholes allows for higher interest rates in the event that the customer agrees to the rate. This preys on people who are desperate for money and will agree to almost anything to get it.

Check-cashing businesses are another species of predator in our neighborhood. Many of my friends do not have bank accounts, so they rely on these businesses to cash their checks or to send and receive money. Fees can run as high as 10 percent of face value to cash a check. I can deposit $100 in my bank account at no charge; my friends using the check-cashing business in our neighborhood walk away with only $90.

Even some of the independent neighborhood businesses are predatory. Dee saved up enough money a few years back to buy a used car. Because she didn't have a car, the easiest way to buy one was to walk to the used car dealer a few blocks away. She bought a 1995 Lincoln Town Car for $2,000. The whole family could fit in the car. They loved the whitewall tires and the radio controls on the steering wheel. On her drive back from singing at a nightclub less than a week after buying the car, she was pulled over by the Minneapolis police. The officer said the plates on the car did not match up with the car she was driving, and he put her in the back of the squad car. Despite her explanation and paperwork showing she had just bought the car from a dealer (who put the plates on), the officer gave her tickets for various offenses, including driving a nonregistered vehicle, driving with a stolen license plate, and driving without insurance (the car was not legally hers). He said he believed her story, but she would have to fight it out in court. They had her car towed and dropped her off at a nearby gas station. It was well after midnight by this time. She was eventually able to get a cab and a $30 ride home.

In order to straighten out this mess, Dee had to take time off work to appear in court twice (riding the bus an hour each way to do it). The car was in the impound lot, and she was not allowed access to get her things from it while the tickets were pending. By the time they were cleared, the car had been sold or salvaged. She lost birthday gifts, a camera, and other personal items.

She was out more than $2,000 and still had no car. The judge allowed the car dealer to pay her money back in payments. Over a year later, she had finally received the full amount she paid for the car, but no compensation for the registration money she paid him when she bought the car, her cab ride, the time she had to take off work to go to court, the full tank of gas she lost, or the personal items that were left in the car. She spent an enormous amount of time and money on *not* having a car. And each time she received another payment from the dealer, there were other bills that needed to be paid. Despite the fact that he was dealing on the shady side of things, the car dealer was not fined or ticketed. The only hardship he suffered was having to pay back money he had unethically taken from Dee for a car he did not have the title to. He is still in business four blocks from my house. She was without a car for a few years afterward.

Cortez recently felt preyed upon when his car was stolen. He had purchased a 1998 Toyota Corolla for $300 and was thrilled to be done with the bus and have the ability to take his son out, get to work quickly, and generally feel the freedom that comes with owning a car. Five months after buying the car, however, it was stolen from the front of his house in the middle of the night. The neighbor's security camera picked up a grainy image of a black man driving off with the car at 2:00 a.m., along with his last thirty dollars, which was in the glove box. When the car was found by the police several days later, it was towed to a city impound lot. In order to even see the car, he had to pay $140 in towing and storage fees. Once he had a chance to check out the car, he found that the battery, headlights, fuel pump, fuel line, and other important parts were missing, and it was not worth what it would cost to repair it. Cortez felt victimized, first, by the thief, whom he felt had been watching him. He used Connie's metaphor of crabs in a bucket as he described what it felt like to watch a black man drive off with his car. He felt victimized, second, by the city lot that charged him so much money for the honor of having his car stolen. Like Dee, Cortez *also* spent a lot of money to *not* have a car.

Ricky and Wesley add to the list the higher prices charged by grocery stores and liquor stores in the city compared to in the suburbs. Journalist Dave Zweifel adds credit card and insurance companies to the list of predators, noting that "insurance companies charge higher premiums to those with low credit scores."[13] The unjust business practices of these predatory companies deepen the divide between rich and poor, burying those who are poor further into debt with higher costs and interest rates than those with financial resources. "Those with the least ability to pay," says Zweifel, "almost always end up being exploited."

Judgment

One result of these completely different beliefs and experiences with money is that the opportunities for misunderstanding and judgment are multiplied.

Anthony* and Mara* were a young couple who had a difficult start to adulthood. Mara was only eighteen and had a two-year-old and an infant. She had recently taken up with Anthony, who had just been released after serving time in prison on drug charges. Anthony was having a hard time finding a job due to the felony on his record. Mara was just trying to survive every day. A few of us in the neighborhood started to get to know the young couple and spent time with them, sometimes helping out with rides and food and other basic needs. The house they were renting was sold, and when they had to move we worked with a friend who owned an apartment building in the neighborhood. She agreed to rent them a two-bedroom apartment for $250 per month. They arrived at this amount based on the income Anthony and Mara had from public assistance and temporary jobs. The usual rent for the unit was $700. We were meeting regularly with the family, trying to build the relationship and make sure their needs were met.

A few weeks after Anthony and Mara moved into their new apartment, we went to visit them. We found that they had contracted with the local cable company for high-speed internet and the most expensive cable television package available. The bill for these services was over $200 per month. When I asked them how they were paying this bill and tried to explain that if they had an extra $200 per month, some of that money should rightly go to paying more rent, they were completely baffled by this idea. No matter how long we talked about this and how many angles I tried, Anthony and Mara didn't understand why their cable bill was anyone's business. They thought if they were savvy enough to get the landlord to give them the apartment that cheap, then all the better for them: now they could get cable.

Similarly, Lisa* moved into our neighborhood and two of her young children started attending our programs at The Lift. She had recently left an abusive relationship and was struggling to go to school and make ends meet. As winter approached, she told us her four kids had no coats or boots. We were able to gather some resources to get their needs met. When Hadley and I went to deliver the winter gear, we found Lisa excited about her new phone with an unlimited data plan. To her, there was no conflict between asking people to help her get coats for her kids, while she spent whatever money she had on a new phone.

Stories like these about Anthony and Mara and Lisa are stories that I cannot tell in most contexts. Middle-class people seem to agree that you do not ask for help for basic needs while you spend your money on luxuries like smartphones and cable television. My neighbors also see it in black and white: if I am smart enough to track down and take advantage of every available resource, why can't I put my money to use in whatever way I want? I have found that the truth is in the gray area. Dee, who understands the urban reality far better than I do, can tend to get irritated at neighbors who seem to be taking advantage of the generosity of others. But for suburban people whose basic needs are more than met, the judgment is more severe. It is as though poor people should not be allowed to have any pleasure at all.

In our volunteer trainings at The Lift, people have expressed disgust at how all the poor people have cell phones. It may be a legitimate question, but it's often asked with a bad attitude. On the subject of phones, suburban people don't seem to realize that cell phones are cheaper than landlines, and when a single mom is often at work or on the bus, a mobile phone is the only way her children, or her children's school, can reach her.

Everyone has an opinion on why poor people are poor. A group of social workers studied the attitudes of social workers in Mississippi to ascertain their views on poverty and the poor. In chapter 5, we saw the difference that faith makes in people's views on the causes of poverty, but in this study *political* views were under the microscope. It found that conservatives tend to see the problems of poverty as "mainly rooted in personal shortcomings," while liberals are "more likely to hold positive attitudes toward poor people," viewing the problems of poverty as emerging from systemic inequalities. The research also found that those who identified with conservativism viewed people in poverty as "lazy, irresponsible, lacking ambition, and otherwise unworthy of assistance."[14]

These are the attitudes those living in poverty bump up against on a regular basis. "Why do poor people make stupid, illogical decisions to buy status symbols?" asks researcher Tressie Cottom, who grew up on the edge of poverty. There are as many answers to this question as there are poor people. Cottom says it is for the same reason that most people buy status symbols: "We want to belong," she says.[15] Essayist Linda Tirado, writing about her own experience of poverty, says that none of her poor financial decisions matter in the long term. She expresses the hopelessness I see so often: "I will never not be poor, so why does it matter?" If you never have enough money, she says, "it ceases to have meaning."[16] A welfare recipient goes on the offensive: "We don't shame people who receive Earned Income Tax Credits, so why shame the ones on cash benefits?"[17] According to the Pew Research Center, there are $1.3 trillion in tax breaks available to businesses and individuals for items such as employer-paid health care, contributions to retirement plans, and mortgage interest deductions, among other things.[18] This is in contrast to the cost of welfare benefits which, according to the *Washington Post* in 2014, cost the federal government $212 billion annually.[19]

These differing views on the people who receive public assistance and judgments about how they should spend their money can be significant barriers to developing reciprocal relationships. I come from a world in which eating out or going out for drinks is a normal activity. About two years after moving into the city, I started a women's group that met in my home every week. It was a very diverse group, both ethnically and socioeconomically. We got into the habit of going out to dinner for group members' birthdays. This turned out to be a very awkward and educational activity for us. If a woman in the group shared that she was struggling to buy groceries and the next week we went out for a birthday dinner, what does everyone do? No one wanted our friend to have to come up with twenty dollars to pay for dinner. Obviously, she didn't want to go out and drink water while watching everyone else eat. If she pulled out twenty dollars and paid for her food, there was the potential for judgment as people might wonder how she could can afford this. People were glad to pitch in to pay for her dinner, but this could create an imbalance in the friendships, especially if white women were always covering the bills of black women. We worked as a group to find better ways to celebrate that didn't emphasize this divide. One celebration took place at a fast-food restaurant where we all ate a ton of French fries. At other times, someone baked a cake and we stayed in. The white women learned that it doesn't need to cost a lot of money to celebrate.

However, this is an ongoing issue in our community. It's very easy for everyone to stay in their own corner: people who can afford it go out and celebrate; people who can't, stay in. But eating together is an important social bonding experience. Memories are made as we celebrate together and share meals. It requires intentionality to create an environment that is hospitable to this. It takes compromise and honest communication. And it requires that people with resources be willing to affirm the right of those in poverty to have a good time without being judged.

Generosity

Amid a great deal of financial struggle in my neighborhood, I am surprised to see a level of generosity here that I haven't seen anywhere else. When I was growing up, I had five brothers and sisters, and one thing we did not share was money. This is in stark contrast to what's always going on with the teens in my neighborhood. It seems logical to me that a situation of scarcity would not breed generosity. To my surprise, the students freely share any money they have with one another, and, even more surprising, they share it with their families. If one student is broke, his friends pitch in so he can participate in whatever they are doing. If mom is short on rent money, all the kids give what they have to make up the difference. Unless it gets really out of hand, the kids don't complain.

Cottom says she watched her elders use what little they had "to help other people make ends meet."[20]

I can't imagine what I would have done if my parents asked me to help pay the mortgage when I was a teen. Our view of money was individualistic. My money is *my* money, and not only will I not give you some of it, but I would rather not even loan you anything. We were private about every aspect of it, and my dad modeled a frugality that saw excessive sharing as irresponsible. Or *any* sharing. I know that some of the sharing in my neighborhood comes out of a lack of knowing what the other options for money are. If money is to be spent and there's nothing right in front of you to buy, you may as well give it to your friend. Ricky explains that when he sees his mom struggling to pay the bills, it's a no-brainer to help if he can. He also says that paying his friend's way into a movie is a good investment, as "you know you'll need it the next time." Cortez agrees: "We're all in the same situation." But I also know that much of the sharing is simply evidence of a generous spirit. I have never seen this in any middle-class neighborhood I've lived in.

Part of the reason I have never seen it is that I come from a culture very different than Ricky and Cortez do. Although the United States is an individualist culture (emphasizing the independence of people from their groups), many minority cultures in the United States embrace collectivism (emphasizing *inter*dependence). In the former, the orientation tends to be toward *me*, while in the latter, the orientation is more often toward *us*. Harry Triandis, a pioneer in the field of cross-cultural psychology, identifies a "generosity rule" that operates among in-group members in collectivist cultures. According to this rule, when you are with your group, everyone shares in whatever resources are available, regardless of who contributed what.[21]

In the midst of the ideal of collectivism and its value of generosity, sharing has also led to some difficult situations: Bailing a relative out of jail instead of paying the rent. Helping a relative in another state instead of paying the rent. Helping your son with college tuition instead of paying the rent. Buying your daughter an iPhone for her birthday instead of paying the rent. It goes on and on—and it's usually the housing that's compromised. There is a set of tribal rules around sharing and generosity that I do not entirely understand. My past self would have pronounced judgment on some of these choices. My current self, however, is hoping some of the generosity rubs off on me.

#

I have tried to capture here the size of the cultural divide related to money. I don't know that I've done it justice. Of all the stories and surprises and aha moments I have experienced over my decade in this context, the majority are in some way related to money. I am still learning. A quick cultural competency or diversity training seminar or having a coworker who is different than you will not bridge this divide. Even though I now understand or can usually figure out why the people around me make the financial choices they do, it's still not the way I do it. And because money is attached to power and freedom, this is much larger than a conversation about why a higher percentage of black people than white people are poor. We turn now, then, to the more substantial topic of freedom: What is it? Who has it? What does it mean?

Notes

1. Douglas Adams, *The Hitchhikers Guide to the Galaxy* (New York: Ballantine, 2005), 3.

2. Karl Marx, *On* The Jewish Question (review of Bruno Bauer, *The Jewish Question*), https://tinyurl.com/y2mfqqom.

3. Karl Marx and Friedrich Engels, *Manifesto of the Communist Party*, 100th ed. (New York: International, 1948), 9.

4. Lee Stringer, "My Life on the Streets," *Salon*, April 18, 2013, https://tinyurl.com/yxqtza2k.

5. Anuj K. Shah, Sendhil Mullainathan, and Eldar Shafir, "Some Consequences of Having Too Little," *Science* 338 (2012): 682.

6. Herbert Marcuse, *One-Dimensional Man: Studies in the Ideology of Advanced Industrial Society* (Boston: Beacon, 1964), 4–6.

7. Paul Willis, *Learning to Labor* (New York: Columbia University Press, 1977), 26.

8. Susan Beacham, "One Marshmallow, or Two?" Parents' Choice Foundation, 2003, https://tinyurl.com/y4nmbc6r.

9. Creola Johnson, "Payday Loans: Shrewd Business or Predatory Lending?" *Minnesota Law Review* 87, no. 1 (2002): 5.

10. "Predatory Turkeys," Behind the Lines, *Multinational Monitor* 25, no. 12 (December 2004): https://tinyurl.com/y45tmlh7.

11. Johnson, "Payday Loans," 2.

12. Johnson, "Payday Loans," 4.

13. Dave Zweifel, "Predatory Business Again Targets Poor," *Madison Capital Times*, June 25, 2007.

14. Tim Rehner, Jane Ishee, Mimi Salloum, and Donna Velasques, "Mississippi Social Workers' Attitudes toward Poverty and the Poor," *Journal of Social Work Education* 33, no. 1 (1997): 131–42.

15. Tressie Mcmillan Cottom, "Why Do Poor People 'Waste' Money on Luxury Goods?" *Talking Points Memo*, November 1, 2013, https://tinyurl.com/y2ecmysq.

16. Linda Tirado, "This Is Why Poor People's Bad Decisions Make Perfect Sense," *HuffPost*, November 22, 2013, https://tinyurl.com/y54a9dkc.

17. Jill Krasny, "Welfare Recipient: Stop Judging the Poor for Blowing Money on Junk," *Business Insider*, July 12, 2012, https://tinyurl.com/y35pnprt.

18. Drew DeSilver, "The Biggest U.S. Tax Breaks," *Pew Research Center*, April 6, 2016, https://tinyurl.com/y4yacho5.

19. Mike Konczal, "No, We Don't Spend $1 Trillion on Welfare Each Year," *Washington Post*, January 12, 2014, https://tinyurl.com/y4kqrvef.

20. Cottom, "Why Do Poor People."

21. Harry C. Triandis, "Individualism and Collectivism: Past, Present, and Future," in *The Handbook of Culture and Psychology*, ed. David Matsumoto (Oxford: Oxford University Press, 2001), 42–44.

7.

Tribal Freedom

> We have been segregated and severed, from each other and even from ourselves. We have been told that freedom is the ability to pursue our petty, trivial desires when true freedom is freedom from these petty, trivial desires.
>
> —Russell Brand[1]

I spent a lot of time on playgrounds as a child, and every time the inevitable conflict would arise, someone would eventually stick their chin out and yell something along the lines of "You can't tell me what to do. This is a free country." And who could argue? Every morning, we all recited the Pledge of Allegiance, which promised "liberty and justice for all."

The stories about money in chapter 6 reveal a marked difference in the rules by which people from different backgrounds manage their money. But I want to say more than that rich people have money and poor people don't, and even more than that rich and poor people view money differently. I want to tie this distinction to the all-American value of freedom. To do this, I will share the story of "Alexa" that I have shared in sermons as I try to help middle-class people understand and *feel* the realties faced by those living in economic poverty. This story is a composite of many of the painful realities I have observed in the past decade in St. Paul. Everything in the story has actually happened (and continues to happen), just not all to the same person—though, as should be evident, it is very easy for such situations to compound in one individual's experience.

Alexa was born to a mom who was sixteen years old. Her mom tried to continue going to school, but it got to be too much, and she dropped out in the middle of her junior year. Alexa's dad dropped out of the picture even earlier than that.

The family had a bit of luck when they qualified for a two-bedroom apartment in public housing for only fifty dollars per month. Other than that, all the basic parts of life were a struggle.

Throughout the sixteen years she lived with her mom, Alexa first witnessed drug deals by her neighbors and then by her mom. She watched men come and go, leaving new babies behind. Three more came after Alexa, all girls.

The family never owned a car, so Alexa's world was very small. In kindergarten, she walked four blocks to the bus stop by herself, because her mom was still sleeping.

When things weren't going well, Alexa took the brunt of her mom's frustrations through screaming and hitting and ultimately tearful and shame-filled apologies by her mom, promising it would never happen again. Until next week when it happened again.

Alexa's favorite thing about first grade was that she sometimes got real grapes in her school lunch. She also liked the volunteer who came and listened to her read out loud.

By the time she was nine, Alexa was spending most of her free time taking care of her three younger sisters. Sometimes there was food and sometimes there wasn't. Even when there was, it was noodles and chips and canned beans from the dollar store.

When Alexa was ten, her mom's boyfriend moved in and things got even worse. He stayed around a lot longer than any of the other men had. Alexa witnessed violent drunken arguments, and after a few months she had to fight off the boyfriend's advances toward her ten-year-old body. When she tried to talk to her mom about this, her mom became angry and accused her of trying to steal her boyfriend.

Alexa started avoiding going home, which was just fine with her mom, who seemed to live in utter fear that her boyfriend would leave. When Alexa was gone from home, she was terrified that something bad would happen to her sisters. She wasn't sure why her mom insisted on keeping the boyfriend around, since he ate their food, made messes, didn't work, and bossed everyone around. But it became normal to Alexa.

The boyfriend finally did leave, but he was followed by a string of boyfriends, most of whom showed Alexa that men are not safe.

Alexa did not know a single married couple, nor did she have even one friend whose father lived with them. Her only information on marriage and intact families came from watching TV. She especially liked reruns of *The Fresh Prince of Bel-Air* and dreamed of moving into a mansion like Will Smith.

The best part of Alexa's life was always school. She was safe there. She loved the lunches, she loved reading, and she loved to write poems and stories. She missed quite a bit of school to watch her sisters, but she did her best to get there as much as she could.

Sometimes, she would get up late and miss the bus, and then was stuck at home for the day unless her mother wanted her out of the house and happened to have five dollars for a cab.

Another struggle was finding a place to do homework. The house was always noisy, and every single surface was covered with papers and junk. They didn't have a desk, so Alexa usually moved the living room lamp into a corner and sat on the floor doing her homework. She got stepped on and her homework got stepped on. Sometimes her homework would disappear while she was sleeping, and she'd have to try to do it again on the bus.

She had a hard time finding pens and pencils that worked and always had to borrow paper from classmates. When she needed to do a project, she was too embarrassed to admit she couldn't afford poster board, or paint, or glue, or whatever was required. Even if she had a dollar or two, she had to walk almost a mile to the closest Walgreens.

When Alexa got into junior high, it seemed to her the game changed. Kids got meaner and people started talking about gangs. She tried to avoid the fights that broke out every day, but it was hard.

What she wore also became more important than ever. You got ridiculed if you weren't wearing the right clothes. Sometimes she babysat, and sometimes her grandma had ten dollars for her, but it was hard to piece together a wardrobe. And it was especially hard to go to school feeling good when there was no laundry detergent.

Or soap. Or toilet paper. Or underwear. Sometimes she just stayed home to avoid ridicule.

Her classrooms were overcrowded, and the books were years out of date. In her eighth-grade math class, there weren't enough desks, and she sometimes had to sit on the floor using a book with no cover that was nearly twenty years old.

More and more, her assignments required computers, printers, and internet access. Alexa could try to get two miles to the library, or she could stay after school and use the computers there, but then she had no way to get home.

By the time Alexa started high school, she had already suffered through abuses from several of her mom's boyfriends. These always caused the worst fights she had with her mom. At the beginning of her junior year, her mom finally kicked her out after accusing her of trying to steal her boyfriend. Alexa started couch hopping, spending a night or two on the couch of friends whose moms were either okay with it or too busy to notice her.

Up to this point, Alexa had defied the odds, getting all of her credits for the first two years of high school without even having to go to summer school. Her English teachers tended to take special notice of her and helped her when they could. She won an award for a poem she wrote, and it was published in a local magazine.

Her school counselor kept the idea of college in front of her. She was involved in a program that helped kids like her get into college, and she started dreaming about living in a dorm room with friends and having three meals a day. In her senior year, she applied and was accepted to a state school three hours from home. She received quite a bit of scholarship money but had to take out a $3,000 student loan for each semester.

The college offered shuttles from her city to the campus, so one day in late August, she climbed on one with three trash bags filled with her stuff and arrived on campus with great expectations.

When she got to school, she was surprised to find that she saw very few nonwhite people—students or teachers. Her roommate was white and had been delivered by her mom and dad along with a car full of furniture and appliances and blankets and decorations.

She watched them arrange everything carefully and then say tearful goodbyes.

Over the next several weeks, two things became clear to Alexa. First, she was in over her head academically. Apparently, her high school was sub-par, because she was not at all prepared to deal with the college workload. Second, she was very far out of her cultural comfort zone. The cafeteria food was bland. All of the people she was meeting were from the suburbs or rural areas. She was the only one who had never learned to drive (and how could she when they didn't own a car and her mom had never learned to drive?). Everyone spoke English, but no one spoke her language. She had never even been out of her state, but she felt like she was in a foreign country.

She went home for Christmas break and never went back. She left all of her clothes and belongings in her dorm room for someone else to deal with. She needed to live in a familiar place. As painful as home was, at least everything made sense. Even the chaos proceeded in a predictable manner. And she needed some food with some flavor.

She found a retail job making minimum wage and had no option but to try living with her mom again. Soon, she was taking responsibility for her three younger sisters in addition to trying to keep her mom sober and get back and forth to work on time. The store she worked at was seven miles from where she lived, but required two buses to get there, which took nearly an hour some days.

Six months later, she started getting notices that she needed to start paying thirty-five dollars per month toward her student loan. In the first year, she was able to make a few payments, but she gave half of the little she brought home to her mom to help with food and rent. She had to pay for her phone and bus fare and the basic necessities of life. There was just never enough to go around.

After another year, she realized her life was going nowhere fast. She decided to try a local technical school to become an LPN. In two years, she could finish the program and be making almost twenty dollars per hour. She felt hope for the first time in a long time.

She was accepted to the program, but she ran into a snag when the school found that she was in default on her previous student loan. With penalties and interest, she now owed much more than the $3,000 she had originally borrowed. The technical college encouraged her to get the loan problem taken care of so that she could enroll in the program.

She called someone about the loan. The lady was very nice and tried to explain how Alexa could get back on track. The problem was that Alexa did not understand anything the woman was saying. She had never had a bank account, never had a credit card, never borrowed money, and neither had her mom. She just didn't understand the words, and $3,000 may as well have been $100,000 as far as she was concerned.

After years of trying to beat the odds, she finally gave in.

Over the next three years, she didn't make any payments on her student loan. She did have two kids, whose daddies didn't stick around too long. She couldn't hold onto her job with no one to take care of her kids, and she couldn't afford daycare on minimum wage. She bounced with her two kids between her mom and her friends.

She qualified for WIC and food stamps, so usually they could at least eat. And she was able to sell some food stamps when she needed cash. She was no longer dreaming of school and jobs and escaping the ghetto. She no longer wrote poems. She was twenty-one.

One day at the local grocery store, she was using her food stamps to buy groceries, and she could see that the well-dressed white lady behind her did not approve. She turned to her and said, "What is your problem?"

The lady responded, "Oh, nothing, except that my tax dollars are apparently buying your groceries today. Why don't you get a job like everybody else? McDonald's is hiring."

In this home of the free and the brave, Alexa certainly qualifies as brave, but is she free?

Freedom Defined

This, of course, depends on what we mean by freedom. I grew up in a social and religious context that thoroughly bought into the ideology of American exceptionalism. If I had been questioned in early elementary school, it is not outside the realm of possibility that I would have said the United States was the only free country in the world. I knew we were free before I knew the alphabet. Not only did I know we were free; I also believed that everyone in my country was as free as I was. I had the privilege of not thinking too much about the meaning of freedom for much of my life.

Social activist and author Maxine Greene questions "whether any person can be free when enslaved."[2] I found that the answer depends, again, on how freedom is defined. The answer might be yes if freedom is merely an abstract concept relating to the ability to reason and have opinions. But Greene does not allow for this sort of definition. A society is not free simply because the laws protect rights and apply equally to all. Rather, Greene argues that freedom cannot exist when these rights are *supposedly* offered to all people, but in fact many of them have not had equal educational, economic, and leadership opportunities. The nineteenth-century French journalist and author Anatole France wrote of "the majestic quality of the law which prohibits the wealthy as well as the poor from sleeping under the bridges, from begging in the streets, and from stealing bread."[3] In the same vein, philosopher and political theorist Sir Isaiah Berlin insisted that to "offer political rights . . . to men who are half-naked, illiterate, underfed, and diseased is to mock their condition."[4] Our society continues to leave basic needs unmet, while supposedly offering self-actualization to all. According to educational reformer John Dewey, this is "a pure absurdity."[5]

Alexa also finds it absurd.

Sociologist Zygmunt Bauman traces the understanding of freedom historically as moving from a communal view of "the right to share in joint determination of the common fate"[6] to an individualistic understanding of freedom as the pursuit of private happiness brought to fruition in today's consumer-driven society. He challenges the common assertion that "this is a free country," arguing, like Greene, that this statement assumes that freedom only requires a lack of prohibition. Bauman introduces here the perspective that perfectly describes Alexa and most of my urban neighbors—they are people who live in a country that allows them to travel by plane, use a credit card, or sign contracts to purchase homes and cars, but who nevertheless lack the means to do these things. It is meaningless to Alexa that she is free to buy groceries.

During my doctoral studies, I experienced enormous changes in my understanding of poverty, freedom, and communal participation, although I cannot now conceive of ever having thought differently. Bauman shows that despite our inability in this social context to even conceive of a person who is not a "free-chooser," this so-called free-chooser is mythological—a local social creation, rarely seen throughout human history. We have equated freedom with consumption and take for granted that it always has been and always will be so, even though it is rooted in a unique and local economic system. Adult education expert Stephen Brookfield writes that our need for consumer goods is "created by the dominant capitalist order and then internalized by us until they are indistinguishable from our most basic desires."[7] Thus a fulfilled life has come to be defined by the attainment of consumer goods. The problem with this, according to social psychologist Erich Fromm, is that consumer goods do not lead to a fulfilled life.

> The observable data show most clearly that our kind of "pursuit of happiness" does not produce well-being. We are a society of notoriously unhappy people: anxious, depressed, destructive, dependent—people who are glad when we have killed the time we are trying so hard to save.[8]

Any evidence of the shortcomings of consumption seems to be continually squelched. Poverty's singular definition (inability to consume) pits it only against the power to purchase rather than the ability to have a voice in the community. This is true to such an extreme degree that the definition of poverty has expanded to include not just those who are objectively poor, but also those who are subjectively poor (lacking the capital to consume at a desired level). As a result, escaping poverty is defined singularly as gaining purchasing power, and participation in the common good has become largely irrelevant. The selfishness of a system rooted in consumption "makes leaders value personal success more highly than social responsibility."[9]

According to Bauman, we have moved so far from including social responsibility and the common good in our definition of freedom that outside controls (that is, government) are almost unnecessary, as the market has become the determiner of freedom. And what does Alexa know of the market? Today, those who can participate fully as consumers are free; those who cannot are unfree. Government has actually become a threat to the "private affair between the consumer and the market."[10] As long as the value of consumption holds up, no further controls are needed. It is in everyone's best interest to get in step with the demands of the market. This view of freedom is thoroughly rooted in late Western reality. For most of history and indeed most of the world today, the unimpeded ability to consume remains a privilege enjoyed by the few.

Throughout his long career, economist Milton Friedman continued to advocate for a market increasingly free of any and all government controls. He argued that this system would benefit people at all levels of society. He asserted that the progress under capitalism "has freed the masses from backbreaking toil and has made available to them products and services that were formerly the monopoly of the upper classes."[11] He advocated for individual charity to help the poor who were not benefitting from the market, as well as for programs that do not "distort the market or impede its functioning."[12] For Friedman, if we can stay the course of an unfettered market, everyone, including Alexa, will benefit. Friedman's magnum opus, *Capitalism and Freedom*, was first published in 1962. Here in the twenty-first century, Alexa is still not faring very well.

Despite this easily observable and well-documented obsession with consumption, my friends describe freedom differently. For

Wesley, freedom is about being comfortable in his own skin. He is free when he can "move around and be the man who was created in God's image." Ricky says freedom is "being without worry." When I asked each of them if they are free, they both immediately said "no." Ernest, who spent twenty years locked up, said that freedom is "to be able to go where I please and do what I please." Keshia speaks of freedom *from* sickness and negative people and freedom *to* vote, speak her mind, and have rights. In the midst of these laudable ideas of freedom, Wesley adds the caveat that he does "want to be free financially." He says that "poor people are born indentured slaves," and it's clear that he identifies with that designation.

I think very few people at any income level would include explicitly the idea of consumption in their definition of freedom when asked. But when I observe what people from all parts of society pursue and value, it seems like most have subconsciously bought into the construct of "freedom as consumption." "What can we buy next?" sings the choir. When they are not overcome by nihilism, my urban neighbors may seek a job or further education, and they describe it to me in terms of increased earning power, as opposed to self-actualization. When DeMarco* talks about learning a trade, he talks only about how much money he can be making in five years. He does not express to me any excitement about the skills he will be learning or about the experience of continuing his education.

When I was a St. Paul police chaplain, an officer with whom I rode along was called to respond to a domestic disturbance. We showed up at the apartment in a rough part of our neighborhood and banged on the door. A man in an undershirt holding a newborn baby answered; he said the woman who had called in the complaint was gone. The officer went inside to make sure she was not in the apartment. I stepped into the entry and could see into the kitchen and living room. The furnishings were limited to a milk crate (on which the man had sat down with the baby) and a 64-inch big-screen television. We couldn't do anything about the domestic complaint since the complainant was nowhere to be found, so we left, and I spent the rest of my ride-along wondering how a person could end up living in an apartment empty other than a milk crate and a TV that cost a few thousand dollars.

The man and his milk crate illustrate Bauman's point that "the less freedom exists in the other spheres of social life, the stronger is the popular pressure on the further extension of consumer freedom—whatever its costs."[13] At some point, this man had to choose whether to buy a chair or buy a TV, to meet basic needs or to consume. While I wanted to indict him for his choice, I now see it as his exercise of today's version of freedom—that is, his desire to participate in a world where he is able to do all of the things that are not prohibited by law. He did not appear to be thinking about carving out a space where he could "share in joint determination of the common fate."[14] He couldn't fix racism, but he could have a TV. And how could I blame him? By today's definitions, he did indeed obtain freedom with his purchase, just not the kind that brings meaning or opportunities to participate in the common good.

The man with the milk crate was freely participating in the free market. He may have even felt that it was working for him. Writing about market efficiency and its relationship to issues of social justice, sociologist Jürgen Habermas says, "A functional justification is not enough to make egregious social differences normatively acceptable in a democratically constituted civil society."[15] Put simply, just because the market is working on some level for some people doesn't make it right. A wealthy man and the milk-crate man can both bring home a TV and place it in their living rooms and be happy about it. This is their private liberty. But the milk-crate man paid a high cost on top of the price of the TV. When he consumed, he was supposedly free, but as I picture him in my mind all these years later, he is still sitting in front of his TV, chained to that milk crate.

When people of means evaluate the market merely by saying, "It works for me," and define freedom as, "I can buy whatever I want," it results in a world where my neighbor Alma* is struggling to feed her three kids, while fifteen miles away my old suburban neighborhood is filled with oversized new homes with empty bedrooms, two new cars in each garage, and pallets of food from a bulk store that could carry a family through the apocalypse. This has been accepted as normative because we still subscribe to the "pull yourself up by your bootstraps" myth, even as we reject the value of equal respect for every person. My urban neighbors, it is thought, have an equal chance to fill their cupboards to over-flowing, regardless of their particular story. If Alexa works hard enough, she can earn the income and she will be rewarded with private liberties. In this understanding, the magical equation can be stated as:

hard work = more money = more freedom

There are several problems with this formula; the one that is most troubling to me is that it assumes poor people do not work hard.

In every stratum of society, there are people who work hard, as well as people who do not. Social researchers Laurent Daloz, Cheryl Keen, James Keen, and Sharon Parks say, "Some work ever harder to purchase things they do not need, while others, working equally hard, cannot secure the basics of food, shelter, and health care."[16] If hard work is defined not by income, but by hours and effort, Kayla* is one example of a hard-working poor person in my neighborhood. She is a single mom with three young children, who runs a daycare out of her home from 6:30 a.m. to 6:30 p.m. many days. She has up to four extra kids in her home on a given day, and she is in constant motion keeping everyone active and safe and fed. Because our neighborhood is filled with people try-ing to make ends meet, it frequently happens that the moms can't pay Kayla at the end of the week. Because our neighbors tend to be transient, she also has children withdrawn from her daycare with no notice—and no payment. She has often worked a full week pro-viding daycare and ended up with very little income to show for it.

Through the many years I have known Dee, I have seen her work jobs that require physical labor, even while injured. I have seen her work two jobs at a time, keeping her away from the many needs of her children at home. She has had unreliable daycare, which has threatened her employment in corporations that are not patient with these kinds of situations. She has been called at work about problems with her children at school, but she cannot leave her job, and even if she could, it would take her an hour on the bus to reach the school.

Kayla and Dee are not poor and unfree because they aren't working hard. This equation is overly simplistic and does not take into account the social structures that work against freedom for so many. The math for Kayla, Dee, and others in my neighborhood just doesn't add up.

Here is how this barrier looks in real life. Some of our Lift events put Kayla and Dee in the same room with a young couple from the suburbs with two children in private school. They live in a $500,000 home and spend the Christmas holiday in South America every year. Mom has stayed home with the kids since they were born. What does the conversation between these parties sound like? And when is there space to develop this relationship further when Dee and Kayla are both single moms working full-time just to survive? Where are the commonalities that make for workable dialogue? In theory, this would be a conversation among equally free people, but the freedom of this suburban family reinforces the shackles that Kayla and Dee intuitively feel are with them all the time.

The barriers to developing a reciprocal relationship confronted by the young suburban couple and my neighbors are primarily related to class as opposed to race. It's hard to answer the question about what dialogue would unite these people from different worlds, because very little has been written about it. When sociologist James Vela-McConnell was researching diverse friendships, the goal for his study "was to have equal numbers of friendships representing several of the major socially constructed boundaries in our society," one of which was the boundary of class. Early on, he found that "identifying and recruiting friends who bridge the social boundary of class was amazingly difficult."[17] Ultimately, he had to remove class as one of the primary aspects of his study of diverse friendships, including it instead among secondary boundaries. With respect to our current topic, the higher your social class, the freer you are.

Corporate and Individual Freedom

In attempting to answer Greene's question about whether a person can be both free and enslaved, I have kept in mind two central aspects of freedom. The first is the *corporate* aspect of whether freedom can be legislated by a society without an infrastructure that levels the playing field and, possibly, without a morality that makes change possible. Without an equitable infrastructure, we end up blaming those who seem less free than we are, or we end up mocking those in need by offering them freedoms they have no ability to take advantage of.

The second aspect of freedom is *individual,* and it relates to Greene's insights about people being free to make their own decisions. I have observed that our society seems to focus on the second question to the exclusion of the first. We assume that we already have the right laws in place (corporate), and these will automatically lead to all citizens having control over their destiny (individual). But freedom will be realized only when we redefine and reinvent the structure and rules by which our society operates, while at the same time addressing ongoing individual racism and classism.

Sometime after we moved into our neighborhood, someone used a baseball metaphor to explain this distinction. Two teams were playing, and one team was far ahead as the seventh inning began. The team that was ahead admitted, at this point, that they had been cheating the entire time. The umpire told them to stop cheating, and, with no disciplinary measures and no correction of the score, the game resumed. Every individual player on the losing team could choose to play or not, but unless there was a mechanism to ensure fair play, that freedom didn't amount to much. In theory, my neighbors are invited to play every game. When they can't play competitively, it is assumed to be their fault or their choice, rather than a direct result of over two hundred years of cheating. Alexa is losing at this game, and it's assumed she is simply an unskilled player.

Abstract vs. Actionable Freedom

Greene and Bauman effectively deconstructed my idea of freedom, and they have helped me construct a new one. In speaking about individual freedoms, Greene argues that central to freedom is the ability to make decisions that are fully one's own. Similarly, educator and civil rights activist Myles Horton includes in his definition of *democracy* the necessity that "people are really free and empowered to make collectively the decisions that affect their lives."[18] Greene and Bauman made me realize that the freedom I grew up learning was available to all was merely an abstract concept and an important idea, whereas freedom must be actionable in order to be real. Abstract freedom versus actionable freedom, if you will.

My middle-class church worshipped the abstract concept of freedom, without any recognition by the worshippers that they were also bequeathed actionable freedom by their circumstances, and without any awareness that many people have never been offered the latter. Among many of my middle-class family and friends, this seems to still be the operating assumption. It seems to me that white privilege allows a large portion of our society to not think about the connection between money, power, and freedom.

The distinction between abstract and actionable freedom, and the fact that this is not a topic of public discourse, adds to the difficulty of crossing socioeconomic boundaries to develop meaningful relationships. According to this value system, rich people view my urban neighbors as worthless based on their lack of economic resources, and my neighbors view the rich as resource hogs who are (perhaps intentionally) limiting the options and freedoms of the poor. To the rich, the world is equitable, and they are where they are because they deserve it. To the poor, the world is fundamentally inequitable.

Because money and freedom are so closely related to power, it is difficult to conceive of reciprocity in whatever relationships do form between people who do not have resources and people who do. A master and slave may live near one another, speak the same language, and have a similar list of desires, but there will never be reciprocity until the terms of the relationship are redefined.

Reciprocity

I have thought a lot about reciprocity and how to get it and keep it in my relationships since moving to the city. By *reciprocity,* I simply mean mutuality and equality. One thing I've learned is that it takes hard work. I once received an email from a young middle-class white couple who had moved into our neighborhood. They really wanted to get to know their neighbors and were seeking advice about how to go about it—how to overcome the barriers and relate across so many differences. They recognized their position of privilege and were concerned to avoid the "savior" mentality that some do-gooders evidence. They asked good questions and operated out of good intentions, but the fundamental misconception—one that I also held at one time—was that their financial resources were the basis for relating to their neighbors. They met a family that was about to be homeless, and on the same day were considering inviting them to live in their basement. Her email was filled with questions about how to help the neighbors they met—one of the neighbors had a teen in trouble; another was an elderly woman taking care of her young grandchildren all by herself; and another was a single mom with three children under four.

When we start by thinking about how we can help our neighbors, we begin from a position of power, which is not the starting point for a reciprocal relationship. From my own experience, I can say that I never moved into a *suburban* neighborhood and immediately started looking for those who needed my help. I assumed equality and built relationships of reciprocity. Every family in every neighborhood has both assets and challenges. When well-meaning and well-resourced people assume that they bring all the assets, and that their economically disadvantaged neighbors have all the challenges and require their help, not only can there be no reciprocity, but there is a high likelihood that damage will be done.

Each of the neighbors described in the email did indeed face challenges. But they also had a lot to offer, whether that's wisdom, a listening ear, comfort, problem-solving, or help putting challenges into perspective. I never once considered the role of power in my relationships with my suburban friends; I think about it constantly in my relationships that cross lines of difference. According to philosopher Michel Foucault, it's wise that I do. Foucault sees power operating at micro levels. It "reaches into the very grain of individuals, touches their bodies and inserts itself into their actions and attitudes, their discourses, learning processes and everyday lives."[19] How often have I unknowingly used my own power as an educated member of the middle class to impose my views on Dee and others? I don't know, and possibly she doesn't either, but it would be naïve to pretend I have not done so.

Greed and Consumption

I am greedy, but it just looks like normal. I want to buy things I don't need. I want to consume without thought of those who can't. I want to get the new iPhone when it comes out even though mine is working fine. I had lunch with Dee a while back and at the end she asked if she could borrow some money because she was short on food and payday was two days away. I gave her the fifteen dollars I had in my wallet. The next day, I arrived early to an appointment and wandered into a store to kill time. There was a dress on the clearance rack for twenty dollars. I tried it on but felt some conflict about buying it. I didn't need another dress, no matter how cheap it was. However, my frugal upbringing makes it hard to pass up a deal. I struck a deal (with the devil? God?) that I would buy the dress but not let Dee pay me back the fifteen dollars. I know what you're thinking: I could have passed up the dress and given her another twenty.

But what I'm thinking is: "What difference would that really make?" Dee would have twenty more dollars in her pocket, and I could be happy about that. But at the end of the day, Dee is still

living under the weight of an unjust system, and I am still benefitting from it. My growing recognition that the things I buy are not
just individual choices that reflect my own desires, but are rather
"needs that are felt as individual but in reality are socially induced"
is a step in the right direction.[20] I can now see that the world is
conspiring in a nefarious plot to make me buy dresses I don't need,
and unfortunately, I'm not the only one.

In order to change the system, we would all have to recognize
the ideology we have bought into. When my children were very
young, we had a ritual that I hoped would help them become at
least a little bit more aware than I was at their age of the daily messages coming at them. Each time they watched a television com-
mercial and recognized something it was telling them to think or
buy or do, they had to point at the TV and yell, "That's a load of
crap." We also had a ritual after watching movies. While we were
driving home, we would identify and "critically evaluate" the messages we heard in the movie. I remember walking out of a Disney
movie when Hadley was four years old, as she rolled her eyes and
said, "Ugh, now we have to 'cwitically' evaluate it."

Even as adults, we don't recognize the messages, and we do
not often critically evaluate either advertising or our choices in
response to it. We consume mindlessly, and our self-definition
appears to be tied up in our ability to consume. We are a society
"centered around things" rather than "around persons."[21] Because
our very identity is at stake, we are alienated, and "must be envious
of those who have more and afraid of those who have less."[22]

Greene talks about the multitude of people whose basic needs
are long met, but who continue to pursue material gain, even
when those pursuits are utterly artificial and superfluous. Freedom,
again, is defined as getting ahead or having more. How many bedrooms do we need in order to be free? How many dresses? Apparently, an awful lot. Fromm says that our society "requires one to
consume ever more, because previous consumption soon loses its
satisfactory character. Modern consumers may identify themselves
by the formula: *I am = what I have and what I consume.*"[23] Own-
ing one more dress is of critical importance in this equation.

Living in close proximity with people who don't have their

basic needs met means that I am regularly buying things I don't need while those around me struggle. The prevailing narrative absolves me of guilt for this. I work hard. I make money. I can spend it on myself. But who gave license to this narrative?

It is no easy task to live in a society while simultaneously step-ping outside of it, critiquing it, living by different values, yet main-taining enough proximity to speak to its needs. I think I live like a "comfortable radical." I have a print hanging on my wall by the artist Brian Andreas with a caption that says, "Of course I want to change the world . . . but I was hoping to do it from the comfort of my regular life." I want to live according to the culture's definition of normal, while at the same time being critical of that definition. I want to be a person who buys dresses she doesn't need, while call-ing for the world to change.

Horton is an example of one person who had some success at finding this perspective. He was born poor in the South in 1905. He graduated from college and seminary but rejected the life of privilege that had become available to him. In 1932, he founded the Highlander Folk School in Tennessee, where he edu-cated activists and community organizers. His school played a major role in the Civil Rights Movement, educating leaders such as Dr. Martin Luther King Jr., Rosa Parks, John Lewis, and Ralph Abernathy.

Horton was able to live in a society that valued power and money, and perpetuated greed, without buying into them. He crit-icized this greed, asking "how love can exist in a society that exploits people," and he asserted that the "violence of poverty" wreaks destruction far beyond physical hunger.[24] According to Horton, we have accepted a "system which assumes that people's lives, the natural resources and everything else exist for the pur-pose of making money."[25] That is, financial gain has become the highest goal there is.

Horton's pedagogy at the Highlander Folk School encouraged risk-taking and challenging the system. A major element of his practice involved bringing together people who shared the same problems in order to solve those problems. He didn't rely on out-side experts for this. He recognized that "the best teachers of poor and working people are the people themselves."[26] He equipped people to analyze their problems and work for change. Through this approach, Horton overcame his own desire to control, and he worked for freedom alongside his friends and neighbors—on their terms. He recognized the greed and the power, challenged it, and lived his life differently than most around him.

Harry F. Ward, a Methodist minister who served as the ACLU's first national chairperson, wrote in 1929:

> The final clash between our current economic morality and the ethic of Jesus is over the nature of man. The capitalist economy rests on the hypothesis that man is a creature who prefers material comforts to moral values, who would rather have an increase in goods than in the quality of existence.[27]

The pull of consumption is not limited to the middle class. According to Ernest, the common occurrence of poor people who live in run-down housing going out in their cars wearing new clothes "is about showing that you are successful, even if you're not. As long as people can see you driving a big old car and you're dressed to the tee and you got this bling on, you look successful." Success here is defined as being tied exclusively to cars and clothing. There may be nothing in your house, he says, but you have to look good when you go out.

When we attended a black church for a while after moving to the city, we were looking forward to attending their annual Black History Month concert. Choirs from many area churches participated, and I was told the building would be overflowing. I knew some of the women in the choir, and they told me they were going shopping for new clothes to wear to the concert. I had known them for a while and had been in some of their homes, and I knew there was usually a shortage of money and food. I knew they had unpaid debts, and that their housing was not stable. When I showed up at the concert, these women were decked out in amazing new outfits. According to Ernest's view of the world, they were not about to stand up in front of the crowds looking anything but their best, regardless of what was going on back home.

Even as he was nearing seventy, Ernest shined his shoes and ironed his jeans every day. He said this kind of care shows that "you are kept." Wesley tried his best to avoid going to school a few years back when it was a de facto requirement that you wear a perfectly white tall tee and tennis shoes without a scuff. He says when he was in school dressed less than his best he sat in the back row and tried to be invisible. He called his school a "fashion show, a place where you don't want to be perceived as poor."

Dee was always taught by her grandfather that appearances matter. He told her not to act poor. She wasn't even allowed to leave the house if her jeans weren't ironed. Clothes and shoes are often the façade that my struggling neighbors hide behind. Wesley says this attitude is "embedded into the black community." When I leave the house in old sweats and a ratty tee shirt, I still hold my head up. For Ernest and Wesley, you just flat-out don't leave the house like that.

The cupboards may be empty at home, where ten people are living in a two-bedroom house with no beds, but no one will know this by looking at you. This is a significant barrier to developing reciprocal relationships. Good friends tend to be in and out of each other's houses. When your house is barely hanging together, you are not going to invite people inside (that's why you go *out* looking good), and you are certainly not going to invite middle-class people in. And if you're black, you are definitely not going to invite white people in. In the suburbs, I made friends with my neighbors and was sitting in their kitchen within days. In my St. Paul neighborhood, it was a very long time before I was invited inside anyone's home. When I do get invited in, I see it as a sign that we've crossed an important barrier. When you are invited into the reality behind the ironed jeans, trust has begun to take hold.

All of these examples show the power of the dominant narrative of consumption to define a person's worth. By presenting a well-dressed self to the world, you are saying, "Look, I can consume, too."

Hopelessness

You can't fool yourself, however. It gets tiring to maintain the façade. When people are told they are free but don't see any real options, it breeds despair. At a Lift event a year or two into my urban tenure, I sat down with the students one at a time and asked a few questions to get a sense of how they were doing. I asked them to share what was going well and what was not going so well. How was school? Family? My final question was, "If you could change one thing about your life, what would it be?" The answer I got from almost every student was a variation on: "Nothing." They said they would change *nothing* about their lives. No wishes that dad would come home, that the cupboards would be full, that their brother would get out of jail, or that mom would stop drinking. No dreams of good grades or a giant truck full of money pulling up in front of their house. Over the years, I have asked this question of various students and sometimes their mothers. The answer is almost always the same: "Nothing." Today, when Cortez is facing an uncertain future in his late twenties, he tells me, "I'm really close to being free. I have no problems right now."

What is going on here? My cultural incompetency was hard at work when I asked the students what they would change. I didn't understand that asking this question likely sounded to them like, "Please list all of the things you will never have." What I think I was running into were the effects of hopelessness. It's painful to list things you are certain will never come to pass. To say the reality out loud can make the poverty more real and more painful than it already is. It makes sense to stay rooted in the here and now when the future holds little promise. Cortez agrees: "You just live: moment-to-moment and day-to-day." Wesley adds that admitting a need "is to admit a weakness."

When the students said they wanted to change "nothing" about their lives, I don't think it was a failure of imagination. All of them have shown themselves capable in less direct circumstances of articulating what they want, whether it's Wesley making a quiet statement on his birthday about wishing his dad were around, or all of the kids getting excited about seeing a Jaguar in our neighborhood. It was merely a statement of hopelessness.

I have several adult friends who did not graduate from high school, which makes it difficult for them to find a job. At various times, they have all said they are planning to take the general equivalency diploma (GED) test. Some of them have been planning this for years. I've given out information on free GED preparation classes, and I've told people where they can take the test. I recently ran into a former Lift student, now in her mid-twenties, and she had recently taken the test and passed it. She was the first of my connections here who actually followed through. She had support from her employer and went through a free program that provided transportation. She is the exception. Nobody takes the test. It takes hope to even bother.

Brazilian educator Paulo Freire writes about the importance of hope for humans and describes the hopelessness of oppression as a kind of silence. His observation aligns with my experience interviewing students who wanted to change nothing about their lives. He sees hopelessness not so much emerging out of "limit-situations," but rather out of the inability to act against the limitations.[28] These stories are about real children and families in my neighborhood who have never seen, and will certainly never be inside of, a mansion on the ocean with towels as heavy as furniture. The mansion may as well not even exist, but what these children see in the media, combined with their day-to-day struggle for survival, makes the mansion both real and irrelevant. Of hope and despair, Freire says:

> It needs to be clear that despair is not a natural human way of being human, but a distortion of hope. I am not at first a being of despair, who needs to be converted by hope. I am, on the contrary, a being of hope, who for any number of reasons loses hope and becomes hopeless. This is the source of our struggles as human beings which should be fought with the aim of reducing the objective reasons for hopelessness which immobilize us.[29]

Magical Thinking

It is not only hope that is needed. There is a practical side of gaining a different future, and most of the students I have come to know are unaware of this practical side of things. On the occasions when our students at The Lift do discuss their hopes for the future, they often display what I call "magical thinking" about money. Because the hard work of earning a living wage has not often, or ever, been modeled for them, some seem to lack an understanding of the *process* of getting out of poverty. They see the ends of a continuum, but they don't understand the various things necessary to move away from the poverty end of things.

With few exceptions, the plans to move toward wealth involve making it big as a sports, music, or movie star. Cortez says that he always thought someone in his family would win the lottery. He sometimes even hoped for a disaster. "I got to the point where I was hoping a car accident would happen to me and I would collect insurance money and I could make something happen. . . . We would be a happy family again." There is no realistic plan to work hard in high school and then work hard in college and then work hard at a job. This is obviously because it has not been modeled within their purview. How could you know the steps of a process if you've never seen anyone take them?

We took a few of Dee's kids to our friends' very nice lake home in northern Minnesota one spring. We all took the motorboat for a ride, and then the kids paddled the paddleboat across the lake. They played in the water with every conceivable beach toy and sat in the hot tub. After a day of this, ten-year-old Ansaya excitedly pronounced that the owners "must have won *Fear Factor*." Her list of possible ways a person might acquire a lake home was limited. This also explains why the guys thought Dave was a hit man. When someone has a lot of stuff, they believe that something secretive, magical, or lucky befell the person. The boring story that people finish school and go to an office for eight or ten hours every day for decades to get their stuff is not a story anyone is telling.

#

In case the point of this chapter has been unclear, I will state it succinctly here. A quick study of our society shows that "ability to consume" is the de facto definition of freedom. People who have more financial resources are able to consume more; therefore, they are more free. People who have fewer financial resources cannot consume at the same level and thus are less free. Accepting this definition as legitimate for just a moment, we must question where it came from and why it has been embraced. Fromm writes: "Unrestricted satisfaction of all desires is not conducive to *well-being*, nor is it the way to happiness or even to maximum pleasure."[30] This definition of freedom doesn't get us anywhere good.

On the other hand, are those in poverty faring any better under Bauman's definition of freedom as "the right to share in joint determination of the common fate"?[31] It seems not, and this is where I believe there is a conspiracy afoot, because regardless of the definition we use, Alexa is not free. Bauman explains it: "The ambitions and hopes of the oppressed were now safely channeled away from the power structure and towards the improvement of their material standards."[32] If a large percentage of struggling black people can be convinced that the goal of life is to consume (which is a high bar when you have no resources), it may cause many to channel their efforts away from things like making sure the voting process is fair, advocating for government programs that help poor families, and running for the school board. And it is *these* things that have the power to move us along toward liberty and justice for all.

According to Marcuse, minorities and those in poverty have been duped by an unjust system. Minimal concessions that do little or nothing to challenge unjust social structures, such as making Martin Luther King Jr.'s birthday a holiday or designating February as Black History Month, create the illusion that things are changing. Marcuse calls this "repressive tolerance."[33] "By allowing a limited amount of protest that is carefully managed, a society pressure valve is created to release into thin air the stream of energy that would otherwise cause the system to make real change."[34] It seems that a large percentage of the population has been silenced by seeing a black news anchor or by the slim possibility of obtaining a big-screen TV.

#

After looking at the many obstacles to having friends who don't look just like us, we now turn to the opportunities we have to overcome such obstacles. In the next chapter, we will look at what to expect as we take steps to build relationships across tribal lines.

Notes

1. Russell Brand, *Revolution* (New York: Ballantine, 2014), 25.

2. Maxine Greene, *The Dialectic of Freedom* (New York: Teachers College, 1988), 65.

3. Anatole France, *The Red Lily* (Gloucester, UK: Dodo, 1894), 64.

4. Isaiah Berlin, *Four Essays on Liberty* (New York: Oxford University Press, 1970), 122.

5. John Dewey, *On Experience, Nature, and Freedom: Representative Selections* (New York: Liberal Arts, 1960), 271.

6. Zygmunt Bauman, *Freedom* (Minneapolis: University of Minnesota Press, 1988), 98.

7. Stephen D. Brookfield, *The Power of Critical Theory: Liberating Adult Learning and Teaching* (San Francisco: Jossey-Bass, 2004), 188.

8. Erich Fromm, *To Have or to Be?* (New York: Continuum, 1976), 4.

9. Fromm, *To Have or to Be?*, 8.

10. Bauman, *Freedom*, 82.

11. Milton Friedman, *Capitalism and Freedom* (Chicago: University of Chicago Press, 1982), 170.

12. Friedman, *Capitalism*, 191.

13. Bauman, *Freedom*, 95.

14. Bauman, *Freedom*, 98.

15. Jürgen Habermas, *The Postnational Constellation: Political Essays* (Cambridge, MA: MIT Press, 2001), 93.

16. Laurent A. Parks Daloz, Cheryl H. Keen, James P. Keen, and Sharon Daloz Parks, *Common Fire: Leading Lives of Commitment in a Complex World* (Boston: Beacon, 1997), 11.

17. James A. Vela-McConnell, *Unlikely Friends: Bridging Ties and Diverse Friendships* (Lanham, MD: Lexington, 2011), 9.

18. Myles Horton, *The Long Haul: An Autobiography*, with Judith Kohl and Herbert Kohl (New York: Anchor, 1997), 169.

19. Michel Foucault, *Power/Knowledge: Selected Interviews & Other Writings* (New York: Pantheon, 1980), 39.

20. Stephen D. Brookfield and John D. Holst, *Radicalizing Learning* (San Francisco: Jossey-Bass, 2011), 27.

21. Fromm, *To Have or to Be?*, 16.

22. Fromm, *To Have or to Be?*, 5.

23. Fromm, *To Have or to Be?*, 23.

24. Horton, *Long Haul*, 27.

25. Horton, *Long Haul*, 172.

26. Horton, *Long Haul*, xx.

27. Quoted in Horton, *Long Haul*, 32.

28. Paulo Freire, *Pedagogy of the Oppressed* (New York: Bloomsbury Academic, 2012), 99.

29. Paulo Freire, *Pedagogia da Autonomia* (Sao Paolo: Paz e Terra, 2000), 81, quoted in Stuart C. Carr and Tod S. Sloan, *Poverty and Psychology: From Global Perspective to Local Practice* (New York: Kluwer Academic, 2003), 77.

30. Fromm, *To Have or to Be?*, 2.

31. Bauman, *Freedom*, 98.

32. Bauman, *Freedom*, 72.

33. Herbert Marcuse, "Repressive Tolerance," in *A Critique of Pure Tolerance*, ed. Robert Paul Wolfe, Barrington Moore Jr., and Herbert Marcuse (Boston: Beacon, 1965), 95.

34. Brookfield and Holst, *Radicalizing Learning*, 28.

II

The Opportunities

8.

Tribal Bridging

> You can't stay in your corner of the Forest waiting for others to come to you. You have to go to them sometimes.
>
> —A. A. Milne[1]

Joseph* called me a few years back and wanted me to find him someone he could help. He was a white person from the suburbs who wanted to work for social justice but didn't know how. I asked some clarifying questions. "I have a lot of resources," he said, "and I have some time in my life to help other people, so I thought of you and figured you could hook me up with someone. It would be good if it were a young man who has finished high school and who likes to play sports. Maybe someone who doesn't have a dad around."

Along the same lines, a group from a suburban church heard me speak about what's going on in my neighborhood and got in touch with me, wanting to know if I knew of a single mom who they could come and babysit for, and maybe clean her house.

At times like these, I feel like I am running a dating service. These people are truly well-meaning. They know that people are poor, they want the world to be different, they see themselves as fortunate, and they want to give something back. These approaches, however, actually treat poor people as a commodity in the business of doing good. The exchange that people are asking me to broker sounds like this: "I have X number of hours and X dollars. What can you get me?"

I believe the missing piece in these good intentions is an understanding and acknowledgment of the humanity of poor people and the centrality of relationships in all aspects of life, including attempts to do good. My neighbors don't want a stranger babysitting their kids or cleaning their house any more than I do. Most don't see themselves as needy, and they do not appreciate the designation or the attendant assumptions.

Given the barriers that I have outlined thus far, developing deeply personal reciprocal relationships that cross lines of race and class is not going to be easy. For starters, I think it's safe to say that asking to be assigned a poor person is not the way to do it.

Deeply Personal Reciprocal Relationships

Before discussing *how* to build "deeply personal reciprocal relationships," I want to be clear about what they are. They involve more than just being neighbors or coworkers or casual acquaintances. Philosopher Laurence Thomas lists three features of friendship. First, he says, friendship emerges when both parties *choose* it; second, when neither party has any authority; and, third, when the parties share an enormous bond of trust. That bond, says Thomas, is "cemented by equal self-disclosure and, for that very reason, is a sign of the very special regard that each has for the other."[2]

Friends trust one another, love one another, and show mutual respect. They basically "enjoy spending time together."[3] Ernest made a distinction between friends and acquaintances. An acquaintance, he said, "is just somebody you hang around with . . . it's not really nothing serious." A friend, on the other hand, he defined as somebody who's got your back, who's there for you.

For my purposes here, one of the most important attributes of friendship is reciprocity. Sociologist James Vela-McConnell captures this in his definition of close friendship as "an active and freely chosen platonic relationship between two *equals* demonstrating a high degree of commitment toward each other and relating to one another in a variety of ways."[4] His research is on diverse friendships, and he sees equality as essential.

Friends also look out for the good of one another. Ernest said his relationships with me and people at The Lift were his first relationships with white people that have felt like equal friendships. When I asked him if he ever felt that anyone in our community looked down on him because of his past, he answered decisively: "No! No one looks down on me! No. No one. No one. No one." And he laughed while he said it. Dee's story is one of growing into reciprocity. She said that when we first met, her thought was "I know they must be judging me." Over those first few years, she grew to a place where she trusted that our relationship was genuine—that it was what it seemed to be. She grew out of her tendency to doubt the legitimacy of the friendship.

Reciprocity

When we talk about our relationships at The Lift, we emphasize the importance of reciprocity. It is our basic understanding as a community that both parties in a relationship have something to offer, as well as various needs or struggles. In my own experience, a relationship is reciprocal only when the person who society would view as the "receiver" in the relationship says it is. In other words, I can say all I want that Dee and I have a reciprocal relationship, but if she sees it otherwise, she's right. Today she says, "Our friendship really taught me how friendships really work. You learn from each other. No matter where you come from, we can all become better people by learning things from someone else."

Laurence Thomas touches on this theme of reciprocity when he talks about friends not being under the authority of one another. This is essential in the formation of the kind of relationships I am describing. When there is a lack of equality, he writes, "the one with the higher station is inclined to think that his utterances have more authority than those of the other."[5] He warns against the tendency in these cases of the one with the higher station to strive to help the other out of pity for their position.

Dee and I talk about this aspect of our relationship. Are we thrown off balance if she needs groceries one week and I help her out? If we are, what are the things that might put us back in balance? How do we weigh the relative value of me buying her groceries versus her being on the board or volunteering at The Lift?

The answer is that you cannot weigh these things. A relationship stays in balance when there is trust and mutual respect, when resources are shared with no sense of pity or power involved. Dee and I, and Ernest and I, are friends partially based on our shared commitment to making the world a more just and equitable place. We all strive to see things like helping out with groceries or rent as a step in the direction of justice and equity, rather than the entrenchment of status quo power in our relationships.

Shared Commitments

The common commitment to justice is another essential component of these types of relationships. Friendship cannot be relegated to a specific activity or timeframe each week. If I am someone's friend, I care that they are experiencing oppression, injustice, and racism. There's a cost to this; being sad about it is not enough. We commit resources and time and passion to the things each of us cares about. Dee and I are allies in seeking justice. Brazilian educator Paulo Freire addresses this issue:

> True solidarity with the oppressed means fighting at their side to transform the objective reality which has made them these "beings for another." The oppressor is solidary with the oppressed only when he stops regarding the oppressed as an abstract category and sees them as persons who have been unjustly dealt with, deprived of their voice, cheated in the sale of their labor—when he stops making pious, sentimental, and individualistic gestures and risks an act of love. True solidarity is found only in the plenitude of this act of love, in its existentiality, in its praxis. To affirm that men and women are persons and as persons should be free, and yet to do nothing tangible to make this affirmation a reality, is a farce.[6]

Shortly after I met Dee and her family, she received an eviction notice from her landlord. She had health problems and hadn't been able to keep up with her rent. She moved to a house about five miles away and continued to be involved at The Lift. Within a year, she received another eviction notice. Dave and I decided, against many of our friends' and family members' better judgment, to buy a house that Dee would rent from us (and rent-to-own if she wanted) in our neighborhood. Dave, Dee, and I found a house that would fit all seven of them, and Dave and I bought it. The day of the closing, she received notice that she would be receiving Section 8 housing assistance after being on the waiting list for over five years. It made us feel like God was in it with us. Section 8 covered about half of her rent, and we agreed that she would cover as much of the other half as she could.

We had a mortgage on the property, and that first year was tough. Dee was working at a drugstore and tore her meniscus from all the stock work she was doing. She had to take time off. Sometimes we received rent, and sometimes we didn't. It was not fun, but during the times when I was stressed and nervous about our decision, I had to keep coming back to the point that Freire makes (even though I didn't yet know who Freire was). There is nothing in my life that makes me more deserving of my middle-class benefits than Dee. It is purely the result of generations of injustice. Yes, we need to change the structures, but in the meantime, if I care about Dee and her kids and their housing stability and have the power to make a difference, it seems like I should. Dee lived in the house for almost three years, and then she moved out of state for a short time. She moved back to St. Paul a year later and is in a more stable place now. The house remains a resource for people in our community who go through times of struggle.

I didn't know this until recently, but this situation of working together to stabilize her housing was when she started to feel that what was going on between us was genuine. That was the time, she says, "when I felt genuinely loved." She says at that moment, "I started to believe what I was scared to believe." Dave and I were looking at this as a financial risk, while Dee was looking at a much deeper kind of risk. She felt loved, she says, "but I was afraid to love back. It was scary. I might get hurt." We were so opposite from one another that until the house, she kept asking herself, "Can this be real?"

I'm not going to pretend to be Mother Teresa in this tale. I was not always patient or happy about the ups and downs of this arrangement, and when our kids started college and the bills started coming, I found myself longing for a "do over." I wanted to revert to the individualism from my past. My world is better if I keep my money. But *the* world is better if I make sure Dee's family has stable housing. Educators Stephen Preskill and Stephen Brookfield admit that the long-term commitment to individualism is an obstacle to building community. Community building, they say, "does require individuals to give up something of themselves to promote the community's goals."[7] And deeply reciprocal relationships that cross lines of race and class also require sacrifice. In *Mere Christianity*, C. S. Lewis declared, "If our charities do not pinch or hamper us, I should say they are too small. There ought to be things we should like to do and cannot do because our charitable expenditure excludes them."[8] If I substitute the word "love" for "charity," I completely agree.

Brookfield and educator John Holst refer to the maxim that "we cannot seek any individual advantage unless that same benefit is sought for all."[9] There is a critical intersection here between the communal and the individual. My purchase of a house for Dee to live in does not solve broad social problems. But *not* purchasing a house for Dee to live in does not solve problems, either. Brookfield and Holst call for a "qualitative change in the way people think, not just a change in external political and economic arrangements," although they are also clearly in favor of a change in external political and economic arrangements.[10]

This tension between the communal and the individual cannot be overstated. I bought a house as an act of love that many people thought was stupid (which it was, according to the dictates of individualism and capitalism). My act cannot change the world since we require radical political and economic overhaul. But this kind of overhaul, preached by many, can only be realized if many people learn to define their individual interests, at least partially, in view of the interests of the whole. I even see tension in Freire's quote above. He calls for an end to individualistic gestures and speaks of the need for an "act of love," but the choice to love seems to me to be an individual one. The oppressors as a category cannot risk an act of love; only individual oppressors can do that.

We meant for the purchase of the house to be an act of love toward Dee and her family. We also wanted it to be part of a larger move toward the overhaul of the social and economic realities that surround us. From one quarter, we hear that we made a stupid economic decision that jeopardized the financial health of our family. From another quarter, we hear that we think of ourselves as messiahs, but our action was just a further entrenchment of our power and privilege. It seems like those in the first group don't care what *we* think or feel about it, and those in the second group don't care what *Dee* thinks or feels about it. Freire says that "love is an act of courage, not of fear."[11] I agree.

This minefield that any person must walk through to try to build trust relationships with those who are different from them reveals the difficulty of the "how." This minefield is further defined by sociologist Xavier de Souza Briggs's categories of bonding and bridging.[12]

Bonding and Bridging

"Bonding" and "bridging" are Briggs's way of classifying relationships. Bonding is forming relationships with people similar to yourself, whereas bridging is forming relationships across social divides. Bonding is the easy one, and we all know how to do it. It's just another way of saying all our friends look like us. Bridging relationships, on the other hand, can be a challenge. Bridging relationships provide perspectives that restrain, as when a black friend helps us see a different perspective on the Black Lives Matter movement. Without bridging relationships, homogeneous groups often work against the common good, combining for "sinister ends."[13] An example of a sinister end would be bringing a group of white people together to discuss issues in an urban school and not engaging any of the black parents. Homophily (having only homogeneous friendships), says Briggs, "limits people's social worlds in a way that has powerful implications for the information they receive, the attitudes they form, and the interactions they experience."[14] These two concepts, bonding and bridging, ideally go together. Our experience of building bonding relationships creates a launching pad to venture outside our comfort zone in an effort to build bridges with those who are different from us.

In the 1990s, the Serbs, Croats, and Bosniaks were the three tightly knit people groups that made up the newly independent nation of Bosnia and Herzegovina. They each formed their own ethnically based political party, and each violently fought the other's for power. Although they shared a relatively small geographic area, they did not mix. Towns and villages were populated by one of the three groups. Ultimately, the Serbs conducted an ethnic cleansing against the Croats and Bosniaks. Public policy experts Robert D. Putnam and Kristin A. Goss insist that "bonding without bridging equals Bosnia."[15]

Bonding and homophily are far easier than bridging. Seriously. I went to lunch with Keshia recently, and she was struggling because her electric service had been turned off and the house she was renting was going to be torn down to widen the road in a few months. These very serious problems were heavy on her mind. They were overwhelming to me. The Lift does not have financial resources to assist people with this level of need. I was pastoral, and I listened and agreed to come to a meeting she was having with a relocation specialist the city had assigned to her. But on the day of my lunch with Keshia, I was pissed because I had just bought a new washing machine, and after about killing myself helping my husband and son drag it up the stairs, it was not working properly. What I wanted to do at lunch that day was bitch about how irritating this situation was. If I had been at lunch with friends from a background similar to mine, I would have had free rein to do that. Since Keshia had no electricity and was close to being homeless, however, I didn't bring it up. And this is not a bad thing. Who of us middle-class types can't benefit from being reminded of our privilege? I needed to put my washing machine problem in perspective, and Keshia helped me do that. But if I'm looking for easy, these kinds of bridging lunches are not it.

Studies have shown that in contemporary society, many people have a hard time forming any kind of close relationships, let alone those that cross lines of race and class.[16] Building these relationships is fluid and chaotic in addition to being time-consuming. However, there are stages that can be identified. In his bestselling book *The Different Drum*, psychiatrist Scott Peck provides a broad description of the steps by which people form communities. His model is equally applicable to the building of individual friendships and it helps explain the difficulty of building them across cultural and other differences. Peck's stages of community-building are pseudocommunity, chaos, emptiness, and true community.[17] Before this process can begin, there needs to be a willingness to welcome chaos and conflict as friends.

The Stages of Building Community

Pseudocommunity

In pseudocommunity, people are extremely pleasant with one another. Conflict is avoided and individual differences are ignored or even denied. Peck asks if there might be many people who don't even realize there is anything beyond pseudocommunity, commenting on the human tendency to conform. If people in homogeneous contexts have not learned to go beyond pseudocommunity, it is unlikely that they will arrive at a place of friendship, as defined above by Briggs, with those from different races and classes. I can reflect on my own arrival in my neighborhood in 2003 and see my naïve assumption that merely meeting my neighbors of diverse backgrounds would lead easily to transformative relationships. I met Dee across the alley and thought, "I gave your kids cookies; let's be best friends."

It seems that black and white people might be particularly susceptible to keeping their relationships with one another in the pseudocommunity stage. Womanist Brittney Cooper says that adult interracial friendships "require a level of risk and vulnerability that many of us would rather simply not deal with."[18] Given the racist past and present in the United States, getting past pseudocommunity to the next stage, chaos, has the potential to be particularly challenging.

Chaos

Peck calls chaos an essential part of the process of forming relationships. In this stage, individual differences are out in the open, and those involved may try to fix or heal one another and bring them around to their own perspective or belief system. Many people despair at this stage, feeling hopeless about the relationship. According to Peck, chaos is preferable to pseudocommunity, as issues are now being confronted openly. There is no pretense. No matter how important this stage may be, people flee from chaos, and perhaps more so when differences of opinion are exacerbated by differences of race and class.

One area of chaos for me when I moved here was when I realized I needed boundaries. I had become the taxi driver, the document printer, the check casher, and, God forbid, the babysitter. It's not that I didn't want to be available to help at times. It's that I didn't want these roles to subsume my reason for being in the neighborhood. As I set up boundaries and told people no sometimes, some of them got frustrated with me. I had to explicitly tell people that I wanted to be their friend but that didn't mean I wanted to drive their kids to school at 7:00 a.m. every time they missed the bus. Many suburban people who have tried to get involved in our neighborhood leave when the chaos comes, missing out on the good that can come from staying in the mess.

Ernest and our whole community experienced a situation of chaos that had nothing to do with race or class. He had come to our Lift service one weekend and asked for prayer for his disabled daughter who lived in another state. She was going to be having surgery on the following Tuesday. The next day, my husband passed out, and we found out he had a tumor in his abdomen. A few hours after that, I destroyed my phone by driving over it in the hospital parking lot. I was in a place of crisis and completely forgot about Ernest's daughter's surgery. Tuesday came and went, and no one called Ernest to find out how the surgery went. He called one of our staff and told her he was done with us. "You all are a bunch of fakes," he said and hung up. I called him, and he was willing to give me a pass due to what was going on with Dave, but everyone else who didn't call was indicted. I asked Ernest if he would do me one last favor and show up at our Saturday meeting and tell everyone what happened and how he felt about it.

And, boy, did he.

He read everyone the riot act and said this isn't how friends do for each other. We apologized individually and as a community and asked if he would give us another chance. He agreed. It was a turning point for all of us. We ran head-on into chaos, and we didn't blow apart. Communities are fragile things, but, ironically, I've found that avoiding chaos makes them weaker rather than stronger.

Disappointments and misunderstandings, says philosopher Lawrence Blum, "can constitute tests of the relationship, which ultimately strengthen the ties and deepen the meaning of the friendship."[19] Cortez said he realized we were going to have an actual relationship when "we had an argument and you didn't kick me out." As a result, our trust grew, as well as Cortez's willingness to be honest. As part of this strengthening process, there is the need for Peck's third stage, which he calls emptiness.

Emptiness

Peck says that emptiness is the hardest part of community formation. In emptiness, participants must let go of the idea that their way is the right way or the only way. People must give up control and embrace the uncertainty inherent in authentic human relationships. Peck says this is painful and compares it to a death that is necessary for rebirth. It is a "fearsome adventure into the unknown."[20] Often during this phase, there is a flight back into pseudocommunity. Emptiness in the Ernest story above was about all of us realizing we had wronged Ernest and apologizing for the hurt we had caused. For Ernest, emptiness was agreeing to give us another chance; he had to put himself in a place where he could be hurt again.

I have had a fifteen-year battle with emptiness. When the original group of teens I met in my neighborhood neared adulthood, they started to pull away. They wanted to be independent, and I was getting in their way. Many of the guys went through a struggle that started in their late teens that involved some run-ins with the law, stints of homelessness, and unemployment, among other things. Every six months or so, one or two of them would come back into the picture and we would talk about how things were going. They would admit that even though they thought they could do it all on their own, they could not. This was generally followed by them again disappearing for several months. I would be disappointed and swear that I would not get my hopes up next time. Then it would happen again. But as these guys enter their mid- and late twenties, things are changing for the good. They have jobs, Ricky is married, and Cortez and Wesley have children. They have stopped disappearing. They had to go through some rough spots and they certainly did, while I had to hold out hope and not get angry at their seeming indifference to me as a person who had grown to love and care for them. It has really felt like emptiness.

It seems like seeds we planted a decade ago are starting to bloom. Cortez is now employed as a program manager for The Lift, and he recently said, "You are the best friend I could have because you can make me think differently about things." He said he has tried over the years to do things that would make me reject him, "to see if it was real," he says. "Nobody loves somebody like that. I seen that it was possible to actually love somebody outside your family." These words make all the chaos and emptiness worth it, but it is still not easy. Emptiness does not feel good.

Emptiness doesn't always happen in ways that are as profound as what I've been through with Cortez, but it still results in meaningful change. For example, I struggled for a long time with my beliefs about time. As I mentioned previously, I had always viewed time to be an absolutely black-and-white reality. It was instilled in me that the handbook for the universe included the rules of the twenty-four-hour day and the correct starting time for activities, as well as the need to arrive ten minutes early to everything. Part of my emptiness was realizing that the way we use time is merely a social construct, and in the world I came from, the way it was used was often destructive. If I had held on to my view of time, it would have been a major obstacle to building relationships here.

At our Lift church service, which in theory starts at 5:00 p.m. every Saturday, you can see the contrasting views of time in action. Everyone arrives at a different time. White suburban people, in general, tend to show up before 5:00. My black urban neighbors tend to show up after 5:00. When we have white visitors, I can often see them getting nervous as 5:00 comes and goes and we still haven't started. We try to start by 5:15, but my growth in this area causes me to say, "Who really cares?" A while back, a woman who had stopped by to ask about our programs earlier in the week showed up with her five kids at 7:00, after the last piece of pizza had been eaten and we were ready to lock up. We ended up staying around for another half hour, getting to know her story, meeting her kids, and making plans to see if there was space in our programs for her older kids. Today's version of me says, "Who cares that she came at seven?" She had to get five kids ready all by herself and who knows what other obstacles stood in her way? But she showed up, she met some people, and her kids got chocolate cake. It was all good. The 2003 version of me would have been irritated that my time was taken up (even though I had nowhere to go) and would not have given any grace.

True Community

According to Peck, if people stay engaged in this process of community formation, they finally arrive at the stage of true community. It is at this stage that a relationship has been formed wherein the participants are "committed to hanging in there through both the agony and joy of community."[21] I experience this as a moment of realization that feels like "We did it." We disagreed, argued, fought, and came through it and still love each other. That's how I felt in the situation of Ernest and his daughter. It was the biggest conflict we'd faced to date, and it proved to be a transformational one for our community.

This doesn't mean we've arrived and no further effort is needed. Relationships are cyclical, falling back into earlier stages and requiring the hard work of emptying all over again. This is why I feel like it's been a decade of emptiness. Peck dissuades his readers from viewing life in community as being easy and comfortable in comparison to life without it. According to him, both the agony and joy of life are greater with community. My hard-fought arrival at a place of true community with people who are different from me has proven that it is a worthwhile journey. The difficulty is getting people to take the first step.

To-Do List for Tribal People

I have woven pieces of my story throughout this chapter, along with theory and quotes from wise people from other times and places. Without many of them as guides, I would not have made the progress I have. I want to join my voice to theirs and hopefully serve as a guide to others on the way by sharing some things I have learned over the past fifteen years about how to build relationships with people who do not look like you.

I certainly did not have a formula when I started on this journey. As I look back over the past decade, I can identify the basic things I have done that have opened up this new world of relationships to me. None of them are particularly profound, but together they created space for reciprocal relationships across lines of race and class.

The first thing I did that was obvious but still needs to be stated is that *I went where there were people who were different than me.* This is a necessary but insufficient step on this journey. I didn't just physically move to a diverse place; I met my neighbors, attended community meetings, joined a black church, and generally put myself in unfamiliar situations. I made mistakes, too. I remember meeting some neighbors down the street who asked about the stuff that was being hauled out of our house. I told them that we were redoing our kitchen. "It was just awful," I told them, "with a ripped-up countertop and plywood cabinets." So, of course, when I went into their house a while later, I found a kitchen with those same features.

Which leads me to another action that was essential for beginning to form friendships: *I had to shut up.* By this, I do not mean that I had to become unwilling to talk about difficult subjects. I mean that I had to be quiet at times and let my new friends lead the way in the formation of our relationship. Will it move slowly or quickly? How much disclosure are we ready for?

I sometimes talk too much, and I realized at the beginning that people weren't listening, and so I tried to stop talking. White people always get the microphone, and I learned that my neighbors here were not especially interested in my opinions on things when they had just met me. I always know we've reached a milestone when a friend asks for my opinion! For me, it means they've decided that we are moving to a new level.

I wouldn't say I'm one to take the safe road, but this whole process of moving to the city required me to *have more courage* than I had previously needed, or maybe it was just a different kind. I was in a place for the first time in my life where I was the minority. I was the Other. I was part of conversations in which I did not always understand the vocabulary. I didn't share similar life experiences with many of the people around me. I had to find a certain fearlessness to walk into these environments. I was in my late thirties and had never experienced anything like this. I realize that many nonwhite people likely start feeling this way as small children, especially in Minnesota where they are often surrounded by people who don't look like them. For me, the learning came late. For anyone like me who wants to get out of their comfort zone, there is a bit of courage needed.

In the midst of trying to be courageous, I also found that *I needed to be open.* Brookfield defines openness as "the willingness to entertain a variety of alternative perspectives, be receptive to contributions from everyone regardless of previous attainment or current status, and create . . . multiple opportunities for diverse voices and opinions to be heard."[22] This is what I needed, but I didn't know it right away. I came in to lead something and found I needed to learn something—a lot of things, actually. Brookfield says leaders who are open "have learned to stop talking and start listening to what others have to say."[23]

I learned early on that the black people in my neighborhood were mostly not looking to be friends with white people. While black and white people shared space in the neighborhood, they didn't much share in each other's lives. This meant that if I wanted to make friends in my new context, *I was going to have to do the pursuing.* I made an effort to meet my neighbors here in the same way I made an effort in my suburban neighborhoods. I learned names, yelled greetings across the alley, and, at least at first, unwittingly created some suspicion.

When I asked Cortez about when we first met, he said, "I did not think I would know you." There would be "no actual relationship," he says. Wesley tells me today that he was surprised that we weren't more afraid or hesitant to engage with him and his family. Within a few months of moving in, I had met most of Dee's kids, but I had not met her. I saw her going out to get the mail one day and made a beeline. We had a polite conversation that lasted just a minute or two. If I had not continued to pursue Dee, she admits that conversation would probably have been the end of it.

One challenge in trying to make friends here was the simple fact that my life was so different from the lives of Dee and other neighbors. It was and still is sometimes hard to *find the common ground* that is so essential for friendship or even for conversation. Many of what would have been "normal" topics for me upon meeting someone didn't work well in this context. Most of the women I met were single moms struggling to get their basic needs met. Many had difficult childhoods, had been homeless, and were unemployed or underemployed. None had graduated from college, and some did not have their high school diploma. My normal topics in the suburbs would have included things like my career, school, vacation plans, tennis successes and failures, or even a new website where I had found great deals on shoes. While Dee and I can talk about these things today, they are not topics that work at the inception of a cross-class relationship. The common ground I found was about our kids. Almost all the adults I met were moms, and everyone likes to talk (and sometimes complain) about their children.

I also learned that *I needed to suspend judgment* about activities that seemed to cross ethical or moral lines. I know moms who smoke weed with their teenagers. I know people who collect benefits they don't qualify for, or whose entire income is under the table and thus untaxed. But I learned that I can't be the morality police. "Will you be my friend, but hang on a minute while I report the dime bag I just saw on your coffee table?" does not work as an invitation to go deeper. Who knows what I would do if I couldn't feed my kids or if my housing was threatened? As I've grown closer to some of my neighbors, they've asked my opinion about some of these activities, and I've had the chance to truthfully engage. It's not that I have felt the need to throw my morals out the window; I have just learned not to impose them on others. I wait to be asked.

Finally, I have learned that *working alongside people*, no matter how different they are from me, is a better way to build a relationship than sitting across the table trying to find topics of conversation. Dee and I used to walk to a neighborhood church together and work in the nursery. She's invited me to various marches for political or social justice issues. We've attended a couple of conferences on urban ministry together, and we have volunteered at various neighborhood organizations. She was instrumental in getting The Lift started. In all of these cases, the common ground that draws us together is our shared commitment to making the world a more just and equitable and peaceful place. I may never be able to discuss vacation plans or new shoes with my neighbors, but how much more valuable it is to have friends who share my worldview and commitment to the common good.

The steps toward building deeply reciprocal relationships across lines of race and class can thus be summarized as:

- Go where people are different than you.

- Shut up.

- Be courageous.

- Be open.

- Pursue.

- Find common ground.

- Suspend judgment.

- Work for common good together.

The step that is commonly left out is that we do not tend to go where people are different than us. Other than that, these are the same actions most people would take to build a friendship in any context. The other steps are necessary but not sufficient without this critical first step. C. S. Lewis describes the awakening of a friendship simply as meeting someone and saying, "What? You too? I thought I was the only one."[24] I found this common ground with people who are radically different from me, and it has been transformational.

Lest I overwhelm people with a task that seems impossible given the reality of their day-to-day lives, I want to clarify that there are small steps everyone can take to begin to open doors to relationships of difference. Many of our adult volunteers at The Lift come from the suburbs, and we obviously don't start our engagement with them by recommending they move to the city and rearrange their entire life around new priorities! We first ask them to attend a daylong training we developed called *Lose Your Comfort Zone*, which is designed (as you may have guessed) to get people out of their comfort zone, where almost everyone looks like them. We start the training with Dee showing up a few minutes late, with me yelling at her for being late and saying some things to her that tap into stereotypes—and her doing the same to me. Something along the lines of "You are always late" and "Well, you are always uptight." At this point, everyone in the room is very uncomfortable. The first time we added this to the training,

Ernest was there, as he pretty much always was. When Dee and I started getting into it, he stood up and said, "Ladies, ladies, you need to calm down." Dee and I started laughing, and we clarified for everyone what was going on. It was interesting to me that even after many years of knowing each other and talking about these topics, Ernest really thought I was capable of subscribing to stereotypes in this way.

Once we get everyone's blood pressure down after the opening, we review and discuss the cultural differences our volunteers may encounter working across differences of class and race. We've also created a list of dos and don'ts along the lines of the steps above, which we illustrate with many of the stories included here. The most critical aspect of this training is that it is taught by Dee, Ricky, and me, and we each bring our unique background and experiences to the training. We only engage in training or conversations about these important topics when we have a diversity of perspectives in the room. In other words, we don't train a room that includes only middle-class white people on how to build relationships that cross lines of race and class.

It is important that anyone wanting to embark on this journey recognize that it is indeed a journey. My path from living a suburban life of homogeneity to a life enriched by diverse friendships had many steps. Depending on a person's life experience, it may be essential to read books or attend a class before jumping into a situation of limited peripheral participation. The journey is too important to rush.

#

After setting forth the importance of deeply reciprocal relationships and charting out a path toward creating them, in the next chapter we will examine how the ways we learn, grow, and change perspectives can help us become leaders in the important task of forming tribes where everyone does not look just like us.

Notes

1. A. A. Milne, *Pooh's Little Instruction Book* (New York: Dutton Children's Books), 52.

2. Laurence Thomas, "Friendship and Other Loves," in *Friendship: A Philosophical Reader*, ed. Neera Kapur Badhwar (Ithaca, NY: Cornell University Press, 1993), 49.

3. Neera Kapur Badhwar, "Introduction: The Nature and Significance of Friendship," in Badhwar, *Friendship*, 3.

4. James A. Vela-McConnell, *Unlikely Friends: Bridging Ties and Diverse Friendships* (Lanham, MD: Lexington, 2011), 18 (emphasis mine).

5. Thomas, "Friendship and Other Loves," 54.

6. Paulo Freire, *Pedagogy of the Oppressed* (New York: Bloomsbury Academic, 2012), 49–50.

7. Stephen Preskill and Stephen D. Brookfield, *Learning as a Way of Leading: Lessons from the Struggle for Social Justice* (San Francisco: Jossey-Bass, 2009), 198.

8. C. S. Lewis, *Mere Christianity* (New York: Macmillan, 1952), 82.

9. Stephen D. Brookfield and John D. Holst, *Radicalizing Learning* (San Francisco: Jossey-Bass, 2011), 26.

10. Brookfield and Holst, *Radicalizing Learning*, 26.

11. Brookfield and Holst, *Radicalizing Learning*, 89.

12. Xavier de Souza Briggs, "'Some of My Best Friends Are . . .': Interracial Friendships, Class, and Segregation in America," *City & Community* 6, no. 4 (2007): 263–90.

13. Robert D. Putnam and Kristin A. Goss, "Introduction," in *Democracies in Flux: The Evolution of Social Capital in Contemporary Society*, ed. Robert D. Putnam (New York: Oxford University Press, 2002), 11.

14. Briggs, "Some of My Best Friends," 265.

15. Putnam and Goss, "Introduction," 12.

16. Robert D. Putnam, *Bowling Alone: The Collapse and Revival of American Community* (New York: Simon & Schuster, 2001).

17. M. Scott Peck, *The Different Drum: Community Making and Peace*

(New York: Simon & Schuster, 1987).

18. Brittney Cooper, "The Politics of Being Friends with White People," *Salon* (August 13, 2013), https://tinyurl.com/yxl6w99s.

19. Lawrence Blum, "Friendship as a Moral Phenomenon," in Badhwar, *Friendship*, 199.

20. Peck, *Different Drum*, 100.

21. Peck, *Different Drum*, 106.

22. Stephen D. Brookfield, "Transformative Learning as Ideology Critique," in *Learning as Transformation: Critical Perspectives on a Theory in Progress*, ed. Jack Mezirow (San Francisco: Jossey-Bass, 2009), 21.

23. Brookfield, "Transformative Learning," 21.

24. C. S. Lewis, "Friendship: The Least Necessary Love," in Badhwar, *Friendship*, 42.

9.

Tribal Learning

Tell me and I forget, teach me and I may remember, involve me and I learn.

—Xun Kuang[1]

I had a call on a Saturday night after our church service. The caller told me that Dina,* the mother of one of our students, who had attended the service that evening, was out front afterwards trying to sell weed to our students. I hung up feeling red hot. I was too mad to call her that night, so I decided to wait until the next day. In the morning, Dina's son called and said, "My mom didn't want me to call, but we don't have any food at home, and I was wondering if you could help." My perspective on what was going on changed so quickly, I experienced worldview whiplash. I walked around all day on Sunday trying to find a category or a label or really any way to tuck this story away somewhere and not think about it.

Instead, it was all I thought about. As I brought groceries over to Dina that day, I wondered to what lengths I would go to feed my children if they were hungry. I wondered if I would choose to unapologetically sell weed in order to care for my family instead of groveling for food in humiliation. I could see myself hustling dime bags. Dina never sold weed at church again that I know of, but in that one incident I learned about myself, my values, my beliefs, my priorities, and my tendency to jump to judgment. After these chapters describing relationships that cross tribal lines, we are going to look at how we can learn to engage in them.

Making New Maps

My views on race and class were formed in my early years without any formal teaching. As children, we begin to create our own map of the world that includes our values and beliefs. This map is influenced by lessons from our parents, our education, our religious training, and, as we get older, our peers and work experience. We consult these maps to solve problems, make decisions, and evaluate the things going on around us. The content of our maps reflects the tribes to which we belong. What happened with Dina and her son blew away a major part of my map—the part that says what's right and wrong, what's good and bad. The part that had been very black and white about things like selling weed after church.

Our maps do not always accurately reflect reality or consider the complexity of the world around us. Social psychologist Erich Fromm speaks of how we can be deceived by our perceptions, not realizing that our view of reality does not always correspond to what is "really real." People are "half-awake, half-dreaming, and are unaware that most of what they hold to be true and self-evident is illusion produced by the suggestive influence of the social world in which they live."[2]

This is not how people see their maps. In order to step back and give our maps a more honest assessment, I created a training exercise that I have used in graduate and seminary classes, with church groups, in my neighborhood, and in training suburban residents who want to volunteer in my community. I give participants a piece of paper and markers and tell them to draw the Twin Cities. The only additional instruction I give is "Draw on the map whatever is important to you." When they are done, we compare our maps. I ask them who included things like schools, stores, churches, rivers, and highways. Then I ask them whose map is "right." I use this mapping exercise as a metaphor for the mental maps we all draw that include the things that are important to us. Things like our view of right and wrong, what we believe about marriage and families, how decisions are best made, which political party is best, whether there is a God, the origin of the universe and life, and so on. We all have a map in our brains that reflects our view of the world.

When we are young, I tell the participants, we think that everyone's map is very similar to our own and that our map accurately represents the territory in the same way that a globe accurately represents the physical world. In other words, we think *our* map is *the* territory, rather than just our own subjective representation of the territory. In the introduction of this book, I described how in my fundamentalist church we believed we were the only ones with the right map. The more we get out of our comfort zones and interact with people who are different from us, the more our maps get challenged. We begin to realize that our map is not *the* territory. It is just *our own map* of the territory.

After I had given this lecture to a mostly white, mostly middle-class college class, a student responded:

> Okay, so to be completely honest, this concept blew my mind. It's not that I haven't thought about how each individual views the world differently before, but I have never seen it put so neatly into an analogy. . . . I guess you could say that it sort of turned my map upside down. Maybe not quite all the way upside down, but it definitely tilted things. . . . So, I guess you could say that mapping forced me to take off my glasses for a little bit in order to see everyone else's—more specifically, so that I could see that everyone else's glasses are different from my own. This was an enormously enlightening step for me. What I found most interesting is that the language of mental mapping created a universally even playing field for discussion. We could start admitting our own faults and frustrations through mapping because everybody has a map.[3]

This student, in her early twenties, is far ahead of where I was at that age. I didn't even realize these kinds of mental maps existed. When I decided to step out from the comfort of my own tribe, I ran headlong into a whole bunch of conflicting maps. Living in this context has afforded me the opportunity to expand my map, and to realize the benefits of learning from others' maps, rather than wasting time arguing that mine is right. Journalist David Berreby says that "experimenters have found that people cling to their perceptual map even when it is wrong."[4] It seems that people have a hard time recognizing that their mental maps of the world are only maps, and not the actual territory.

During my years in this urban context, my map has changed in the areas of time, money, child-rearing, welfare, religion, and right and wrong. The story of Dina did not cause me to begin suggesting that people sell drugs or break laws in order to feed their families, but it messed with my map so thoroughly that I became obsessed. I wrote an essay called "Sinning on the Sidewalk after Church," about how often in my own history I had seen or participated in things like talking negatively about the sermon or someone's clothing after the church service. Or going out after church for a lunch that cost far too much. Or shopping on Sunday afternoon and buying things I didn't need while others were hungry. I argued both sides of whether selling weed or gossiping and gorging cause more damage to the human race. On the maps of my past, this would not even have been a question. The road that led to hell on that map was paved in weed. My map was challenged and revised because I lived up close to a person whose map was different than mine. The people from my fundamentalist past would not see this as a good thing. They would say I was becoming liberal, or that I had begun the slide down the slippery slope of relativism. It may show how far I've slid that I see this as a good thing, and I believe I have a better map than I had before, thanks to Dina.

Whether it's learning the meaning of the word "swag," learning to view time differently, learning to love someone who's different than you, or learning why you would even want to, it is indeed a process of *learning*. Most people can't jump across cultures and fit in immediately.

So how do we learn?

Adult Learning Theory

Once we've created maps, it can take a major shakeup to change them, especially in critical areas. I can say definitively that our maps do not change merely because someone tells us stuff. Our maps are made up of more than information. I can tell my own story, give alarming statistics related to race and class, and appeal to people's religious and moral views, but I often still find myself hitting a wall in terms of getting people to take a step outside of their comfort zone. When I speak with suburban groups about The Lift, people lean in and express a lot of interest in what I do and what is going on with urban youth and families. People have given donations of money or clothing, but they don't often take steps to engage at a deeper level by volunteering. The information I share is not quite compelling enough. Something more is needed, and, ultimately, that something is time spent with people whose maps differ from ours. The very thing that has the power to change our maps is the thing we avoid.

Citing Jerome Bruner of New York University, scientists and researchers John Brown and Paul Duguid explain the difference between "learning about" and "learning to be."[5] Classroom learning or even conversations *about* diversity or poverty or engaging the other are not on par with the learning that can happen by spending time in a communal or relational context with people who are racially or socioeconomically different than you. Learning is about more than information—and, without contact, information is all that is left. Learning is social, and when we engage with the other in authentic ways, we arrive at a new level of understanding that enables us to overcome stereotypes and prejudices. Social activist and educator Myles Horton founded the Highlander Folk School on these principles and, through his experiences, learned that "learning which came from a group effort was superior to learning achieved through individual efforts."[6]

Anthropologist Jean Lave and educational researcher Étienne Wenger assert that "learning and a sense of identity are inseparable: They are aspects of the same phenomenon."[7] This means that a decision to engage in this form of social learning has the potential to cut to the very core of people's sense of who they are. Educators Stephen Brookfield and John Holst talk of people learning "a whole new way of being—a way of thinking, acting, feeling and creating—that moves from acquisition to creative fulfillment in association with others."[8] This is in sharp contrast to learning that is "narrowly defined as efforts to add compatible ideas to elaborate our fixed frame of reference."[9]

In corporate America, there are significant efforts to change people's thinking about race. However, corporations have launched many diversity training programs over the past decades, and they have shown inconsistent results at best. Researchers Frank Dobbin, Alexandra Kalev, and Erin Kelly say, "Our research shows that certain programs do increase diversity in management jobs—the best test of whether a program works—but that others do little or nothing."[10] Programs that have formal mentoring components show better results, likely because mentoring is a form of social learning, which is much more effective at changing our frames of reference than merely doling out information.

New history books have been written that reveal our nation's hidden past, but these revised histories tend to be embraced by people who do not need convincing. All in all, sociologists Joe Feagin, Hernan Vera, and Pinar Batur seem accurate in their assessment that white people tend to live in a "spatial and psychological 'bubble,' separated for the most part from the world of African Americans."[11] And they seem comfortable staying in the bubble. And they are privileged to be able to do so.

Transformative Adult Learning

The field of adult learning theory can help us understand why some approaches do not work and why patterns of separation and disunity remain entrenched. Transformative adult learning has been defined as "a process by which previously uncritically assimilated assumptions, beliefs, values, and perspectives are questioned and thereby become more open, permeable, and better validated."[12] This learning approach is associated with sociologist Jack Mezirow, whose Transformation Theory identifies the principles of how adults successfully change their fundamental frames of reference.

It is important to define what we mean by "transformation." Brookfield is careful to state that transformation is a change in "perspective, in a frame of reference, in a personal paradigm, and in a habit of mind together with its resulting point of view," as opposed to "any instance in which reflection leads to a deeper more nuanced understanding of assumptions."[13] Another way of saying this is that transformation is closer to a 180- than a 90-degree change. It is not a small thing, and one sign of it to me is changed *behavior* to go along with the new frame of reference.

Our frames of reference, according to Mezirow, are frames "through which meaning is construed and all learning takes place,"[14] not unlike the maps I described above. We use our frames of reference to explain and understand our experiences. In transformative learning, new frames are established that enable us to "reinterpret an old experience (or a new one) from a new set of expectations, thus giving a new meaning and perspective to the old experience."[15]

Experiencing transformative learning causes us to critically reflect on our frames of reference, making them more open and flexible, and ultimately transforming them. It enables us to develop beliefs that are more reliable as guides to action. Mezirow describes learning as "using a prior interpretation to construe a new or revised interpretation of the meaning of one's experience as a guide to future action."[16]

My journey started with a new understanding of my own assumptions, driven by a process of critical reflection. This kind of reflection, according to Brookfield, is a necessary but insufficient condition for transformation. In order to qualify as transformation, there must be a "shift in the tectonic plates of one's assumptive clusters," and not merely progress toward a deeper understanding of an idea or assumption. When I landed in this unfamiliar neighborhood, I became more aware of my inner dialogue, which provides constant commentary on everything that is happening. I noticed that I thought everyone needed something from me, and a lot of my inner processing was trying to determine what it was. When I met Dee at her mailbox, I wanted to connect and be friends, but I also "knew" she needed my help. Through the many steps of the journey articulated throughout these chapters, I have arrived at a place where that assumption is gone. I am able now to enter conversations with people who are very different from me and see them as people rather than as people in need. The process of critical reflection on my inner dialogue over time, resulted in what I view as transformation. My tectonic plates shifted.

Community is an important element in adult learning. For Mezirow, learning is embedded in relationship. Human beings, he asserts, are "essentially relational":

> Our identity is formed in webs of affiliation within a shared life world. Human reality is intersubjective; our life histories and language are bound up with those of others. It is within the context of these relationships, governed by existing and changing cultural paradigms, that we become the persons we are. Transformative learning involves liberating ourselves from reified forms of thought that are no longer dependable.[17]

Brookfield agrees, asserting, "Any critically reflective effort we undertake can only be accomplished with the help of critical friends."[18] And according to educators Bradley Courtenay, Sharan Merriam, and Patricia Reeves, the "catalytic events" that transform us "emanate from a support system of family and friends, support groups, and/or spirituality."[19]

In line with these catalytic events, Mezirow posits that the process of liberating ourselves from entrenched forms of thought often begins with what he calls a "disorienting dilemma."[20] This kind of learning is often precipitated by an "intensely threatening emotional experience,"[21] and so it is quite possible that adults intentionally or unintentionally avoid circumstances that may bring about disorienting dilemmas. Without the dilemma, we miss out on the series of steps that have the potential to bring us to the place of real transformation, where we integrate our new learning and embrace our new perspectives.

My first year in my urban neighborhood was basically a string of disorienting dilemmas. The first one I remember was when I met Dee and found out she did not have a car. A coworker picked her up for work each day, but other than that, she relied on the bus. I had never met a family that did not own a car. At the time, Dee had five kids in school and one preschooler. All of her kids went to schools that were at least five miles from her house. I couldn't make sense of how this could work. What if they missed the bus? What if they got sick at school and she was at work with no car? What about parent-teacher conferences and sporting events?

Learning that my friends don't have food at home is an ongoing disorienting dilemma. I was about to preach at a church one weekend when Jaleesa* casually mentioned that the only food she had left at home was cabbage. I never cease to be challenged by the thought that someone I see regularly and consider a friend has empty cupboards. I have never experienced it, and until I moved here, I had never had friends who experienced it.

Having regular contact with people who do not have transportation or enough food or stable housing and who are victims of society's unjust structures forces me to continually revisit my assumptions and engage in the task of critical reflection. Brief contact may have caused me to see them as victims, but prolonged contact helped me to see them as human beings. I began to care about them and enter their hopelessness. It mattered to me that Dee did not have a car. It started me on a new journey. Brookfield says, "The overall purpose of adult development is to realize one's agency through increasingly expanding awareness and critical reflection," with a goal toward that shift of tectonic plates.[22] The trio of awareness, reflection, and agency that I experienced captures my own journey of transformation as an adult learner over these past fifteen years.

Legitimate Peripheral Participation

Over the years, our Saturday church services at The Lift have been the context for a lot of learning. We've had people wander in high or drunk and then either be disruptive or sleep through the service. Several times, people have asked for prayer to find a church. What we do is unrecognizable to some people as church, so they come to The Lift on Saturday nights and attend a "real" church on Sunday mornings. People have taken phone calls and had entire conversations during the church service. Occasionally, during our dinner following our service, someone who is hungry will take far more than their share of food. We've had money stolen during church services. One of our youth wanted to sing a solo for us one week. We didn't vet him at all, however, and he stood up front wearing headphones singing something about "an angel sleeping next to me." Apparently, the word "angel" qualified it as a song appropriate for church. One of my favorite moments was when The Lift first started, and we were renting space in a local church. The pastor of that church came out of his office during our prayer time and played a Whitney Houston song on the piano to accompany us. I could go on. We are an odd community in a variety of ways.

Lave and Wenger's theory of legitimate peripheral participation addresses how people learn and describes how we accidentally created our odd learning community at The Lift and in our neighborhood. Whatever else The Lift has been, it has certainly been a place of learning. Lave and Wenger's theory "concerns the process by which newcomers become part of a community of practice."[23] Like Mezirow, they argue that learning is always situated, and that knowledge and learning are inherently relational. They even refer to the "dilemma-driven" nature of learning, bringing to mind Mezirow's disorienting dilemma. They are not advocating the creation of dilemmas for the purpose of learning; they are merely pointing out the power that dilemmas have to force learning.[24] I can attest to the power of dilemmas to reshape perspectives!

Situated learning, they assert, takes place regardless of whether any education is intended. Their description of organic relationship formation describes what happens in my community on a regular basis. We have various programs, meetings, and events at The Lift where people who do not look like one another come together. These are opportunities for people to "accidentally" learn enough to take the next step toward relationships that cross the boundaries of race and class. People may visit our informal Saturday church service several times before they are even ready to stay after for the dinner. They observe the dynamics in the room to see if they can see themselves taking part. They may experience a dilemma due to something unexpected happening, and they must decide what to do with it. Eventually, they may stay for dinner and join in the conversation. A while later, they might start volunteering at The Lift's programs or mentoring a student.

Lave and Wenger explain that a newcomer's legitimate peripherality to a learning environment provides more than a third-party perspective, or "'observational' lookout post":

> It crucially involves *participation* as a way of learning—of both absorbing and being absorbed in—the "culture of practice." An extended period of legitimate peripherality provides learners with opportunities to make the culture of practice theirs.[25]

In other words, if adults are to learn, it requires looking beyond didactic methods or mere observation. It requires that they enter a community of practice that will challenge their assumptions and show them new ways of seeing the world. This is in contrast with "learning as internalization"; the focus is on the "whole person acting in the world."[26]

Before we moved to St. Paul, I had spent several years serving the poor and engaging in social justice projects before I established relationships with people who could potentially be the beneficiaries of my activities (as I would have phrased it then). It was not until I moved into this neighborhood and started participating, tentatively at first, in a community different than my own that I experienced a profound change in myself. I would say that I used to *do* things for purposes of justice, but moving here started me on the road of *being* a just person.

Dee's experience was similar to mine. "Being a part of The Lift," she says, "is really what changed my thoughts." She said she had never developed intimate friendships with people that went beyond the surface. At The Lift, she really got to know people, and many people were from a background different than hers. She got to know people's children and learned when everyone's birthday was, learned about their hurts and their childhoods. She found enough similarities to begin to build relationships across lines of difference.

Dee's and my experiences are examples of Lave and Wenger's thesis in action. Dee says it took a few years for her to work her way into her place in this diverse community. She says, "There was never a time when I was like, 'I get it.' I didn't get it; there was just little 'get its' at a time. Little bits. Just a little bit of this and a little bit of that."

While we may exemplify Lave and Wenger's model, we also stretch it. We were really forming a new community of diversity in those early years, and *everyone* was on the periphery. I think my family, Dee, and Ernest navigated how to become friends and, as we made progress, our periphery grew. A few of Dee's friends and family members came to see what was going on, some of my suburban friends showed up, some of Dee's and my mutual neighbors came because they wanted their kids involved in something good. We grew into Lave and Wenger's model as a core of relationships formed that was outside of the norms in our neighborhood.

There are many challenges in applying this approach to learning more broadly for purposes of building friendships between people who don't look alike. To name just two: First, Mezirow's disorienting dilemma that may lead to new ways of seeing the Other is unlikely to happen in our segregated and stratified context. Lave and Wenger point out that access to communities of practice, while essential, is also problematic in multiple ways. In other words, where does one go stand on the periphery of a community where black and white, rich and poor are friends?

Second, it does not appear that most adults of any class are very interested in going through an "intensely threatening emotional experience" that would require them to radically reorient their lives and values and learn a new way of seeing the world. In my own context, this has been exemplified by what seems to me to be fear on the part of conservative people to engage the Other, especially the Other who is poor. Some have seemed suspicious that what we are doing is an inherently liberal activity, and they have to protect their ideology by staying away. This ties in with Brookfield and Holst's understanding of transformative learning. They see "adult education for democracy" as coterminous with "adult education for socialism."[27] Their point as it relates to my story is that my political journey from the world of conservative Baptists to a liberal perspective on social justice is not meaningful unless it includes a new understanding of economics. These few sentences would strike fear into many of the conservative people I know. They are not looking for a disorienting dilemma. They do not want to be emotionally threatened. They do not want to become socialists. They do not want anyone to say the word "socialism." In chapter 10, I will talk about the positive side of starting on this journey and why the disorienting dilemmas and intensely threatening emotional experiences are worth it.

My story of moving into a diverse community, forming new friendships, and starting The Lift is very much about creating a context where disorienting dilemmas are likely to happen, and where there are knowledgeable people from various races and classes who have been through it who can serve as guides for those who are brave enough to stick around. But we are small. We have space for a limited number of legitimate peripheral participants. I sometimes feel hopeless about this reality, and I have to remind myself that it's better to do something small than nothing at all.

I don't want to beat a dead horse, but this type of social learning requires a willingness to be uncomfortable: to be confronted head-on with the realities of white privilege and racism, to engage in conversations where you feel the outsider, to run into rituals that are unfamiliar and can sometimes feel threatening. My daughter was explaining to a friend what this book was going to be about, and when she got to the subtitle, *Why Do All Our Friends Look Just Like Us?*, her friend's response was, "Well, I'm not a racist."

If white people can feel threatened so easily, the barriers begin to seem insurmountable. Because more than a mere subtitle, building relationships of difference is time consuming and can feel threatening. It also requires a long-term commitment. Educator and researcher Laurent Daloz studied social commitment and found "no instance of transformation as a result of an isolated, epochal event."[28] Brookfield and Stephen Preskill agree, stating,

"It takes a great deal of time and energy to bring people together regularly enough for long-term relationships to form."[29]

One thing we have found at The Lift is that disorienting dilemmas can be kind of fun when you have them with other people. When there is mutual trust, Dee and I can be disoriented together, albeit usually for different reasons. My white coworkers Julie and Aaron and I can slap our foreheads together when we realize how many things we viewed naïvely or incorrectly in the past. And we can celebrate together when we see the growth in ourselves and our community.

Imagination

The celebrations are frequently mixed in with frustration. A white woman from Minneapolis called me recently. She had heard that we lived in St. Paul and had created a nonprofit with community support and input. She and her husband had moved into the city with the hope they could do something similar, but she felt like they were not making any progress. I asked her to tell me about their experience, and she described having other white friends over and walking around the neighborhood trying to meet people. She described going up to groups of black people and trying to start conversations. She said they all just looked at them like they were aliens.

And in a way, they were. I advised her to just meet her next-door neighbors (as she likely had done when living in the suburbs) and to ask questions about their kids and family. To view her task as making friends rather than helping people. This came as a relief to her. It can be difficult when we think we are in charge of situations we know nothing about.

If Mezirow is correct that learning is embedded in relationship, the first step is that relationships start to form—relationships that go beyond mere proximity. Social researchers Laurent Daloz, Cheryl Keen, James Keen, and Sharon Parks argue that this kind of engagement is "not achieved simply by mere proximity to the other nor by sharing an enjoyment of the other's folklore, cuisine, or art."[30] Rather, a real connection consists of recognizing that we all share the essential human feelings of fear, joy, yearning, delight, suffering, hope, and love. The woman in Minneapolis was looking for something to share, but she was not yet culturally competent or patient enough to see it happen. This kind of connection takes a long time to form across the divisions of race and class.

An important step, then, is being open to difference. People from backgrounds different than our own can be threatening when we see our own culture and preference as "right" and all others as suspect. This requires what one of the authors' subjects calls "connected knowing," in which people very deliberately "imagine themselves" into the world of the other, attempting to truly experience living in that world, especially the feelings it entails.[31] Mezirow concurs with the importance of imagination, saying that it is "indispensable to understanding the unknown. We imagine alternative ways of seeing and interpreting."[32]

Educators and researchers Mary Belenky, Blythe Clinchy, Nancy Goldberger, and Jill Tarule call this a woman's way of knowing. They say that women believe that if they listen carefully enough, they will be able to do the "right thing" and will "get along with others." In contrast to men's "emphasis on separation and autonomy," they say, women share a "rootedness in a sense of connection."[33] Whether it's based in gender or just learning things the hard way, this kind of knowing is critical to building relationships across lines of difference.

When Dee does something I don't understand, like not showing up for something she said she was coming to, I try to imagine myself into her reality. Just imagining it is overwhelming. If I were dealing with six kids, no husband, and not enough money, I don't know that I would be functional. So when she doesn't show up, I ask what the reasons might be. Does she have gas in her car (when she has one)? Does she maybe have a sick child? Is she exhausted from working two jobs and juggling the schedules and needs of all her kids?

Recently, a group from The Lift was giving a baby shower, and Dee didn't show up. In the past, I would have been irritated. But I checked in with her the next day and found out that she had taken her son to the emergency room the night before the shower, and she had ended up at the doctor's office herself that afternoon with a major health problem. Her phone service had been suspended, so she had no way of contacting us about the shower. The real problem was not that Dee didn't show up for the shower; it was that Dee was in crisis. Those in my community who are willing and able to imagine themselves into the life of the Other take a step toward reciprocal relationships. Those who are not don't make much progress.

The Hudsons* are a wealthy suburban family that was involved at The Lift for over two years. They came and immediately voiced their commitment to social justice and their willingness to be learners. They even talked of the possibility of selling their suburban home at some point in the future and moving to our neighborhood. They were gung-ho. After a while, though, another side emerged. They started to regularly express frustration to me about the "dumb decisions" people in our neighborhood made—about money, time, parenting, and so on. I did my best to help them understand the cultural and social differences that could lead them to see the world so differently than my neighbors.

In one case, they were irritated that a woman at The Lift was not keeping up with her gas and electric bill and seemed to constantly be in crisis. I asked them how they thought that this single mom with three kids at home who had a monthly income that was approximately the same as their car payment could better manage her finances to meet her obligations. Our conversations centered on The Lift's core commitment to social justice. Working for social justice often involves engaging with people in dire financial straits. Rather than judging them or being frustrated by choices that we don't understand, we try to see the situation through the broader lens of a society with a history of social injustice. This history has led my neighbors to this place of financial need, and when we don't recognize that, we may unfairly judge individual behaviors. It seemed that the Hudsons expected to drive in from their wealthy suburb and find people just like them. They were perhaps lacking in imagination.

According to Daloz, deeper encounters with those who differ from us are essential, as superficial encounters often lead to stereotyping and exacerbating misunderstandings, rather than helping to resolve them. In the case of the Hudsons, however, even a long-term encounter was not enough. As sociologist Xavier Briggs points out, encounters of this kind are rare, and research on people who have these deeper encounters has been limited, leaving a lack of understanding about how they are formed and why they sometimes *don't* form. Why did the Hudsons leave frustrated and with their stereotypes further entrenched after two years, while others end up transformed?

Once we have rearranged our maps and engaged in learning experiences that are disorienting and transformative, we have the opportunity and the responsibility to lead others as they embark on this journey.

A Vision for Tribal Leadership

Throughout my years in higher education, I read books and articles on transformational leadership, leading change, strategic leadership, church leadership, the challenges of leadership, the dark side of leadership, leading teams, empowering leadership, the laws of leadership, the levels of leadership, and the importance of leverage for leaders. While I learned important principles from many of these readings, there was little there to prepare me for the kind of leadership that I have needed to exercise in my current context. When I think about leadership, I think about leading *people*. Most leadership books, while they talk about leading people, are focused on leading *organizations*.

On the topic of creating a diverse workforce, educators Flannery Stevens, Victoria Plaut, and Jeffrey Sanchez-Burks say this task requires an approach that "maximizes inclusion and minimizes resistance."[34] Their goal in helping employers create this kind of environment is for them to gain a competitive advantage in the marketplace. This is an example of a common view on developing and leading diversity, wherein the employees (in this case diverse ones) are seen as instruments toward a greater end, such as competitive advantage, rather than as the essence of what I believe should be the focus of an organization.

The kind of leadership that is essential in a context of diversity of race and class is not easily described, and it is nearly impossible to quantify. The best description I can come up with is that such leadership requires the same skills that are necessary to be a very good friend. When I think about my own leadership, I don't think about the organization; I think about the people. And I don't think about leading the people; I think about loving the people. We don't use titles much at The Lift (although we have them for practical purposes), and we don't refer to people as leaders or followers. We have learned that when people feel loved and included, they will get on board with whatever is going on. Educator and philosopher Nel Noddings says, "Children will work harder and do things—even odd things like adding fractions—for people they love and trust."[35] This is not just true of children; it is true of everyone.

I will include here three principles of leadership that our community is implicitly built around. I may be accused of being naïve, but I will refer my detractors to my fifteen-year track record of leading, in collaboration with others, a community of people that includes men and women; teens and elders; the financially rich and poor; black, white, Hispanic, and Hmong; married, single, and divorced; conservative and liberal; urban and suburban residents; and the usual diversity of thought and opinion that exists in any community.

First, leadership is not about power. You cannot effectively lead a community that includes disempowered people by relying on power that is rooted in title, position, or social status. In our context, hierarchy is one of the things we are trying to work against, and it cannot be perpetuated in how our community is structured. In *Servant Leadership*, management researcher Robert Greenleaf comes closest to outlining the type of leadership I am describing when he makes servanthood central to the task. He says, "To the worldly, servant-leaders may seem naïve; and they may not adapt readily to prevailing institutional structures."[36] We reject those prevailing structures, as they are what got us to this racially inequitable place.

Second, this means we only lead as people are willing to follow. I've heard it said that the way you know if you are a leader is to look behind you. While this may seem to refer to a positional sort of arrangement, there is something very true about it. Greenleaf writes of the difference between formal authority and moral authority. Formal authority exists due to a position within an organization. Moral authority is earned as leaders prove themselves to be sacrificial, committed, focused on means and not only ends, and interdependent with those in their community. I don't want anyone following me because of a formal position. I am someone's pastor because *they* see me as such, and not because I call myself their pastor. I am surprised every time Keshia proudly introduces me to someone as her pastor. It's not a title I have ever claimed, but for her, it's an important aspect of our relationship.

Third, the primary role of a leader is to love people. It has been my experience in all of the various places I have lived and led that people are looking for love and belonging, not for someone to follow. Greenleaf says, "Showing deep respect and love to others" is part of the essence of moral authority.[37] Once a group has been formed in which people feel loved and included, there is tremendous potential. Near the end of Ernest's life, when he was dragging a heavy oxygen tank around with him, he refused to miss a board meeting or a church service. Six days before he died, he was late for a meeting. When I called to see if he was coming, he said he was already in his pajamas. Nevertheless, fifteen minutes later, he was there. Ernest gave every last piece of himself to our community to the very last minute, and it was because he belonged.

I believe the reason this kind of leadership works in this context is that forming a diverse group should not be seen as a means to an end; it should be seen as the primary reason for the endeavor. The existence of a healthy community is a legitimate end in and of itself. However, I would argue that once that kind of community exists, there are many possibilities for maximizing the community to accomplish more measurable goals. It seems backwards to start with measurable goals as the priority and then try to create a diverse community to accomplish them. Systems scientist Peter Senge defines leadership as "the capacity of a human community to shape its future."[38] It seems that this definition requires, first, the formation of a community that will, second, together work to shape its future.

The topic of leadership is, of course, the topic of many, many books. It is of critical importance in the work for social justice and in modeling the kind of relationships I am writing about. And I believe it requires a type of leadership that has not been fully explored in the literature. Even Greenleaf, in his excellent description of servant leadership, defines the task of leadership in terms of "institution building."[39] Leadership, to me, is about "people building" regardless of whether there is any institution involved at all.

#

After exploring the barriers to reciprocal cross-race and cross-class relationships, and setting forth some educational, relational, and leadership principles for how to establish them, in chapter 10, I will make my best case for why building these relationships is a worthwhile endeavor, both for the individual and for society.

Notes

1. Xun Kuang, *Xunzi*, Book 8, 818 CE. This quote is often falsely attributed to Benjamin Franklin.

2. Erich Fromm, *To Have or to Be?* (New York: Continuum, 1976), 33.

3. Email message to author, April 8, 2013.

4. David Berreby, *Us & Them: The Science of Identity* (Chicago: University of Chicago Press, 2008), 73.

5. John Seely Brown and Paul Duguid, *The Social Life of Information* (Boston: Harvard Business School Press, 2000), 128.

6. Myles Horton, *The Long Haul: An Autobiography*, with Judith Kohl and Herbert Kohl (New York: Anchor, 1997), 47.

7. Jean Lave and Étienne Wenger, *Situated Learning: Legitimate*

Peripheral Participation (New York: Cambridge University Press, 1991), 115.

8. Stephen D. Brookfield and John D. Holst, *Radicalizing Learning* (San Francisco: Jossey-Bass, 2011), 34.

9. Jack Mezirow, "Learning to Think Like an Adult: Core Concepts of Transformation Theory," in *Learning as Transformation: Critical Perspectives on a Theory in Progress*, ed. Jack Mezirow (San Francisco: Jossey-Bass, 2000), 18.

10. Frank Dobbin, Alexandra Kalev, and Erin Kelly, "Diversity Management in Corporate America," *Contexts* 6, no. 4 (Fall 2007): 21–27, https://tinyurl.com/y3bdzxl7.

11. Joe R. Feagin, Hernan Vera, and Pinar Batur, *White Racism*, 2nd ed. (New York: Routledge, 2001), 35.

12. Patricia Cranton, "Transformative Learning," in *International Encyclopedia of Adult Education*, ed. Leona M. English (New York: Palgrave Macmillan, 2008), 628.

13. Stephen D. Brookfield, "Transformative Learning as Ideology Critique," in Mezirow, *Learning as Transformation*, 139.

14. Jack Mezirow, *Transformative Dimensions of Adult Learning* (San Francisco: Jossey-Bass, 1991), 4.

15. Mezirow, *Transformative Dimensions*, 11.

16. Mezirow, "Learning to Think," 5.

17. Mezirow, "Learning to Think," 27.

18. Brookfield, "Transformative Learning as Ideology Critique," 146.

19. Bradley Courtenay, Sharan Merriam, and Patricia Reeves, "The Centrality of Meaning-Making in Transformational Learning: How HIV-Positive Adults Make Sense of Their Lives," *Adult Education Quarterly* 48, no. 2 (1998): 78.

20. Mezirow, "Learning to Think," 22.

21. Mezirow, "Learning to Think," 6.

22. Brookfield, "Transformative Learning," 142.

23. Lave and Wenger, *Situated Learning*, 29.

24. Lave and Wenger, *Situated Learning*, 40.

25. Lave and Wenger, *Situated Learning*, 95.

26. Lave and Wenger, *Situated Learning*, 49.

27. Brookfield and Holst, *Radicalizing Learning*, 5.

28. Laurent A. Parks Daloz, "Transformative Learning for the Common Good," in Mezirow, *Learning as Transformation*, 106.

29. Stephen Preskill and Stephen D. Brookfield, *Learning as a Way of Leading: Lessons from the Struggle for Social Justice* (San Francisco: Jossey-Bass, 2009), 198.

30. Laurent A. Parks Daloz, Cheryl H. Keen, James P. Keen, and Sharon Daloz Parks, *Common Fire: Leading Lives of Commitment in a Complex World* (Boston: Beacon, 1996), 70.

31. Daloz et al., *Common Fire*, 113.

32. Mezirow, *Transformative Dimensions*, 83.

33. Mary Field Belenky, Blythe McVicker Clinchy, Nancy Rull Goldberger, and Jill Mattuck Tarule, *Women's Ways of Knowing: The Development of Self, Voice, and Mind* (New York: Basic, 1997), 44–45.

34. Flannery G. Stevens, Victoria C. Plaut, and Jeffrey Sanchez-Burks, "Unlocking the Benefits of Diversity: All-Inclusive Multi-Culturalism and Positive Organizational Change," in *Leading Organizations: Perspectives for a New Era*, ed. Gill R. Hickman (Thousand Oaks, CA: Sage, 2010), 411.

35. Nel Noddings, "Schools Face 'Crisis in Caring,'" *Education Week* 8, no. 14 (1988): 32, https://tinyurl.com/y2qrgzoo.

36. Robert Greenleaf, *Servant Leadership: A Journey into the Nature of Legitimate Power & Greatness* (Mahwah, NJ: Paulist, 1977), 341.

37. Greenleaf, *Servant Leadership*, 6.

38. Peter Senge, "My Definition of Leadership," December 18, 2012, YouTube video, 1:51, https://tinyurl.com/y2zsd7s9.

39. Greenleaf, *Servant Leadership*, 35.

10.

Tribal Unity

> It is time for parents to teach young people early on that in diversity there is beauty and there is strength.
>
> —Maya Angelou[1]

When I lived in the suburbs and made friends with my neighbors who looked just like me, I learned a lot of things that I didn't know I was learning. I learned that to have a really nice kitchen, you must have stainless steel appliances. I learned that good people have fancy landscaping that they regularly maintain. I learned that your furniture and dishes should all match, and that beds don't belong on porches or in entryways or, God forbid, in the living room. I learned that each household should have its own lawn-mower and, at least in Minnesota, its own snowblower. I learned that all kitchens simply must have a dishwasher.

Then I moved into my urban neighborhood and learned that not everyone believed these things. With more reflection than I had ever given to these types of issues, I realized that none of these things were essentially true. They were constructs of my suburban context that we suburbanites had all silently agreed upon, and these constructs were constantly reinforced by the media and by the fleeting feelings of joy we had when the new furniture was delivered.

How willing are we to have these constructs challenged? Do I want to become a person who can overlook mismatched furniture and dishes? Pea-green refrigerators? Beds in the living room? After examining the significant barriers to engaging in deeply reciprocal friendships that cross lines of race and class and looking at the hard work required to overcome these barriers, it is not unfair

223

to ask, "Why even bother?" It is commonplace to ask of almost any endeavor, "What's in it for me?"

In this final chapter, I will attempt to provide answers. The answers are both communal and individual. What are the benefits for the world we live in, and what are the benefits for me as an individual? Although these are two very different questions, the answers intersect in important ways. Sociologist James Vela-McConnell writes: "Patterns of homogeneity in our personal relationships actually determine the amount of social stratification existing in a society."[2] Having all of our friends look just like us contributes to social division. And Briggs writes: "Connections among socially dissimilar persons have been shown to have a broad impact on society, expanding social identities, working against insular thinking, containing conflicts and reducing inequalities." Cross-tribal connections can provide lower-status groups with "keys to economic access and attainment."[3] In other words, *not* having all our friends look just like us has a lot of benefits for society.

Briggs is exactly describing my experience in my neighborhood with friends from diverse backgrounds in terms of the benefits to "lower-status" groups. However, he doesn't get around to describing the benefits to the "higher-status" groups, which is the larger point I am making. Reciprocal relationships, by definition, include benefits for both parties. The power and benefits are shared equally, making a positive impact on society as a whole. Lower-status groups benefit, society benefits, and higher-status groups benefit as well. This is a point that is often missed. While my ultimate focus will be on these personal benefits, I will start by briefly discussing the communal benefits.

Communal Benefits

Sociologist Kathleen Korgen writes: "In our increasingly racially and ethnically diverse society, the ability to form cross-racial and cross-cultural relationships is vital for the well-being and stability of the nation."[4] Although most people might nod in agreement with this statement, I am not sure many would be able to answer *how* these relationships are vital to national stability. It is politically correct to agree, but it is difficult to define.

Although far from being fully realized, I see three primary ways that reciprocal relationships of the kind I have been discussing can potentially benefit society: first, they improve the commons; second, they contribute to an increase in the generosity of those with financial assets; and, third, they help heal the brokenness that is part and parcel of how our country was founded and how it currently operates.

Improving the Commons

According to social researchers Laurent Daloz, Cheryl Keen, James Keen, and Sharon Parks, in an earlier time, "the commons" referred to "a shared public space of the sort that anchored the American vision of democracy." This was often a town hall or square, a county courthouse, a park, or Main Street. Regardless of the form it took, "it marked the center of a shared world."[5] Today, we have to work harder to develop a commons, which includes educating people about what it is and why it is needed. Sociologist and philosopher Jürgen Habermas says that public opinion that formerly emerged from the commons "has partly decomposed into the informal opinions of private citizens without a public."[6] With the emergence of social media, it could be argued that it has further decomposed into informal opinions of *anonymous* citizens. This is a great loss as "only in the light of the public sphere did that which existed become revealed, did everything become visible to all."[7] On Twitter, it could be said that everything has become visible, but it is often scurrilous arguments about things that don't matter or should not be visible rather than reasoned dialogue between peers for the benefit of society, although I wouldn't go so far as to say reasoned dialogue does not exist at all in this sphere.

The center of our shared world has been obscured. Globalism has increased the complexity of the world, seemingly expanding the commons to include seven billion people. In discussing Habermas, Stephen Brookfield says that "society has become too vast and complicated for everyone to sit round the table and talk about how they wish to arrange things."[8] At the same time, rampant individualism has caused people to prioritize their own needs, with the good of the whole coming only as an afterthought.

Today, it may be more helpful to think of the "common good" as opposed to the commons. There are still many people willing to work for the common good, but there are unfortunately few spaces where "the diverse parts of a community could come together and hold a conversation within a shared sense of participation and responsibility."[9] In today's world, the town square is often more ornamental than functional. Public spaces are places of anonymity: coffee shops, restaurants, malls, high-rises—and, increasingly, Twitter.

Embracing the common good is about making a commitment to the good of all the diverse parts of a community. In their long-ranging qualitative study on the subject of the common good, Daloz et al. make the case that middle- and upper-class people are increasingly realizing that their well-being "depends not only upon their talent, initiative, and ability to work hard, but also upon the quality of our common life."[10] Our individual realities are bound up with the whole. The erosion of the commons impacts everyone.

How do deeply reciprocal relationships that cross lines of race and class contribute to the common good? How might my friendship with Dee or Ernest create shared benefits? I will turn to three recent researchers for answers: first, Vela-McConnell claims that diverse friendships have the ability to "strengthen social affinity";[11] second, Briggs adds that relationships that bridge social boundaries can "reduce inequality directly";[12] and, third, economist Scott Page contends that diversity helps us develop better solutions to social problems.[13]

Let's start with social affinity, which is strengthened as a community of people come to share values, ideals, and a commitment to a common cause. In their study of the formation and sustenance of the common good, Daloz et al. reported:

We have learned that a constructive encounter with others who are significantly different from oneself is key to the development of a capacity for trustworthy belonging and confident agency in a diverse and complex world, a capacity that transcends the traps of individualism and tribalism and enables people to become at home in the new commons.[14]

This captures the essence of the type of community we are trying to nurture at The Lift.

Vanessa*, who is a single mom living below the poverty line, tells her story of getting a flat tire on Christmas Day in subzero temperatures. She left her car at the gas station, and a stranger gave her a ride home. Facing the reality of not being able to get to any family Christmas events, she hesitantly called Aaron, who is white and middle class and who had recently moved into our neighborhood with his family. Aaron and his father-in-law fixed her flat tire and returned her car to her with a full tank of gas. The following week at The Lift, Vanessa was sharing this story with tears in her eyes. The story was not about her embarrassment at not being able to solve her own problem, nor was it about a wonderful stranger who helped her out, but rather about how meaningful it was to have a friend close by who was willing and able to offer assistance.

Later that same week, with temperatures now twenty-five below zero, Dee's fifteen-year-old car refused to start because she had so little gas in the tank that condensation built up and caused her fuel line to freeze. Neighborhood friends from The Lift went to add some gas and try to get it started. Inspired by Vanessa's story of Aaron, they went beyond the two gallons they needed to add and filled it up. These stories strengthened our community, met needs, built trust, and added to our shared story of going deeper despite our differences. They increased our social affinity. As these types of friendships catch on and stories are told, the growth of good will is not just additive, but exponential.

In addition to strengthening social affinity, relationships that cross tribal lines also have the potential to reduce inequality. In late 2016, Dee was accepted into an innovative program at a local consulting company that some of us at The Lift learned about. The program is designed for people who have had barriers to entering or reentering the workforce. Being a single mom of six kids, sometimes lacking reliable transportation, and having her education interrupted several times meant she had spent most of her adult life merely trying to hold a job rather than build a career. She went through several months of training in project management and was placed at a local Fortune 500 company for on-the-job training. That company picked up Dee's contract following the completion of her training, and she is now on track to begin making far more money than she ever dreamed she would.

In the past, Dee says, she worked only to survive. She never had a thought of having an actual career. In a very short time, Dee has moved from poverty to having a middle-class income and a professional job. This will have benefits for Dee's entire family. It changes the future for Dee, her kids, and her grandkids. Of course, one family getting out of poverty does not change society overnight. But this is where Briggs's observation about reducing inequality helps frame the situation. He asks us to look beyond the individual and see how the expansion of social networks in such opportunities does more than help this individual get a job or that individual be accepted into a training program. Rather, the hope is that people who are networked to resources will interact with those who are not.

The potential benefits Briggs lists of relationships that cross social boundaries include "improving access by lower-status outgroups to information vouching (recommendations and other social endorsements), preparation, mentoring, and other keys to economic success and attainment."[15] This exactly describes what happened with Dee, who says that without her friends at The Lift, "I would never have known about this opportunity."

Finally, Scott Page contends that relationships that cross lines of race and class help us develop better solutions for the world in which we live. In 2005, Hurricane Katrina decimated the Gulf Coast, leaving thousands of people stranded and homeless. In an attempt to meet basic needs quickly, the Federal Emergency Management Agency (FEMA) handed out $2,000 debit cards to those who were in the most dire need: those living in shelters, those without insurance, and those without transportation. A few days after the cards were issued, stories began circulating that cards had been used to purchase $800 purses, visits to strip clubs, tattoos, an engagement ring, a Caribbean cruise, NFL football tickets, and casino and massage parlor visits. These stories were later confirmed by the Government Accountability Office (GAO), which estimates that $600 million to $1.4 billion of the handouts were used for purchases that were not in line with the intended uses for the cards.[16]

When news started to break about these abuses, many of my east-side neighbors laughed out loud and expressed neither surprise nor judgment. They seemed baffled that anyone would be surprised. To them, getting handed a no-strings-attached $2,000 gift card would be seen as license to have fun in the midst of a lot of personal hardship. My thought was that if any one of my neighbors (or millions of others who regularly survive severe hardships) had been invited in on the decision-making process, this never would have happened. Dee said, "They needed to just give them vouchers for their specific needs." She anticipated that people who were already poor and who were then hit with a hurricane would not necessarily be in a position to make the best decisions. Using vouchers to make sure the assistance went for housing or food or transportation is just common sense to my neighbors.

This is Page's point. His research shows that diversity always trumps homogeneity in problem-solving. "Collections of people with diverse perspectives and heuristics outperform collections of people who rely on homogeneous perspectives and heuristics." We might sum this up by saying that "two heads are better than one," but Page stipulates that the two heads must be *from different backgrounds and circumstances*. Even more, he claims, diversity even trumps *ability*: "Random collections of intelligent problem solvers can outperform collections of the best individual problem solvers."[17] That is, in order to solve problems, two heads are better than one *regardless of intelligence or expertise*.

For our purposes, Page has three relevant findings. First, diversity in a group "does not magically translate into benefits. . . . For diverse groups to function in practice, the people in them must get along."[18] Throwing diverse people into a work team at the office will not necessarily provide the desired result; those people also need to work well together.

Page's second relevant point is that *identity* diversity (that is, cultural, ethnic, gender, and sexual diversity) produces improved outcomes indirectly. (Page also explored many types of diversity beyond identity diversity: cognitive, perspective, preference, heuristic, and so on.) The connection between identity diversity and benefits requires two links, he says: "The first link connects identity diversity to cognitive diversity. The second link connects these diverse talents to relevant problems."[19] The first link means that identity diversity is not enough to produce benefits all by itself. "Identity-diverse people can think alike."[20] What is needed are identity-diverse people *who think differently* from one another. The second link means that better outcomes will only be realized if the problems to be solved *are appropriate to the type of diversity* represented. In the case of Hurricane Katrina, both of these links should have been present. A group that included educated, connected people with power *and* those who had experienced hardship and received public benefits would have come to a much better solution than either one of those groups acting alone.

Page's third point is that diverse groups of the type we are talking about must be well managed. Due to the very real possibility of competing values, these types of groups should expect conflict. As with any conflict-laden context, good leadership is essential for anything to get done.

Our shared commons would certainly be improved by reduced inequality, stronger social ties, and better solutions. By bringing diverse perspectives and varied resources together, relationships that cross lines of race and class contribute to all of these realities.

Increasing Generosity

Ken Stern quotes research that shows that "exposure to need drives generous behavior" and also that "insulation from people in need may dampen the charitable impulse."[21] He also notes that the wealthiest Americans (those in the top 20 percent) contribute on average 1.3 percent of their income to charitable causes, compared with the bottom 20 percent, who donate 3.2 percent of their income. However, when wealthy people were shown a video on child poverty, their willingness to help others increased to almost equal those in the bottom 20 percent of earners. This raises the possibility that "greater exposure to and identification with the challenges of meeting basic needs has created 'high empathy' among lower-income donors."[22] Low-income donors give proportionately more because they closely identify with the struggles to meet basic needs.

Exposure may also influence where their charitable donations go. While lower-income people tend to give to serving organizations, the wealthy give to universities (that cater to the wealthy), medical facilities, conservancies, and museums. Not one of the fifty largest charitable donations in 2012 went to a charity that serves the poor. It is estimated by the Congressional Budget Office that $33 billion of last year's $39 billion in total charitable deductions went to the richest 20 percent of Americans, of whom the richest 1 percent reaped the lion's share.[23] Again, this is because the elite universities, museums, operas, symphonies, and prep schools that are the beneficiaries of their charity are primarily organizations that also cater to the wealthy.

Economist Robert Reich says these are not charities "as most people understand the term." He reinforces my point about segregation: "Increasingly, being rich in America means not having to come across anyone who's not."[24] But Stern offers hope, showing that exposure can move dollars in another direction. Even the minimal contact created by the wealthy living in socioeconomically diverse surroundings makes a measurable difference in how much is given and to whom. Actual relationships between those from different socioeconomic backgrounds would be an even more powerful incentive to give more and to give to organizations that meet the needs of the poor rather than the rich.

Healing the Brokenness

As I wrote in chapter 4, my experience over the past decade has made it clear to me that the work of the Civil Rights Movement is not done. Racism, hatred, antagonism, and ignorance persist. There is a lot to be done to put our diverse country right. I believe that the development of relationships across the borders of black and white, rich and poor is an important part of healing. Vela-McConnell writes:

> These friendships that cross social boundaries have the potential to decrease the misunderstandings between diverse groups of people and significantly move us along the path toward healing the corresponding divisions within society that shape our attitudes and behavior with regard to those who are different from ourselves.[25]

African American journalist Patricia Raybon has personally lived the experience of healing and writes about spending most of her life silently hating white people:

> "White people" as a category embodied in my view a clear and certain evil—an arrogant malevolence—that had done unspeakable things that I couldn't ignore because I knew the facts of these things. Names and dates and numbers. And the facts haunted me and the numbers justified my hate for all the evil that I believed white people had done.[26]

She could not let these things go, although she politely walked through a white world as "the most agreeable hater."[27]

She writes of learning a love that transcends self: "It must certainly transcend race. It doesn't trivialize race; it rewrites its context. And the effect of that shift, of course, is to liberate the most compelling emotional force—human love."[28] Allan Boesak and Curtiss DeYoung have worked and written extensively in the field of reconciliation and describe it as "exchanging places with 'the other,' overcoming alienation through identification, solidarity, restoring relationships, positive change, new frameworks, and a rich togetherness that is both spiritual and political."[29] There is healing power in love and forgiveness.

But it takes a lot of work on both sides. Journalist Tanner Colby writes: "Interracial friendships . . . across the color line are a key factor in putting the sins of America's past behind us. But it's not something that's accomplished by white people knowing a lot of black people. It helps if white people know how to be better white people."[30] The European-American Collaborative Challenging Whiteness asks white people to strive "on a daily basis to take actions that challenge racism and white hegemony" while also remembering that "even as we challenge white privilege, we are still immersed in it."[31] Healing requires a level of maturity from all of the parties involved, in which they are willing to examine themselves, be honest about history, forgive, and make a conscious decision to work for a new reality.

Dee has spoken of her family members with ties to the Black Panthers and the way their perspectives on society and race shaped her beliefs. Over these many years of building relationships with people very different from herself, healing has taken place, which has had a ripple effect on her kids and extended family members. Healing is specific and concrete. It has to start somewhere and when it does, like social affinity, its growth is exponential.

Individual Benefits

In a series of conversations with friends and family, I sought to understand how they viewed the benefits of their relationships with people at The Lift, specifically with those who are different from those whom they viewed as close friends. I asked, "How would you describe the impact these relationships have had on your life?" and "What, if anything, have you learned from these relationships?"

My Black Friends

I realize this subheading may be jarring. In trying to capture the differences between how individuals on all sides of the black-and-white, rich-and-poor divides see themselves benefitting from these relationships, it made the most sense to group them by tribe of origin. But what to call them? Calling people "poor" or "lower-class" or "under-resourced" seems disrespectful. Calling people black seems like a normal designation, though even that comes with baggage ("I have a lot of black friends"). I asked Dee for ideas about subheadings. We talked again about how it sometimes feels unsafe for white people to even say the word "black." She approved of my headings, despite the baggage, and helped me write this paragraph.

Typically, this first group of people are presumed to be the ones with the most to gain from relationships with those with financial resources or those with higher social standing. Although I entered these conversations knowing that was not the case, I was still surprised by what they did *not* say. But we'll get to that.

Ernest led the way in the formation of many of the cross-race and cross-class relationships at The Lift. When I asked him how he benefitted, two of his answers stood out. First, he said that he had pretty much been alone all his life, and he had learned in the past decade "what it meant to be really loved." He said he now had people who cared about him. Second, he said that if he hadn't met us, he was sure he'd "still be selling drugs of some sort." When I asked him if he was saying that his friends were deterrents to criminal behavior, he did not hesitate: "Yeah," he said, "very much so."

When Ernest died in May of 2013, over two hundred people gathered to mourn him. Some family members came from down south, most of whom had not seen him in decades. Associates from his previous life of crime and incarceration showed up. All of these people from Ernest's past life seemed genuinely shocked, both at the number and at the diversity of people at his funeral. They arrived to find a weeping throng of black and white people from varied backgrounds, and an obituary that listed his Lift board membership and volunteer service in our community. Ernest's last ten years were radically different than his first sixty. I'm almost positive he would list having a large group of diverse friends attend his funeral as a benefit.

Dee's son Wesley spoke of himself and his family as experiencing a true sense of community for the first time, and of his surprise that it was with white people. His previous experience had convinced him that white people were judgmental and saw themselves as superior, assuming it was their job to try to bring others up to their level. He didn't want to be looked down on and had a hard time believing that what he was experiencing could be trusted, but ultimately he decided it could.

Dee also led the way in forming these relationships and found that one benefit of having relationships with people different from her was realizing that the differences are actually helpful; they aren't something bad. She believes now that "differences make us better people." One of the major areas she sees this betterment is in conflict resolution. When dealing with difference, "conflict cannot be avoided." She believes having friends across difference also makes us more patient and understanding, as we learn to deal with different perspectives. She sees people who don't have these experiences as missing out. Like Wesley, she speaks of her experience at The Lift as being her first experience of true community. Her relationships prior to her experience at The Lift had existed mostly on the surface of things, but now she looks around her and seems surprised at both the depth of her relationships and the diversity of them.

When I asked Keshia about the impact of these relationships, she spoke specifically of her relationship with me. "There's not too many people that I can sit down and talk to that don't judge me." Our relationship, she says, has helped her have boundaries and "not let people run over me." She feels that she is a better person as a result, especially in the area of patience. I help her make plans and encourage her, and she says, "You are the only person who does."

Cortez, who moved in with our family as a teenager, says we showed him a way of life that was entirely foreign to him. Living with our family, he says, modeled for him things like having a stable job and having basic needs met. He noticed that we think about the future quite a bit. He says our relationship taught him to "think in a different direction . . . to think as an adult." He also said we taught him what a family is, and that it should be "a place to engage and have an opinion." He was initially surprised at the egalitarian nature of our communication with our kids. We debated and discussed and disagreed with them. In his world, what the parent says goes and is never questioned or debated. He learned that he had a voice in our relationship.

Ricky says our relationship was "refreshing, awkward, and weird" at the beginning, but he could see that we were genuine, and he was in a place where he felt like not many people cared about him. Through our relationship, Ricky learned a new way of thinking. When the guys were rapping behind me in the grocery store and the manager asked if I needed help, he said my response ("These are my friends!") caused him to reflect on the racist responses he regularly experiences and views as "normal." "Maybe we *shouldn't* be questioned everywhere we go," he said after that experience. He felt empowered realizing, "We don't have to take this."

After these conversations, I was trying to identify the themes that emerged. But I was surprised at what was *not* mentioned: No one said anything about money! No one talked about the benefits of getting help with rent or transportation or food. No one spoke of backpacks and school supplies or Christmas presents. I don't know why I thought they would, but I was surprised that they did not. In fact, they listed the same kinds of things most people list when talking about the benefits of their close relationships: they feel loved, they make better choices, they learn, they gain a different perspective, they are accepted as they are.

Why did I think they would list financial benefits? Likely because I had bought into the message of our times, which is that money is what matters. Although relationships do in fact open the doors to resources and opportunity, this appears to be an *effect* of cross-race friendships rather than a *motivation* for them.

My White Friends

The typical script has my white, resourced friends providing the benefits in these relationships and receiving something in return along the lines of "feeling good because I helped others." Thankfully, my interviewees see themselves benefitting far beyond that.

Aaron was our youth director at The Lift for a decade and has lived in our neighborhood for most of the past ten years. He and his wife bought a house a couple of blocks away from us. When I questioned him about the benefits of the cross-race and cross-class friendships he has developed, he says they have enabled him "to have a much more accurate picture of the world." He has been challenged to see things differently. His experiences in our neighborhood have opened his eyes to the "systemic racism present today." He says it has made him aware of "biases and stereotypes" that he didn't even know he had. Like me, he has also realized that a lack of financial resources is not the root problem in impoverished communities; it is often a symptom of deeper issues.

Aaron met his wife Hannah when he was living in a rundown apartment building in our neighborhood. It was not her favorite place to visit, and we all wondered if Aaron would soon be moving with Hannah to a better and safer community. In the past several years, however, they have not only bought a house in our neighborhood, but Hannah has developed meaningful relationships with people very different from her, which she says have helped her "become a more well-rounded and grounded individual." She says putting real faces to the stories of poverty that circulate means you can no longer live in denial or ignorance. She has been awakened to a new "reality of life," and it has moved her from an inward focus to an outward focus.

Julie has lived in our neighborhood for almost twenty-five years, arriving here well before The Lift was even conceived of. She says the relationships she has formed at The Lift have saved her "from an arrogant and judgmental point of view." She can no longer stay silent to avoid confrontation when people make disparaging remarks about ex-cons or single mothers or young men walking down the middle of the street blocking traffic. These categories of people have been transformed into individuals she loves. On a lighter note, she says that relationships of diversity "make life more interesting and exciting."

Rob and his family have been involved at The Lift for several years. They are one of the few long-term committed families who drive in from the suburbs on a regular basis to be involved. "I am a child of the self-reliant, earn your own way, hard work leads to success culture of America today," he says. "I never had difficulty getting a job or being successful, and I always thought it was because I earned everything I was given through my own individual hard work and talent." Once he started making friends from different social, racial, and ethnic backgrounds, he says, "I started to realize that worldly success really has very little to do with hard work or talent. This was true of my friends from higher up the ladder and lower down the ladder equally. I knew lazy, untalented rich people as well as hard-working and talented poor people." This has helped him to reject self-reliance and judgment, and prioritize "unconditional love, community, and mutual reliance."

Jeremy and Shannon helped us start The Lift as a young couple, and they now have two young children. They bought a house in our neighborhood several years ago. Jeremy says his experiences with friends from different backgrounds have made the world both bigger and smaller for him: "The diversity experienced at The Lift is a constant reminder that the world is bigger and more complex than I allow, while simultaneously reminding me of its smallness, specifically seen in the common connections, dreams, hopes, loves, and fears that we all share." Of his friends from different backgrounds he says, "They help me see Jesus." Jesus spent time with "the widow, the orphan, the lowly, and the other," and through my participation at The Lift, I have been able to "discover the ones God loves."

In looking through the answers my friends gave, the two themes that emerge are love and learning. The answers of my black friends tend more toward love, and the answers of my white friends tend more toward learning. Although I know my friends well enough to know that they would all say they feel loved in our community and that they have all learned something, this difference stood out to me. Raybon may offer a partial answer. She tells of generations of poverty and racism and struggle in her family. Her grandmother, who grew up in the South in the early part of the twentieth century, had a different sort of parenting philosophy: "Children could die here. You just trained them and whipped them and prayed." Raybon says there was an "austere harshness" to the environment she emerged from: "We can blame lynching and white citizens councils and KKK night riders for killing us by the thousands, but nobody knows how many more of us have died in our hearts instead from homes without unconditional warmth and love."[32]

Raybon is not, of course, saying that black people do not know how to love. She is describing her own reality in a culture that experienced every sort of hardship in the struggle to survive. The cultural enemies on the outside profoundly impacted what was happening on the inside. She summarizes: "Try granting acceptance when an entire nation is conspiring against the idea of that. There's no time for such foolishness."[33]

Dee believes there is truth in Raybon's point as she has seen this reality play out in families over the years. Her own childhood was not idyllic, as her family lacked financial resources, they moved a great deal, and her dad was not around, but she feels fortunate that she always felt loved by her mother.

It seems from my limited research that part of creating reciprocal relationships may involve white people learning about the things that have brought us to this broken place and replacing their ignorance with love that is healing for everyone.

My Family

My husband, Dave, spent the first twelve years of his life in an urban context, and the next thirty in the suburbs. During our fifteen years in this urban setting, he has come to realize that without having a diversity of friends, you will never be as well rounded as you can be. "Socially, ethically, spiritually, economically, sexually—every type of diversity you can add to your friendship circle makes you that much more well-rounded." He speaks of having his thoughts challenged by people different from himself. When we had a discussion at The Lift about the history of slavery, Ansaya became very upset because the reality of it had just sunk in. Dave realized that it is very different for a black child to come to the realization of our history than for a white person: "It sucks to us, but it's not personal."

Dave also sees service differently as a result of his friendships. "You need to serve a person," he says, "*not* a demographic." If you don't actually know the people you are serving, "you are only placating your own self."

He also talks about the benefits to our own children. He believes that the diversity in which they have been immersed has forced them to see themselves and understand who they are in a broader context. It "made them better people because they understood the world at a deeper level at a younger age." They also learned that they can handle stuff outside the safe suburban bubble they began life in.

My son Connor is now twenty-nine years old. He had just turned fourteen when we moved to the city. With some distance from his teen years, Connor can now articulate how the relationships here have changed him. "I feel like I have a better understanding of the world," he says. "I feel like it helped me understand the importance of taking into account other people's feelings and emotions." Like me, he has also learned there is no they: "those people" over there became "these people" right here.

This has been a long process for him as his main interests in high school were acting and writing; he was not into rap music and sports, which dominated the lives of Ricky, Wesley, Cortez, and other teen boys we got to know. As they have all grown older, however, Connor has had some breakthroughs. His years of at least living up close to people different from himself, even if not becoming best friends right away, gave him a foundation to build off of. During the past few years, he worked at The Lift alongside Cortez, and he found that their shared history (from the time Cortez lived with our family as a teen) made conversation easier. Also, despite their many differences, they have things in common as young men trying to figure out where their lives are heading. He found that talking to Cortez, or to the young people in The Lift's job skills programs, has become as natural as talking to any of his friends who come from a background more similar to his own.

Hadley had just turned eleven when we made the move from the suburbs to the city. Today at twenty-six, she says that living among diversity and building relationships with those different from herself made her a much more compassionate person. She and Ernest built a close relationship. She says he helped her put things into perspective: "He told me not to sweat the small stuff and brought me down to earth." Given all the difficult things he had overcome in his life, when he told her to calm down, stop worrying about tests, and quit biting her nails, she took it seriously. He made her feel special, and he invested in her in a fatherly way. He showed his love for her and pride in her in ways that were different than anything she had experienced: she featured him in her college essay, and after she was accepted, he mailed copies of it to relatives all over the United States. He handwrote her letters while she was in college and called to let her know she needed to write back.

Like many others I interviewed, Hadley spoke of her relationships in our urban neighborhood as helping her see other people's perspectives. We had two teenage girls living with us while Hadley was in high school. One of them was her age, and today Hadley still describes the experience as "surreal." Here was a girl her age with no support system other than an older sister with a baby. This reality helped her learn not to take things for granted. "It sounds like a cliché," she says, "but it was for real."

Me

Before I started formulating my own answer to the question of how these relationships have benefitted me, I asked several of my urban friends what they think the middle-class people involved at The Lift get out of these relationships, and more specifically, how they think I have benefitted from these relationships. Both Ernest and Dee expressed their hope that white middle-class people had learned to see people like them as valuable and good. Ernest hoped that people would realize from knowing him that his past "doesn't make me a bad person" and that, by extension, others with a criminal record should not be judged.

Ernest said he believed I have benefitted by learning to put my phone down and be fully present. He believed that those who have decided to move from the suburbs to our neighborhood have benefitted because they substantially reduced their living expenses and put themselves in positions to meet people who are different from themselves. "Once you and that other person have a better understanding of each other," says Ernest, "life is smooth."

Keshia specifically spoke about me and shared her opinion that I have learned from these relationships not to immediately see people as being from a different race than me; I have learned to just live here and have friends no matter who they are or what they look like.

When I asked Cortez a few years ago how he thought I had been impacted by my relationship with him and others, he was at a loss. He thought about it for a while and started talking several times but in the end could not come up with anything. I asked him again recently, and he said that these relationships helped me gain "street smarts." He says I am now "more in tune with the shit people can pull."

Similarly, Ricky's first answer to the question of how I have benefitted from knowing him was "I don't know." Upon further thought, he decided that I have benefitted by learning about a culture other than my own. "Every culture has strengths," he said, so we all grow when we learn about others. Wesley says I learned a good deal about myself by "being in uncomfortable situations. You stepped outside your comfort zone and learned about a culture that was foreign to you."

But now it's time for *me* to say how I think I have been impacted by these years of living in my urban neighborhood. I approach this task with fear and trembling for two reasons. One, it's hard to remember what I didn't know. Life here in this neighborhood with these friends has become normal. What did I think before? How would I have responded fifteen years ago? I can't always remember. Two, I believe to the core of my being that I have changed nearly as much as it's possible for a human to change as an adult, and I am unsure about how I feel trying to put it into words on a paper that others will read. I use strong words to describe what has happened to me in a spirit of thankfulness and humility.

Brookfield says that ideologies are "sets of values, beliefs, myths, explanations, and justifications that appear self-evidently true and morally desirable." The process of critical reflection causes us to see how these ideologies are embedded in our "inclinations, biases, hunches, and apparently intuitive ways of experiencing reality that we think are unique to us."[34] My decade and a half in this neighborhood has unearthed my ideologies, sometimes in painful ways, and changed my thinking on almost everything. This has been a valuable, if difficult, classroom. Previous classrooms have taught me to "know." This one has taught me to "be."

Daloz et al. and Briggs describe reciprocal relationships that cross boundaries as providing nonmaterial benefits such as new perspectives, better decision-making, diverse experiences, and an increased capacity for belonging. I have experienced all these benefits, but there is a level beyond practicalities that I want to communicate. It is not an overstatement to say that my experience in cross-race and cross-class friendships has caused a fundamental change in who I am as a person. Brookfield and John Holst say that transformative adult learning causes us to "alter how we see ourselves, our purpose in the world, and the way that purpose can be realized."[35] My east-side neighborhood has been my classroom.

Everything I have learned I am still learning. The overused metaphor of life being a journey can be inserted here. It is sometimes less true that I have learned these things, and more true that I have learned that I need to learn these things. And the benefits go far beyond mere learning. Three of the gifts that my friendships on the east side have given me are love, emptiness, and presence.

Love

Like Dee and Ernest have said about their experience in this community, I have been loved. Throughout my life, I have always been loved. I have been fortunate to have had loving friends and family. I was not, like Ernest, going through life with mere acquaintances before I moved here. But this love is something else. This is love that is forged with so much hard work from everyone involved. The hard work is about attempting to understand the things that are foreign to each of us, looking past the history of blacks and whites in this country, and making an effort beyond what is expected or even reasonable.

It's a love that grows as each party realizes over time that they are a different person because of this other person. It is a love born of chaos and emptiness on the part of both parties. It has been paradoxical for me: I met Ernest and saw that he needed to be loved. I chose to love him and was loved in return, which was transformative for me. It can't be measured or quantified, but its effects can be seen. The power of this love has given me hope, helped me become less self-absorbed, taught me to listen better, taught me to grieve for injustices that impact my friends, and given me patience with people who move at a different pace than I had been accustomed to.

This is a conversation I had with Ernest several times each week when I called him on the phone:

Ernest: Hello.

Sandra: It's me.

Ernest: Yay!

It's a small thing, but where do you go to find a friend who is that glad to hear from you? Ernest is the only person who has ever cheered just because he heard my voice. I took it as an expression of love.

Emptiness

I have also learned from my friends here the critical importance of emptiness. It is a human tendency to try to control people and things, and I was raised in a context in which controlling what other people believed and how they behaved was central. When eternity is hanging in the balance, it's important to force your views on all of your hell-bound neighbors. When all of your friends share your views, it becomes a homogeneous army of arrogant and socially awkward people who think everything they do is what God told them to do. This was my world.

Worrying about (and correcting) the beliefs and behavior of others causes an enormous amount of stress because both the worry and the correction are unproductive and destructive. Being surrounded by so many kinds of diversity forced me first to make major revisions to my map, as referenced in chapter 9, and eventually to throw much of it away and start over. For some, this means letting go of the faith of their childhood altogether. For me, it meant reshaping it into something I could live by and embrace, rather than just describe. Once I got a new map that was not about controlling others, the way was opened for the relationships I had been forming to go to a deeper place.

It's hard to measure this kind of thing, but, every once in a while, a story from my past life comes to mind and I realize how much I have changed. I recall sitting with a church group in 1998, about five years before moving into the city. The discussion turned to meditation, and a group member told us all he was practicing a form of Eastern meditation. He had a chronically ill family member, and he said the meditation was helping him deal with the stress. In the evangelical context we were all a part of, anything associated with Eastern religions was considered pagan and off-limits to true Christians. I recall speaking up during our group meeting and telling him that this kind of meditation was not a good thing to be involved in.

From where I sit now, I am embarrassed by my opinions and behavior. They seem to me to be rooted in the fear of the Other or the unknown that was a huge part of my upbringing. It was a judgment both on this friend and on Eastern religions. It is deeply rooted in arrogance about ownership of the truth, and it is endemic in the conservative evangelical subculture in which I was raised. My move to the city in 2003 removed me from a world of cultural, social, and religious homogeneity and landed me in a world of diversity. It was impossible to control, and it became necessary to become empty. It's freeing to realize you are not in charge of the universe.

Presence

The final area of impact these relationships have had on me is in the area of presence. In the introduction, I shared a quote from Henri Nouwen that summed up the kind of life I want to lead. I want to be present. This is an ongoing struggle, and many of Ernest's and my arguments started with him confronting me about looking at my phone too much or needing to rush off to something else. Ernest lived life at a pace that made time for long drives, responding to anyone in need, and watching *NCIS* faithfully every week. He did not have a computer, cell phone, or internet. When he was with you, he was all the way there. When you needed him, he showed up. I remember helping a teen who was trying to move out of his mom's friend's house, where she had abandoned him several months earlier. The friend was not letting him remove some of his possessions from the house. I was trying to intervene and help resolve the conflict, but she wouldn't talk to me. There were about ten black adults in the house, and they were all looking at my white coworker and me in ways that made it clear we were not welcome. It was 8:00 p.m. and getting dark. I called Ernest from the curb and simply said, "We need a black man over here." I gave him the address, and he squealed up minutes later. He exercised his great gift of leadership and badass-ness, and we all left in one piece with the teen's possessions. Whenever I needed Ernest, he was present, both physically and emotionally.

Simply watching Ernest live made me realize the tornado in which I was living. I always had one hundred things going on at once, combined with a phone that constantly buzzed, beeped, and rang. I don't have any problem saying no to things I don't want to do—there are just too many things I want to do! Ernest was a consistent voice in my ear about this. Even though he has since passed away, I can still hear him, and he is right. I still have work to do on this one, but as I look back, I can recognize my progress.

I shared earlier that I have become more relaxed about time. I have also become better about dealing with interruptions. In the midst of a very busy week that involved writing a grant, starting a new program, and trying to complete a research project, I had a call from a neighbor whose partner was in a hospice care facility. Her partner was agitated and finally agreed to have me come and pray with him. A decade ago, this unplanned interruption would have caused me stress. I would have gone, but I would have entered his space and brought anxiety with me. My new self saw this as a sacred trust more important than absolutely anything on my calendar or to-do list. I was honored to be invited to sit with a person nearing death and be fully present.

Sometimes these occasions feel like out-of-body experiences because I don't feel quite like myself. I float above and watch and wonder why I am not anxious or grouchy or rushing or yelling. I am still those things at times, but less often. Hopefully, all adults find themselves growing and maturing in some of these ways. I've set goals in my life to be more patient or less grouchy, and then I've proceeded to try hard to get there. The difference for me over these past fifteen years is that I didn't set these goals or try hard to change. I lived a life that presented different challenges and perspectives than I had ever faced, and, in the process of facing them, I changed. This is the organic beauty of the kind of relationships I am talking about. I began to see the world in a different way, and, in the process, I became a different person.

The politically correct thing to say about my relationships is that I have gained more than I have given—that I have been changed as much as or more than anyone else. In this case, the politically correct thing is also the true thing. I am certain that Dee, Ernest, and Keshia were telling the truth about the benefits they have experienced, but when I met them, all three were already so much more able than I was to be empty and present. They were patient with me as I learned these important things from them. We grew to love one another and have impacted each other in ways big and small.

One underlying difference between blacks and whites when thinking about the benefits each experience in cross-race friendships is the fact that black people are already required to understand white culture in order to survive. Korgen says whites "do not generally feel pressure to understand the cultures of people of color or recognize white privilege. They have no need to learn a culture or perspective other than their own to advance in U.S.

society."[36] Thus the benefit these friendships provide of learning another culture primarily advantages white people.

Several of my friends did speak of these relationships helping them see the world more accurately. Korgen explains, "Those around us provide our immediate outlook on the world. . . . If the majority of people with whom we socialize are prosperous and content, we will tend to believe that our society is just."[37] While it may be easier to maintain this perspective, it would be hard to argue that remaining ignorant is a suitable life goal.

Conclusion

In order to accept my argument that these sometimes-challenging relationships are worth whatever investments need to be made, it requires that we agree that things like improved perspectives, understanding a new culture, gaining a more accurate picture of reality, being present, and letting go of control are things that are worth pursuing. It is possible that many people would prefer to isolate themselves from difference and remain ignorant about the ongoing struggles faced by those from different races and classes than themselves. It's possible that these same people would prefer to maintain control and avoid ever being empty. In the process, I would argue that these are people who are limiting their ability to give and receive love.

Certainly, the barriers to experiencing this love are many. In these chapters, I have talked about the barrier of tribalism that reveals itself in segregation, classism, and racism. I have explained how conflicting views of money and the absence of true freedom create almost impenetrable barriers. I have written about the church's missteps toward reconciliation. I have shown the difficulties of finding a place to experience relationships of diversity and being willing to deal with the chaos and submit to the emptiness required.

But I hope that my ultimate contribution to the ongoing dialogue about our broken society is found in the stories of transformation of Dee and her family, of Keshia, of Cortez, of my own family, of myself, and of Ernest. I think if Ernest were able to read this book and see in print our story of friendship, of hard-fought love, and of the turnout for his funeral, he would say, "Yay!" He would celebrate the fact that before he died, he experienced for the first time a transforming love with the ability to heal an evil broken-ness. "Dear," he would say to me, "now that you've finally got this book finished, go sit on the porch and do nothing for a minute."

Notes

1. Maya Angelou, *Rainbow in the Cloud: The Wisdom and Spirit of Maya Angelou* (New York: Random House, 2014), 6.

2. James A. Vela-McConnell, *Unlikely Friends: Bridging Ties and Diverse Friendships* (Lanham, MD: Lexington, 2011), 21.

3. Xavier de Souza Briggs, "'Some of My Best Friends Are . . .': Inter-racial Friendships, Class, and Segregation in America," *City & Community* 6, no. 4 (2007): 266.

4. Kathleen Korgen, *Crossing the Racial Divide: Close Friendships betwee Black and White Americans* (Westport, CT: Praeger, 2002), xi.

5. Laurent A. Parks Daloz, Cheryl H. Keen, James P. Keen, and Sharon Daloz Parks, *Common Fire: Leading Lives of Commit-ment in a Complex World* (Boston: Beacon, 1996), 2.

6. Jürgen Habermas, *The Structural Transformation of the Public Sphere: An Inquiry into a Category of Bourgeois Society* (Cambridge, MA: MIT Press, 1989), 247.

7. Daloz et al., *Common Fire*, 4.

8. Stephen D. Brookfield, *The Power of Critical Theory: Liberating Adult Learning and Teaching* (San Francisco: Jossey-Bass, 2004), 230.

9. Daloz et al., *Common Fire*, 2.

10. Daloz et al., *Common Fire*, 10.

11. Vela-McConnell, *Unlikely Friends*, 36.

12. Briggs, "'Some of My Best Friends,'" 266.

13. Scott E. Page, *The Difference: How the Power of Diversity Creates Better Groups, Firms, Schools, and Societies* (Princeton, NJ: Princeton University Press, 2007).

14. Daloz et al., *Common Fire*, 54.

15. Briggs, "'Some of My Best Friends,'" 266.

16. Jordan Weissmann, "Did Katrina Victims Really Spend Their Relief Money on Gucci Bags and Massage Parlors?" *The Atlantic*, October 31, 2012, https://tinyurl.com/y3uwyllt.

17. Page, *The Difference*, 10.

18. Page, *The Difference*, xxiii.

19. Page, *The Difference*, 13.

20. Page, *The Difference*, 14.

21. Ken Stern, "Why the Rich Don't Give to Charity," *The Atlantic*, April 2013, https://tinyurl.com/yy2ouv3e.

22. Ken Stern, "Why the Rich Don't Give to Charity."

23. Robert Reich, "Rich People's Idea of Charity: Giving to Elite Schools and Operas," *Salon*, December 14, 2013, https://tinyurl.com/yyxpoynv.

24. Reich, "Rich People's Idea of Charity."

25. Vela-McConnell, *Unlikely Friends*, 38.

26. Patricia Raybon, *My First White Friend: Confessions on Race, Love, and Forgiveness* (New York: Penguin, 1996), 3.

27. Raybon, *My First White Friend*, 11.

28. Raybon, *My First White Friend*, 12.

29. Allan Aubrey Boesak and Curtiss Paul DeYoung, *Radical Reconciliation: Beyond Political Pietism and Christian Quietism* (Maryknoll, NY: Orbis, 2012), 12.

30. Tanner Colby, "Why Don't Whites Have Black Friends?" *CNN*, August 19, 2013, https://tinyurl.com/y62x8qzd.

31. European-American Collaborative Challenging Whiteness, "White on White: Developing Capacity to Communicate about Race with Critical Humility," in *Handbook on Race: A Dialogue between Adult and Higher Education Scholars*, eds. Vanessa Sheared, Stephen D. Brookfield, Scipio A. J. Colin III, Juanita Johnson-

Bailey, and Elizabeth Peterson (San Francisco: Jossey-Bass, 2010), 155.

32. Raybon, *My First White Friend*, 28, 29.

33. Raybon, *My First White Friend*, 29.

34. Stephen D. Brookfield, "Transformative Learning as Ideology Critique," in *Learning as Transformation: Critical Perspectives on a Theory in Progress*, ed. Jack Mezirow (San Francisco: Jossey-Bass, 2009), 129.

35. Stephen D. Brookfield and John D. Holst, *Radicalizing Learning* (San Francisco: Jossey-Bass, 2011), 32.

36. Korgen, *Crossing the Racial Divide*, 67.

37. Korgen, *Crossing the Racial Divide*, 15–16.

Recommended Reading List

Alexander, Michelle, *The New Jim Crow: Mass Incarceration in the Age of Colorblindness.* Rev. ed. New York: New Press, 2010.

Armstrong, Chris R. "Fundamentalism: Contemporary." In *Encyclopedia of Religion in America*, rev. ed., edited by Charles H. Lippy and Peter W. Williams, 886–94. Washington, DC: CQ, 2010.

Badhwar, Neera Kapur, ed. *Friendship: A Philosophical Reader.* Ithaca, NY: Cornell University Press, 1993.

Bauman, Zygmunt. *Freedom.* Minneapolis: University of Minnesota Press, 1988.

Berreby, David. *Us & Them: The Science of Identity.* Chicago: University of Chicago Press, 2008.

Boesak, Allan Aubrey, and Curtiss Paul DeYoung. *Radical Reconciliation: Beyond Political Pietism and Christian Quietism.* Maryknoll, NY: Orbis, 2012.

Bourdieu, Pierre. *Distinction: A Social Critique of the Judgment of Taste.* Translated by Richard Nice. Cambridge, MA: Harvard University Press, 1984.

Brookfield, Stephen D., and John D. Holst. *Radicalizing Learning.* San Francisco: Jossey-Bass, 2011.

Carbado, Devon, and Mitu Gulati. *Acting White? Rethinking Race in "Post-Racial" America.* New York: Oxford University Press, 2013.

Daloz, Laurent A. Parks, Cheryl H. Keen, James P. Keen, and Sharon Daloz Parks. *Common Fire: Leading Lives of Commitment in a Complex World.* Boston: Beacon, 1996.

Davis, Angela Y. *Women, Culture & Politics.* New York: Vintage, 1990.

Delgado, Richard, and Jean Stefancic. *Critical Race Theory: An Introduction.* New York: New York University Press, 2012.

Emerson, Michael O., and Christian Smith. *Divided by Faith: Evangelical Religion and the Problem of Race in America.* New York: Oxford University Press, 2000.

Feagin, Joe R., Hernan Vera, and Pinar Batur. *White Racism.* 2nd ed. New York: Routledge, 2001.

Freire, Paulo. *Pedagogy of the Oppressed.* New York: Bloomsbury Academic, 2012.

Fromm, Erich. *The Art of Loving.* New York: HarperCollins, 1956.

Goffman, Erving. *The Presentation of Self in Everyday Life.* Garden City, NY: Doubleday, 1959.

Greene, Maxine. *The Dialectic of Freedom*. New York: Teachers College Press, 1988.

Horton, Myles. *The Long Haul: An Autobiography*. With Judith Kohl and Herbert Kohl. New York: Anchor, 1997.

Korgen, Kathleen. *Crossing the Racial Divide: Close Friendships between Black and White Americans*. Westport, CT: Praeger, 2002.

Lave, Jean, and Étienne Wenger. *Situated Learning: Legitimate Peripheral Participation*. New York: Cambridge University Press, 1991.

Loewen, James. *Lies My Teacher Told Me: Everything Your American History Textbook Got Wrong*. New York: Touchstone, 1995.

Marcuse, Herbert. *One-Dimensional Man: Studies in the Ideology of Advanced Industrial Society*. Boston: Beacon, 1964.

Massey, Douglas S., and Nancy A. Denton. *American Apartheid: Segregation and the Making of the Underclass*. Cambridge, MA: Harvard University Press, 1993.

Mezirow, Jack. *Transformative Dimensions of Adult Learning*. San Francisco: Jossey-Bass, 1991.

Ockholm, Dennis L., ed. *The Gospel in Black & White: Theological Resources for Racial Reconciliation*. Downers Grove, IL: InterVarsity, 1997.

Page, Scott E. *The Difference: How the Power of Diversity Creates Better Groups, Firms, Schools, and Societies*. Princeton, NJ: Princeton University Press, 2007.

Peck, M. Scott. *The Different Drum: Community Making and Peace*. New York: Simon & Schuster, 1987.

Preskill, Stephen, and Stephen D. Brookfield. *Learning as a Way of Leading: Lessons from the Struggle for Social Justice*. San Francisco: Jossey-Bass, 2009.

Raybon, Patricia. *My First White Friend: Confessions on Race, Love, and Forgiveness*. New York: Penguin, 1996.

Rothenberg, Paula S., ed. *White Privilege: Essential Readings on the Other Side of Racism*. New York: Worth, 2008.

Sennett, Richard. *Together: The Rituals, Pleasures and Politics of Cooperation*. New Haven, CT: Yale University Press, 2012.

Sherif, Muzafer. *Social Interaction: Process and Products*. Chicago: Aldine, 1967.

Sider, Ronald J. *Rich Christians in an Age of Hunger: Moving from Affluence to Generosity*. Dallas: Word, 1997.

———. *The Scandal of the Evangelical Conscience: Why Are Christians Living Just Like the Rest of the World?* Grand Rapids: Baker, 2005.

Smith, David Livingstone. *Less Than Human: Why We Demean, Enslave, and Exterminate Others*. New York: St. Martin's, 2011.

Sue, Derald Wing. *Microaggressions in Everyday Life: Race, Gender and Sexual Orientation*. Hoboken, NJ: John Wiley, 2010.

Tatum, Beverly Daniel. *Why Are All the Black Kids Sitting Together in the Cafeteria? And Other Conversations about Race*. New York: Basic, 2003.

Tutu, Desmond. *God Is Not a Christian*. New York: HarperOne, 2011.

Vela-McConnell, James A. *Unlikely Friends: Bridging Ties and Diverse Friendships*. Lanham, MD: Lexington, 2011.

Yancy, George. *Black Bodies, White Gazes: The Continuing Significance of Race*. Lanham, MD: Rowan & Littlefield, 2008.

Zinn, Howard. *A People's History of the United States: 1492 to Present*. New York: HarperCollins, 2003.

Index